THE MURDER OF MARY BEAN

and Other Stories

TRUE CRIME HISTORY SERIES
Albert Borowitz, Editor

THE
MURDER
OF
MARY BEAN
AND OTHER STORIES

Elizabeth A. De Wolfe

The Kent State University Press

KENT, OHIO

To the next generation and the stories they will tell:

Wendy, Emma, and Allison;

Erik, Alex, Ian, and Will

© 2007 by The Kent State University Press, Kent, Ohio 44242
ALL RIGHTS RESERVED
Library of Congress Catalog Card Number 2007021836
ISBN 978-0-87338-918-1
Manufactured in the United States of America

The author gratefully acknowledges permission for use of the following material:
The texts of Miss J.A.B., *Thrilling and Exciting Account of the Horrible Murder of Mary Bean* (Rulison, 1852), and George Hamilton, *A Full and Complete Confession of the Horrid Transactions in the Life of George Hamilton* (J. Merone, 1852), are used with the permission of the Borowitz Crime Collection, Department of Special Collections and Archives, Kent State University Libraries and Media Services.
John Badger Batchelder, *Saco and Biddeford, Me. Sketched by Nature* (Boston, Mass.: J. H. Bufford Lithographer, 1855); A. F. Walling, *Map of Saco and Biddeford* (Boston: n.p., 1851); and images of news items and advertisements from the *Saco Maine Democrat* are used with the permission of the Dyer Library/Saco Museum, Saco, Maine.
Illustrations of the "Regulations . . . of the Amoskeag Manufacturing Company" and the cover of *A Thrilling and Exciting Account of the Murder of Mary Bean* are used courtesy of the New Hampshire Historical Society.
The photograph of Nathan Clifford is used courtesy of the Library of Congress.
The photograph of Berengera Dalton Caswell is used courtesy of Susan Reynolds-Phaneuf.

LIBRARY OF CONGRESS CATALOGING-IN-PUBLICATION DATA

De Wolfe, Elizabeth A., 1961–
    The murder of Mary Bean and other stories / Elizabeth A. De Wolfe.
        p.   cm. — (True crime series)
    Includes bibliographical references and index.
    ISBN-13: 978-0-87338-918-1 (pbk. : alk. paper) ∞
    1. Caswell, Berengera Dalton, 1828–1850. 2. Murder—Maine—Saco—History—Case studies.
3. Murder in literature. 4. Saco (Me.)—History—19th century. I. Title.
HV6533.M2D48 2007
364.152'3092—dc22   2007021836

British Library Cataloging-in-Publication data are available.

11   5 4 3 2

CONTENTS

ACKNOWLEDGMENTS

I'd like to thank the National Endowment for the Humanities for declining to fund my proposed sabbatical project in 2002. Although I have been the fortunate, and very appreciative, recipient of NEH funding for past projects, I was more fortunate this time to receive the letter that began "we regret to inform you." While initially I found myself in a research quandary—do I proceed with expensive project A with limited funding or do I look for plan B—fate and good fortune intervened when a copy of the *Life of George Hamilton* found its way to a local antiquarian bookstore and provided me with this intriguing project at a moment when I had long blocks of time to pursue it.

Many individuals and institutions have been instrumental in allowing me to tell this story. First and foremost I am very grateful to Kent State University and the Albert and Helen Borowitz Crime Collection for permission to reproduce *Mary Bean, The Factory Girl* and the *Life of George Hamilton*. Cara Gilgenbach, curator and University Archivist at Kent State University, made me most welcome during my visit to the Borowitz Crime Collection. For her assistance then and her support as this project continued, I would like to most sincerely thank her. In Maine, I drew on the resources of several repositories and I thank here the helpful and knowledgeable staff and volunteers at the Saco Museum and Dyer Library; the Saco Area Historical Society; the Alfred Historical Society; the Maine Historical Society; the Maine State Archives; De Wolfe and Wood Books of Alfred, Maine; and the Portland, Maine, Public Library. I thank Don Sharland, Gerald Moran, Peter Morelli, Roy Fairfield, Frank P. Wood, and Scott F. De Wolfe for their help with research resources and Captain Moreau of the York County, Maine, Sheriff's Office for facilitating my examination of the 1850s register recording the arrival and departure of inmates in the York County jail. Librarians and archivists at several institutions were also helpful in locating manuscripts and suggesting new avenues of exploration; thank you to Martha Mayo at the

Center for Lowell History, Eileen O'Brien at the Manchester Historical Society, David Smolen at the New Hampshire Historical Society, Tom Hardiman at the Portsmouth Atheneum, and Brenda Austin, interlibrary loan coordinator at the University of New England. A number of genealogists were eager to help and generously shared information from their own family history research. I'm especially grateful to Jackie Sleeper and Jill Jakeman for the detailed materials both shared.

The quest to identify the mystery woman in the ambrotype led me to numerous scholars, art historians, and collectors, all generous with their time and expertise. Each contributed a bit of the answer to the puzzle of the unlabeled photograph and I'd like to thank them for their enthusiastic participation: Allison Perkins and Darsie Alexander at the Baltimore Museum of Art, Shirley T. Wajda at Kent State University, Holly Hurd-Forsyth and Ryan Nutting at the Maine Historical Society, and independent scholar Jacqueline Field. I'm very grateful to Cacie Miller and her fleet fingers for transcribing the two fictional texts. I'm equally appreciative of the assistance I received creating the illustrations; my thanks to Holly Haywood and Dick Buhr at the University of New England and Peter Morelli, City of Saco. As always, I am fortunate to benefit from the advice, critique, and interest in my work my colleagues and friends have offered. I'd especially like to thank Dr. Terri Vanderlinde, DO; Candace Kanes; Jennifer Tuttle; David Kuchta; Holly Haywood; Kari Wagner; and the collegial members of UNE's Seeds group whose collective wisdom provided the constructive criticism that helped me see the bigger story of this story. Scott De Wolfe remains my best critic, best friend, and best supplier of old newspapers. Pearl Lynn kept me good company. As the Mary Bean tales moralized, home is indeed a very good place to be.

Historical research takes much time and some money and I have been very fortunate in receiving both. I was honored to receive the Dyer Library and Saco Area Historical Society's 2004 Fairfield Award for Saco History which helped fund this research. The University of New England faculty development fund and College of Arts and Sciences research grants were also key in continuing my study, as well as UNE's much-appreciated gift of time in the form of a 2002–2003 sabbatical during which research for this book commenced. When I returned to campus I was fortunate to have the support and assistance of many in the UNE community. I'm thankful for the administrative assistance of Elaine Brouillette and for the thought-provoking comments and ideas students raised in several of my history classes over the past few years. I would also like to thank the UNE library staff and Steve Price and Dick Buhr in the Office of Communications for their help at opposite ends of this project: the librarians for their able assistance in the gathering of research materials and the communications office for sharing the results of my labors with the wider community at and beyond UNE. The latter brought some early media attention to this project and I'm grateful for the opportunities I had to share Berengera Caswell's story through newspapers, radio, TV, and other venues. I would particularly like to thank Bill Green at WCSH-6 (Portland) for his interest in this project and his penetrating questions, one of which—who helped Smith carry Caswell's body to the brook?—remains unanswered. Clearly there are yet more stories that remain to be told.

Fate intervened again in the course of this project, this time in a chance online encounter between this historian and Berengera Caswell's great-great-grandniece. I would most sincerely like to thank Susan Reynolds-Phaneuf for her generous sharing of resources, her enthusiastic support of this project, and especially for welcoming me into her family's lives, present and past. Without her interest and insights, this story would be a far less interesting one to tell.

ILLUSTRATIONS

PART ONE

THE

DEATH

OF

BERENGERA
CASWELL

"SUPPOSED MURDER OF ANOTHER FACTORY GIRL"

On a sunny April afternoon in 1850, in the coastal town of Saco, Maine, young Osgood Stevens made a gruesome discovery. Helping his neighbor clear a clogged brook, the fourteen-year-old boy, with great effort, turned over a wooden plank that had become wedged in the culvert that ran beneath Storer Street. Much to his horror, he discovered tied to the plank the icy, rat-chewed remains of a young woman. A crowd gathered as Osgood's neighbors pulled the body from the water and carefully placed it on the ground. Someone ran for the constable and the coroner. The shocking news spread fast, and more people, on their way back to work after their midday meals, arrived to gaze at the victim. Saco was a growing town with a recent rise in crime, but until now, murder had been unheard of there. The weather reflected the mood of concern; by midafternoon the skies had darkened and the mild spring day had become wintry. The coroner called for an investigation, and the constable quickly convened an inquest jury, appointing several of the adult men who had gathered to watch this unexpected and lurid event. Despite the approaching snow, the jury members began their threefold duty: to determine who the victim was, how she died, and at whose hand.

With the weather turning and the crowd pressing, Constable James J. Wiggin moved the body to the nearby barn of Nathaniel Brooks. Here the jurors could begin their solemn task. The victim rested on a whitewashed plank, six feet long, to which someone had tied her at the ankles and neck. Her hands had been bound so tightly that the cotton rag used to secure them left indentations on her wrists. She was scantily clad, wearing blue stockings (newly footed), a light shift, a nightcap, and a child's checked calico apron tied over her face in "turban form."[1] Coroner Thomas P. Tufts called Dr. Edwin Hall, a trained physician and surgeon with a Main Street office, to the scene. As the day's light was fading, Hall gave the body a preliminary examination. He ruled out suicide and accident. This woman, he concluded, had obviously come to her death at the hand of another. The evidence indicated that she had recently been pregnant and had died as a consequence of abortion. The inquest jury suspected that the victim of this murder—for death during abortion was considered murder—was likely one of the many factory girls at work in the nearby textile mills, and as frequent newspaper stories and numerous true-crime accounts made clear, it was not unlikely for a factory girl to die in just this way. With the short examination concluded in the failing light, the inquest jury knew *how*, but they did not yet know the answer to the twin questions of *who*. The snow increased to an April blizzard and darkness fell.

By the spring of 1850, textile mills had stimulated tremendous growth in Saco and its neighbor across the river, Biddeford. The mills brought economic prosperity, a building boom, and a rapid rise in population, all of which changed Saco from a rural agricultural hamlet to a burgeoning city. As the populace grew and shifted, moving from one town to another as opportunity called, residents found that they no longer knew their neighbors—and an unidentified dead body in an icy stream epitomized the worries and fears these changing times encompassed. What seemed a straightforward story about a murdered girl became a much more complicated tale that brought into question the very foundation of Saco's economic success and that of other New England towns: the labor of the young women in the textile factories.

This one death generated many stories—found in newspapers across New England; court records; and two short novels, cheap pamphlet-length fiction that used the local Saco tragedy to warn a wider audience of the dangers inherent in mid-nineteenth-century urban life. At first glance the story of the body in the brook appeared to be the familiar one of an innocent girl who fell victim to a cruel and cunning criminal. Most readers saw this event through the "murder" lens, a familiar format featuring a passive victim and an active aggressor. The moral of this story was clear: young girls could best be protected at home, away from the temptations and dangers of factory life. But as more information was uncovered, the tale became much more complicated, resisting the attempts of newspaper editors and lawyers to make it fit the expected model of victim and villain, of good and evil. But the imagined solution to urban danger was untenable: if all girls remained at home, who would fill the bobbins and tend the factory looms? And for those inevitable factory girls, how could they be best protected from the many horrors parents feared: dangerous textile machinery, lustful men, frivolous spending of time and money? As the ever-changing story unfolded, residents and newspaper readers grappled with the meaning of this death. It was partly about crime and criminals but a key element concerned the changing opportunities for women to earn wages; live independently; and make their own decisions, some of which may have had tragic consequences. This dead body symbolized the growing separation between sexuality and reproduction, a theme that pervaded literature in the 1840s and brought a great deal of discomfort to those determined to keep alive the ideal of the passionless proper woman.[2] The varying stories told in newspaper reports, court testimony, and novels taught readers cultural lessons about gender roles and behavior and provided a venue for articulating and working out fears about the stability of identity—knowing your neighbor—that the midcentury brought. From the turgid legalese of court documents to the racy text of sensational novels, writing and reading about this shocking crime was a way for authors to put forth a cultural agenda and for readers to work out difficult issues of gender, identity, and social change and ultimately to make sense of their world.[3] It is this complicated, multilayered story that Osgood Stevens uncovered in Woodbury Brook that April Saturday in 1850 and it is these stories, all of which begin with reading a body, that I as a historian investigate here, creating yet another—the latest retelling of the death of this unfortunate young woman.

The bruised and battered body pulled from the brook displayed the worst possible consequence of female independence—a young girl, virtue lost, dying a lonely and anonymous death. As news of the gruesome discovery spread, rumors ran wild and inaccuracies were relayed as fact: one newspaper claimed the victim was from Belmont, Maine; another that her name was Nancy Stafford, Stratford, or perhaps Shattuck. Worried parents wrote to the Saco constable seeking information, hoping that the body was not that of their missing daughter. One paper claimed she was found in a brook, another stated she was found in a pond. Yet another report asserted that the stench of the decomposing body led to its discovery. The *Eastern Argus* claimed their information came from "reliable sources" and promised its Portland, Maine, readers "to keep pace with any thing in regard to [the case] that may appear."[4]

Most nineteenth-century inquests were completed in a matter of hours, but the number of unknowns in this mystery kept the investigation, and newspaper reporters, active for several days. Coroner Tufts took possession of the body and led the coroner's inquest. He, like the constables, was neither a professional nor a medical man. This was an appointed position, rotated among adult men in the community. Tufts was an attorney by trade and also ran Tufts Hotel, a temperance boardinghouse and inn, where, coincidentally, Constable Wiggin resided. It was Tufts's duty to solve the who and how of the case. The why was left up to the trial jury, should the case go that far. Neither Tufts nor the constables had any special tools or techniques to uncover the killer or modus operandi in homicide cases; professional, trained "detectives" or "medical examiners" were still decades in the future. Once the inquest jury reached a decision, it would make a written report, which the coroner and his jury would sign. This decision would then be sent to the constable.

The inquest jury began its investigation with the body in Nathaniel Brooks's barn. The six jurors were a cross section of Saco men: farmer Joseph Hill; millman Gideon Tucker; botanic physician Nathaniel Brooks, in whose barn the body lay; grocer Edward Stiles; currier James Beatty; and the president of Manufacturers' Bank, Tristam Jordan Jr.—the last three, members who worked on Main Street, alerted to the tragedy by Osgood Stevens's cries for assistance. Tufts called in local physicians to assist in an autopsy. Dr. Hall needed several pails of water to remove months of dirt and debris carried by the brook which drained rain and household sewage from the heavily populated area.[5] Once the body was clean, Constable Wiggin removed the victim's clothing and the ropes that had secured her to the plank and placed the items in a pail for safe keeping. Dr. Hall then began his investigation. Since there was a rope around her neck, some speculated the woman had been strangled, but Hall saw no signs of violence on the exterior of the body. He continued his preliminary examination, but the poorly lighted barn made it difficult to see. With evening fast approaching and the body quickly thawing, the constable moved the proceedings to the town engine house. The sexton and town undertaker, David McCullock, arrived at 4:30 and half an hour later buried the body. The inquest jurors met at Tufts's home to consider what they knew so far and how to proceed in their investigation. They had a body and a board, and gossip had already begun to fly. By Monday, April 15, the rumors became investigative leads and the jury tentatively identified the victim as Mary Bean. The newspapers offered various theories: she was one of the local mill girls and she had been identified by a scar on her wrist that a boardinghouse owner recognized, or her identity was discovered by way of a missing tooth a local man claimed to have removed. But most newspapers reported that ultimately she had been identified by the "extraordinary length and beauty of her hair."[6] Bean was not a Saco native, and nothing was known about her except that she had been last seen living with Dr. James Smith and his family on Storer Street. Smith's house was only a short distance from where the body was found.

Had Mary Bean come to Saco in 1830, instead of 1850, she would have seen a vastly different place. There had been several attempts to begin manufacturing on the Saco River, but it was not until Samuel Batchelder's 1831 arrival that the industry began in earnest. With the support of wealthy Boston backers, Batchelder organized the York Manufacturing Company, and the mill began operation in 1832 with Batchelder as its director. The mill buildings were ideally located on islands in the Saco River, between Saco and Biddeford. A series of bridges connected the two towns to Gooch and Cutts Islands, where in addition to the textile mills, employee boardinghouses, stores, and public halls were erected. By 1840, the York Manufacturing Company was a one-million-dollar operation with a thousand employees, 80 percent of them women.[7]

Building and rapid growth continued throughout the 1840s. As the *Saco Union* reported in 1849, the 1840s "gave a new impulse to the prosperity of our place. . . . The hand of industry, directed by the skill and energy of enterprise, has made improvements, which have outstripped the expectations of the most sanguine of our citizens. . . . New streets have been opened, vallies [*sic*] filled, hills cut down, and churches, school houses, factories, stores, dwelling houses, and other buildings have multiplied."[8] The train arrived in the fall of 1842, shortening the trip to Boston to just five hours.[9] Stagecoaches made multiple runs to Portland, interior Maine, and Portsmouth, New Hampshire; and in Saco, the Saco House and the Thornton House offered visitors food and fine places to stay.[10] Opportunity abounded. Hotel manager Asa Wentworth wrote to a friend in New Hampshire: "Business is going to be first rate here this season. They are putting in three mills very large. There is not a store to be hired here nor a tenement hardly to live in."[11] Entrepreneurs poured into town, eager to make their own success.

The population also grew dramatically, and Mary Bean became one of thousands of new residents of this formerly sleepy town. In 1830 the combined population of Saco and Biddeford was 5,213; by 1850 it had risen to 11,891, more than doubling in two decades. With the addition of the farmers and families who lived on the outskirts of town, the total population rose to near 14,000. The growth of Biddeford, where many of the mill workers lived, was especially rapid, a 137 percent increase in the 1840s alone.[12] With people coming and going with "many removals and constant changes," by 1849 the twin towns found it desirable "in a place like ours, where progress is the order of the day," to publish a Saco-Biddeford city directory, containing the name, employment, and

Saco, and Biddeford, Me. Sketched from Nature by J. B. Batchelder (1855). In this celebratory bird's-eye view local residents in the center foreground observe the textile factories situated on Saco River islands between Saco (left) and Biddeford (right). The train from Boston enters the scene from the lower right, connecting this formerly small coastal town to the economy and industry beyond Maine. From the collection of the Dyer Library/Saco Museum, Saco, Maine.

place of residence of each of their citizens, an attempt to stabilize, in print at least, the very fluid population.[13] The directory indicated the extent of the vibrant town; there were nine school districts in Saco, two fire companies, with well over a hundred volunteer firemen, and a wide variety of churches representing several Protestant sects. There were lodges, associations, and societies, including chapters of the International Order of Odd Fellows and the Sons of Temperance. Reflecting the high literacy rates of mid-nineteenth-century America, three literary societies offered reading material. Newsstands and bookshops provided books, pamphlets, and newspapers as well.

As a newcomer to Saco, Mary Bean would have walked in the shadow of the textile mills that had brought the community prosperity and problems. Saco boasted three banks, a fire insurance company, a new cemetery, and two weekly newspapers advertising a host of items to buy at the numerous shops and a variety of entertainments at venues like Cutts Hall, which seated 600 people. In the evening, crowds gathered in Pepperell Square to shop, gossip, and see and be seen. Growth brought new dangers to Saco, and the increasing population brought a greater need for governmental control. For years, Saco citizens had relied on themselves for governing—the community held annual town meetings, and three selectmen shepherded the town through necessary decisions while a town clerk, treasurer, and tax collector assisted. People knew their neighbors, or at least felt as if they did. Like most towns at midcentury, Saco did not have a professional, paid police force. Town control was managed by several part-time positions, rotated among various men in the community. The safety of Saco relied on watchmen and three constables, all of whom held other occupations to make a living. The watchmen patrolled the streets at night, on the alert for fires, fights, or other trouble. The constables worked on a fee-for-service basis—serving warrants or papers, attending court, and transferring or watching prisoners. Mostly they maintained public order by dealing with drunkenness, assault and battery (frequently alcohol-induced), and lewd or lascivious behavior. A covered bridge built between Saco and Factory Island in 1838 was the source of numerous complaints, from the stench of urine to the dark interior that provided a good cover for a variety of crimes.[14] Blocking the entrance to the post office, making rude comments to women, and harassing Irish immigrants were frequent offenses to the public peace. Counterfeiters, shoplifters, and rowdy boys in the streets kept the constables busy. As Saco grew and disorder became increasingly visible and public, the older, more informal ways of dealing with problems were simply no longer adequate.[15] Other dangers struck at home: fires destroyed houses, livelihoods, and property, and diseases such as whooping cough, tuberculosis, dysentery, smallpox, typhoid, and cholera claimed the lives of residents. Saco vital records recall a wide variety of accidental deaths from such things as falls, drownings, and horses' kicks. Death from complications of childbirth took both women and children.[16] And in 1850, Saco added murder to its worries.

But for all the perceived dangers and potential sorrows, life in Saco and Biddeford was bright at midcentury and the source of that optimism was the 2,750 young women employed in the mills, each name carefully recorded in the 1849 Saco-Biddeford directory.[17] Like their better-known colleagues at work in the mills of Lowell, Massachusetts, Mary Bean and the factory girls in Saco and Biddeford enjoyed a freedom and independence that previous generations of women had not. The textile mills offered a chance to participate directly in the economy, earn money by the labor of one's own hands, and do with that money what one pleased. Developing in the 1820s and growing rapidly in the 1830s, textile mills flourished in areas of New England with access to water power—such as Lowell and Lawrence, Massachusetts; Manchester, New Hampshire; and Saco and Biddeford, Maine. Mill agents sought a reliable labor force: young women—the daughters of Protestant New England farmers, well-schooled in duty and, with the increasing availability of consumer goods, without a crucial role to play at home. Where girls in past generations spent their days spinning thread, weaving, and making candles and other household products, these tasks were no longer necessary in more settled areas where goods, including factory-produced cloth, were affordable and readily available for purchase. Girls' household labor became superfluous, and without critical tasks to perform, girls, especially those from large families, drained family resources. Factory work thus provided a venue where young women could make good use of their time and contribute to the household economy by earning wages. The agents assured worried parents that their daughters would be safe under the watchful eyes of a boardinghouse keeper, an older woman who fed the girls, denied access to inappropriate visitors, kept a strict curfew, and made sure her charges attended worship services and other edifying events (as the girls' mill contracts often required).

Typically, factory girls were single, in their late teens or early twenties. Most worked no longer than three years before leaving the mills for marriage or other opportunities. The phrase "factory girl" reflected the cultural belief in the temporary nature of their time in the paid wage workforce, a transitional time between youthful childhood and the mature duties of motherhood.[18] The mills ran on a strict timetable with bells tolling for the opening of the mill gates at the beginning of the day, for dinner at midday, and once again for the mill's closing at the end of the day. This was very different from farm work, where the sun and the seasons, not ringing bells, dictated the tasks—cows were milked when their udders were full, eggs gathered after chickens had laid them, vegetables prepared as they ripened in the garden. Factory girls (also known as "operatives") undertook a number of jobs, increasing in complexity and rate of pay as a worker gained experience. From raw cotton to finished printed cloth, the entire textile operation occurred under one roof. By the late 1840s, textile mill employees worked on average twelve hours a day for a fixed hourly wage, which they were paid once a month. The cost of room and board in company-owned boardinghouses was subtracted from the operatives' pay, and the balance was theirs to keep. In Lowell, an average weekly wage for females was $3.25, including the $1.25 for board; male workers averaged $6.55 per week.[19]

Factory work was dangerous. The noise of power looms was deafening, and fast-moving equipment trapped limbs, dresses, and long hair, often with gruesome, if not fatal, consequences. And the long-term effects of breathing in cotton and wool fibers included debilitating respiratory diseases. Still, factory work provided a very lucrative opportunity for young women to make money. Some girls quite dutifully sent their wages back home to help out their families. Yet most mill girls working from 1836 to 1850 were not from poor families; the majority of young women working in the mills prior to 1850 sought such work for the novelty of it, to experience urban living, or to improve their own economic standing, particularly before marriage. As young women began to realize their own economic value, they spent their wages on themselves, first for necessary items such as shoes or winter clothing but later, as often noted in the press, on gewgaws like hair combs, ribbons, and jewelry. Marion Hopkins, working in the Amoskeag Mill in Manchester, New Hampshire, kept a careful record of her expenses, noting in her diary a wide array of purchases including velvet ribbon, hair oil, puff combs, ink, paper and pencils, apples, calico and other fabric, soap, and a marking plate. On November 6, 1854, Marion, who earned her money weaving cloth, noted with evident pride that she "bought me a dress," the finished product of her hard labor.[20]

In addition to spending money, young women enjoyed the freedom of being relatively on their own. As a group, mill girls married later than other New England young women, and they tended not to marry hometown farmers. Those who returned home after their mill experience often delayed marriage until after the age of thirty, causing no small degree of worry for parents. Opportunities from monies earned at the mills, including going to college or even medical school, offered to the women of Mary Bean's generation a wealth of possibilities beyond marriage. These same possibilities, though, brought uncertainty about the future of middle-class motherhood. What would become of society if her best daughters veered away from the path of marriage and motherhood? Factory life presented other dangers to young girls, especially their virtue. Out from under the protective eye of watchful parents, the young factory operatives struck up new relationships with ease. On one of her evening strolls, Marion Hopkins noted that a strange man approached her and asked if she were walking alone.[21] Although this encounter ended when Marion quickly returned to her boardinghouse, for factory girls other chance meetings produced different results. Perhaps like Marion Hopkins, Mary Bean had encountered a strange man. Perhaps she did not flee to her home, however, and instead, willingly walked with him. As a racy midcentury literature frequently suggested, it was a short walk from virtue to vice, especially for factory girls out of the protective sphere of parents and neighbors.

Some girls did take that short walk, and their horrid deaths made good reading in true-crime literature, newspapers, and sensational novels—all enormously popular in the 1830s, 1840s, and 1850s.[22] Those who discovered Mary Bean's body probably understood her death through the lens of these tragic stories. In the 1830s, readers followed the tale of Massachusetts mill girl Sarah Cornell, who died in 1832 of an apparent suicide after the local minister Ephraim Avery allegedly impregnated her. Or was it murder? Several pamphlets offered opinions on this case, with both the prosecution and Avery's defenders replaying the trial testimony for public consumption. Pilgrims traveled to her grave site and a play about the tragedy made its case to New York audiences in 1833.[23] In January 1849, twenty-five-year-old Orrilla Durrell, jilted by her lover, threw herself into a Lowell mill canal and drowned. This news item was immortalized in newspapers across New England, dramatic poems, and a sensational text, *Love and Suicide; or, A Victim of Seduction.*[24] In early 1850, just a few weeks before the revelation of the Saco tragedy, newspaper readers followed the case of eighteen-year-old Caroline Adams, whose body had been discovered in Lawrence, Massachusetts. In this "Horrible Mystery" the newspapers reported how "the murdered body of a young Girl [was] found sewed up in a sack!" The coroner's inquest revealed she died from a blow to the head and suffocation following an attempted abortion.[25]

The discovery of Mary Bean's body brought similar attention, with local newspaper headlines urgently exclaiming, "Excitement in Saco! Dead Body Found!"[26] The big city papers were more blasé, reflecting the relative frequency of such deaths. The headline of the Boston *Daily Evening Traveller* read "Supposed Murder of Another Factory Girl."[27] Boston readers may have taken the death of yet another young woman in stride, but in Saco, this event shocked the community. The town was abuzz with suspicions: if Mary Bean was the victim of murder, then who was the murderer? Was it Dr. James Smith, whose home was but a few short yards away from the ghastly grave?

Born in Vermont around 1810, James Hervey Smith was one of the newcomers to Saco, arriving around the end of 1844, and part of the influx of people eager to find a niche in the bustling, growing town. Little is known about his life. His place of birth is variously listed as Montpelier or Woodstock. He spent time in New York State and in Newburyport, Massachusetts, before moving to Maine. For a while he lived at the York Hotel and carried out his medical practice. While several Saco doctors had town offices and cared for Saco residents, Smith frequently traveled to nearby villages to treat his patients. His daybook shows he attended to a variety of ailments including coughs, sore lips, kidney disease, and visiting the blind. Smith bought his medicinal supplies from Dr. Joseph P. Grant, which he then dispensed as needed. On occasion, he met with patients in the tavern of the York Hotel, mostly to settle bills. At the hotel, Smith made the acquaintance of Henry Wentworth, the manager of the hotel stable. Each man would be accused of murder by the end of the decade.

In the summer of 1845, Smith married Sarah "Sally" Dresser of Scarborough, Maine. By 1850 he lived on Storer Street with his wife and two young children, four-year-old James and two-year-old Sarah. The Smiths kept a dairy cow and sold milk to neighbors. James Smith was listed in the 1849 city directory as a "botanic" physician. He espoused herbal remedies and treatments much less harsh to the body than the dramatic purgatives and bleedings the "regular" or allopathic physicians prescribed. Benjamin Colby's botanic practice, for example, advertised "roots and herbs of various power to nourish nature and to cure."[28] Mid-century, there were several competing medical philosophies at work,

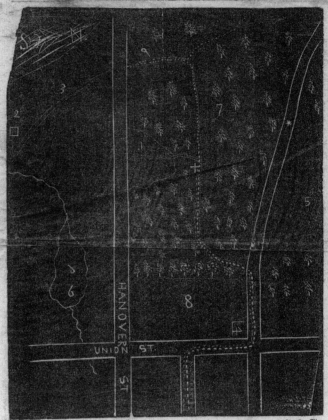

Manchester American.
EXTRA.

MANCHESTER, TUESDAY, APRIL 1st, 1845.

The above is a view of the spot, and surrounding grounds where Mr. Parker was murdered. The following is an explanation.

X Where the body of Mr. Parker was found. 1. A spot of cleared land. 2. House of Mr. Potter, within about 30 rods of the place of murder. 3. The old Rowell Road. 4. School House. 5. The Old Rye field. * Where the young man was when he first heard the cry of murder. 6. Reservoir. ..... The dotted line, the route which Mr. Parker and the murderer took. 7. The Pine woods. 8. An open space. 9. Where the murderer retraced his steps.

Full particulars of the Horrid MURDER of Jonas L. Parker, of this town, on Wednesday night last.

There were found upon Mr. Parker's person, several extensive wounds; one entering at the angle of the jaw, on the right side, and passing into the cavity of the mouth, at the root of the tongue, which severed the external jugular vein. Another commencing by five or six cuts, a little to the left side of the windpipe, and passing obliquely upwards and around the right side of the

Manchester (N.H.) American Extra, April 1, 1845. The shocking murder of Manchester tax collector Jonas Parker stunned the city and generated media frenzy. This *Extra* presented the latest information and a hand-drawn map, with an X indicating the location of Parker's body. From the author's collection.

and the diversity of health care providers in Saco reflects the intense competition. Smith was one of ten physicians identified in the Saco directory; two were botanic, one Thompsonian, and seven allopathic. Saco also had an apothecary, a number of physicians identified as physician/apothecary, and a dentist who doubled as a daguerreotypist.

James Smith came to Saco to seize opportunity, yet wealth and respect seemed just beyond his reach. No records survive to indicate the extent of his medical practice, but it does not seem to have been profitable. A twentieth-century newspaper interview with Smith's children, by then both in their eighties, reported that Smith's "heart and practice were far larger than his enthusiasm for bookkeeping and bill collecting."[29] Saco town records reveal a less nostalgic portrait of a man in and out of trouble. In 1849, 1850, and again in 1854 Smith appears in local records selling household goods to pay his debts, and his money problems appear perennial. In 1850, Smith was sued for $80 for failure to pay a bill.[30] More seriously, in 1849 Smith and brothers Henry and Asa Wentworth, along with Asa's wife, Eliza, were arrested for the 1845 murder of Jonas Parker, the Manchester, New Hampshire, tax collector.

Like James Smith, Jonas Parker had come to Saco in the winter of 1845 seeking opportunity. Parker hoped to buy property with the profits from the recent sale of his Manchester bowling saloon. While in Maine, he ill-advisedly spoke about his habit of carrying large amounts of money. In fact, he had with him several thousand dollars, a combination of collected taxes and his personal funds. A few days later, on the evening of March 26, a man knocked on the door of Parker's Manchester home, to which he had just returned, and told Parker that a "Mrs. Bean" wanted to see him on important business. Parker tried to put off this visitor, but the caller insisted and offered to travel to Bean's house with Parker, who was afraid to go out into the dark. Parker knew that "Bean" was code for a secret meeting among his associates, who included Henry Wentworth. Parker set out into the night carrying a lantern. The light from the lantern was poor. A few moments later, screams were heard; someone cried out, "No! no! murder!" and the next day, Parker's very bloody body was discovered in the woods, his throat slit, nearly decapitated. The wallet containing the town taxes was still at the scene; Parker's personal money was gone.

The crime went unsolved for five years, but in 1849 investigators found a new lead that pointed directly to Saco. Smith and Wentworth were investigated in a hearing before the Saco Municipal Court. The Wentworth brothers had been under a cloud of suspicion for years, having been in financial difficulties when living in Manchester, but suddenly flush after moving to Maine. In New Hampshire, Henry Wentworth had been in and out of trouble with the law, and to avoid arrest, he hid out at his father-in-law's house dressed in women's clothing. To escape a perjury charge, in 1844 Wentworth fled New Hampshire dressed as "Mrs. Bean," easily crossing state lines without suspicion. During the 1849 examination, Smith was able to produce a good alibi: statements from patients as well as his own daybook with records of house calls made. The court was not impressed with Smith's record keeping, referring to his daybook "for what it was worth." They were more impressed with the records of Dr. Joseph Grant whose business register showed James Smith purchasing medicine in Saco on the very day Parker was murdered a hundred miles away in Manchester. The hearing introduced Saco readers to an interconnected group of people who in responding to the charge of accessory to murder slung accusations at each other: perjury, bigamy, and cross-dressing.[31] The March 1849 examination could not turn up enough evidence to indict Smith or any of the Wentworths, and everyone was released. However, the case was far from over. As the *Maine Democrat* wrote, "They were discharged from arrest, but not discharged from the suspicions of the authorities of Manchester."[32]

Smith's shaky finances and questionable friends only fueled suspicion of his connection to the body of Mary Bean. For several years, there had been gossip around town about the nature of Smith's medical practice and in view of the proximity of his house to the location of the body, James Smith was an obvious focus for the investigation. Smith, it was believed, had "been in the habit of administering medicine to females for the purpose of procuring abortion."[33] In one case, the *Farmer's Cabinet* alleged, a patient had died but "the authorities . . . did not see fit to investigate the crime."[34] Constable T. K. Lane visited Smith's house to search for evidence. Lane, who lived on Storer Street near Smith, asked Smith about Mary Bean, but Smith blithely asserted that he wasn't afraid of such questions because Lane was "his friend." Smith told Lane that Mary Bean had lived with his family but claimed that she had died of typhoid, reminding his wife of that fact when the constable walked into their home. At some point during the winter, Smith had claimed Bean had drowned after falling through the winter ice, although that defense made little sense now, considering the body was tied to a board. While the constables focused on Smith, the coroner's inquest jury began to interview people who might have knowledge of the events leading up to Bean's demise. Smith's hired girl, a twelve-year-old Irish immigrant named Ann Coveny, was called for an interview, but she was terribly frightened and swore she knew nothing. Afraid to return to the Smith household, Coveny ran to Biddeford to her brothers' home. The jurors walked up and down Storer Street asking Smith's neighbors what they had seen or heard at the Smiths' residence four months previously. Some neighbors talked to the newspapers as well, which continued to print stories widely varying in their accuracy. One paper reported that Smith had once boasted of his abortion practice, but another indicated (erroneously) that facing the prospect of jail, Smith had decamped—run away from friends and family.

Three days after Bean's autopsy and subsequent burial, the sexton disinterred the body so the physicians could continue their investigation. Dr. Hall removed Bean's reproductive and other organs and placed this medical evidence in glass jars, which were taken to Dr. Hall's office for further study. Four physicians observed the detailed autopsy, which revealed the extent of her internal injuries. McCullock reburied the body, only to disinter it one final time to determine whether it were possible that she had died from typhoid as Smith claimed.

On Tuesday, three days after the discovery of the body, the constables linked Mary Bean's corpse to James Smith's residence. It was not the constables' responsibility to solve this crime, and there was no fee to be made for doing so. Yet the newspapers later commended Constable Wiggin for performing this duty. Perhaps the heinous nature of the crime and the cruel burial motivated Wiggin to restore some semblance of order in his blighted community. Or perhaps he believed the stories that one or more of Smith's patients had died in just the same manner as Mary Bean and thus was determined to end this practice. Whatever the motivation, Wiggin secured key physical evidence that enabled an arrest: the plank to which the body had been tied. J. L. Stevens, Osgood's father, had watched as the body was removed from the brook. He noticed the unusual whitewash on the plank and realized he had seen that pattern before in James Smith's barn. At the request of the coroner's jury, Constable Wiggin, J. L. Stevens, and local carpenter D. F. Ricker walked over to Smith's stable, discovering that one stall was missing a plank. They took the plank found in the brook and placed it in the gap in the stall and found a perfect fit, right down to the marks made by the cleat that had formerly held the plank in place. The next morning, Wiggin arrested

James Smith for the murder of Mary Bean. Saco had no jail so he held Smith at the Saco House, where Constable Lane kept watch for a fee of $3 per day (plus eight nights' room, board, fire, and lights). The coroner's jury released their official verdict late Thursday night, each juror signing the document. Edward Stiles's signature was elegant; Joseph Hill's was more of a chicken scratch, while James Beatty underlined both his first and last name, emphasizing his participation in this difficult civic duty. At 11:00 p.m., their work concluded, they announced that Mary Bean had died from peritoneal or puerperal inflammation, a massive infection resulting from an abortion performed by Dr. James Smith.[35]

There were rumors around Saco that Smith was living under an assumed name, reinventing himself to escape previous wrongdoings in another state. The *Saco Union* described Smith as "a person who has had a doubtful reputation here as kind of a quack practitioner of medicine."[36] Here was an example of the possibilities and the problems of midcentury mobility. In this age of migration, where men headed west for gold and youth headed to the cities for opportunities, anyone could become whoever he or she wanted to be. In the following decades, this idea would be emblematic in the story of Abraham Lincoln's rise to the presidency and Horatio Alger's plucky Ragged Dick's transformation from rags to riches. Yet, this ability to move at will also opened the door to the possibility of masking who one really was and that ability to reinvent oneself, and to hide the less desirable truths about oneself, was a worrisome aspect of these lively times.[37] But as this strange story unfolded, it turned out that it was the victim, Mary Bean, who had been living under an alias. As the investigation into her death widened, William Augustus Nason Long was identified as Bean's paramour.[38] When officials contacted Long, a twenty-one-year-old machinist working on Factory Island, he admitted that the previous fall he had approached Smith about terminating a girl's pregnancy. But Long's concern was with a girl named Berengera Caswell, not Mary Bean. The constables had a new puzzle that reflected these new times: Were Mary Bean and Berengera Caswell one and the same? In fact, they were, but this answer only led to more questions. Why would Caswell take on the persona of Mary Bean? Who *was* Berengera Caswell?

William Long couldn't answer why Caswell became Bean at Smith's residence, but, at the urging of the constables, he could offer some insight into Berengera's brief life. William Long and Berengera Caswell had met in Manchester, where Berengera, a native of Brompton, Quebec, had sought

With her long brown hair, high forehead, and trademark drop earrings, this enchant-
ing woman may be Berengera Dalton Caswell. Ambrotype from the collection of
Susan Reynolds-Phaneuf.

work in the New England textile factories. With two of her sisters—Ruth
(born 1826) and Thais Elizabeth (1830)—Berengera had left the Canadian
farm where they all had been raised, daughters of American parents who
had migrated to the Eastern Townships in the early 1820s. She was said to
have been "a good looking girl," five feet four and a half inches tall, with
fair skin, pierced ears, long dark brown hair, and her teeth, Dr. Hall later
testified, "were the handsomest I ever saw, being complete, uniform and

perfect."[39] As mill owners required of their operatives, Berengera had been vaccinated against smallpox. Berengera's unusual name (derived from Queen Berengera, wife of Richard the Lionhearted) reflected Caswell family connections. Berengera Dalton Caswell, born February 17, 1828, was named for her cousin Berengera Dalton, daughter of her mother's sister Luzetta Dalton. Young Berengera Dalton died at age two in August of 1827, just a few months before her namesake was born.[40]

When Berengera Caswell and her sisters set out for the textile factories of New England in the 1840s, women's lives were changing in new and, to some observers, unsettling ways. Women had been working as mill girls for nearly two decades, but the nature of their relationship with their mill-owner supervisors had grown from paternalistic to increasingly antagonistic. Mill girls undertook some of the first labor strikes in the United States, walking away from their spindles and bobbins and looms in hopes of better pay and shorter hours. In the 1840s there was almost continuous agitation in Lowell and beyond, as the operatives responded to the "speed ups" of machines, the "stretch outs" (slowing machines down but giving operatives additional machines to work, then gradually speeding up), and the reduction in the piece-wage rate.[41] The Ten Hour Movement sought to make ten hours the legal length of a working day; thousands of mill girls added their signatures to a petition asking for a ten-hour workday and invoking the language of independence as the daughters of free men, but the Massachusetts Legislature rejected the petition. New Hampshire passed a ten-hour-workday resolution in 1847 but gave mill owners the opportunity to require more hours in times of need or by mutual agreement. Biddeford mill girls held a strike in 1841, protesting the lack of better wages and company restrictions on where workers could live. Five hundred workers walked off the job, parading through the streets, chanting, "We are not slaves."[42] Although it resulted in little change in their working conditions, the strike, or "turn out" (as others had before), illustrated to men that women could and would understand and act on their perceptions of their own economic value. Folk songs such as "The Lowell Factory Girl" captured the operatives' frustrations with wearying work and decreasing wages.[43] Other girls turned to the media to voice concerns. Signing herself "A Female Operative," one Biddeford factory girl in 1850 used the power of the press to voice her observation that the *Saco Union* inevitably sided with management against the concerns of the workers.[44] The combination of economic self-worth, the reform era, literacy, and the availability of the newspaper was a potent one, and these very public disputes between workers and mill owners upset the image of the dutiful, compliant female worker.

Berengera's experience with mill work was quite typical. Drawn by opportunity and novelty, around 1847 Berengera and her sisters traveled south seeking work in the mills, following a well-trod route for northern girls and a journey sisters commonly took together. The Caswell sisters worked first in Lowell, Massachusetts, the largest of the textile centers. By 1848 Ruth had married William Straw, one of a group of young men from the Brompton region who worked in the textile industry. As with many girls who found marriage in the mills, Ruth would settle in New England and not return to her rural home. Berengera worked in Lowell for just a few months, then moved on to Manchester, New Hampshire. Thais followed a month later. By early 1848, Thais and Berengera were employed at the Amoskeag Mill in Manchester, where they alternated between periods of work and visiting home. Berengera returned to Canada in August 1848 for a visit; by June of 1849 she was back working at Amoskeag with Thais.

The Caswell sisters roomed together in their boardinghouse but worked in different departments at the factory. Berengera worked in the carding room, where raw cotton was cleaned and transformed into thread. Amoskeag payroll records indicated she averaged fifty-four cents per day pay during 1848. When she returned to the mill in June 1849 after a ten-month absence, her average daily pay dropped to fifty cents. Thais Caswell worked in the weaving department from late February 1848 until at least the end of January 1850, when the available payroll records end. Weaving was a much better paid occupation, notably because the weaver had a more intense involvement in the quality of the final product. The weaving looms were automated, yet Thais had to watch carefully for broken or irregular threads and to repair quickly any damage and re-place empty bobbins. Weavers were paid by the "cut," a specific length of woven cloth. The rate of pay varied according to the width and complexity of the weaving as well as the speed of the looms. Thais became skilled quickly. She began her employment making eighty-nine cuts per pay period at fourteen and a half cents per cut, earning an average of fifty-four cents a day, the same as Berengera in the carding department. Within three months, Thais was weaving well over a hundred cuts and earning seventy-four cents per day. A year later, April 1849, Thais wove fewer cuts but was paid thirty-three and a half cents per cut, keeping her daily average wage near sixty-five cents a day. A few months later,

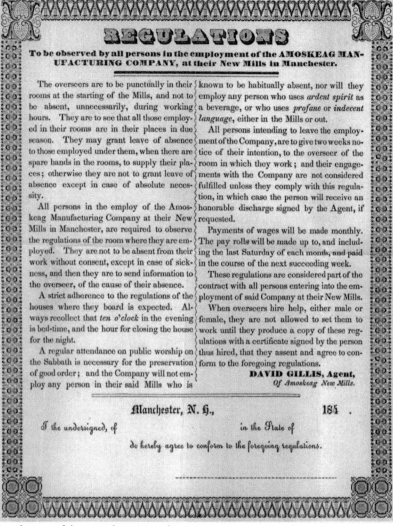

REGULATIONS

To be observed by all persons in the employment of the AMOSKEAG MAN-UFACTURING COMPANY, at their New Mills in Manchester.

The overseers are to be punctually in their rooms at the starting of the Mills, and not to be absent, unnecessarily, during working hours. They are to see that all those employed in their rooms are in their places in due season. They may grant leave of absence to those employed under them, when there are spare hands in the rooms, to supply their places; otherwise they are not to grant leave of absence except in case of absolute necessity.

All persons in the employ of the Amoskeag Manufacturing Company at their New Mills in Manchester, are required to observe the regulations of the room where they are employed. They are not to be absent from their work without consent, except in case of sickness, and then they are to send information to the overseer, of the cause of their absence.

A strict adherence to the regulations of the houses where they board is expected. Always recollect that *ten o'clock* in the evening is bed-time, and the hour for closing the house for the night.

A regular attendance on public worship on the Sabbath is necessary for the preservation of good order; and the Company will not employ any person in their said Mills who is known to be habitually absent, nor will they employ any person who uses *ardent spirit* as a beverage, or who uses *profane* or *indecent language*, either in the Mills or out.

All persons intending to leave the employment of the Company, are to give two weeks notice of their intention, to the overseer of the room in which they work; and their engagements with the Company are not considered fulfilled unless they comply with this regulation, in which case the person will receive an honorable discharge signed by the Agent, if requested.

Payments of wages will be made monthly. The pay rolls will be made up to, and including the last Saturday of each month, and paid in the course of the next succeeding week.

These regulations are considered part of the contract with all persons entering into the employment of said Company at their New Mills.

When overseers hire help, either male or female, they are not allowed to set them to work until they produce a copy of these regulations with a certificate signed by the person thus hired, that they assent and agree to conform to the foregoing regulations.

DAVID GILLIS, Agent,
Of Amoskeag New Mills.

Manchester, N. H.,   184 .

I the undersigned, of   in the State of do hereby agree to conform to the foregoing regulations.

Regulations of the Amoskeag Manufacturing Company, Manchester, N.H., ca. 1840s. The Caswell sisters would have signed this agreement, which stipulated rules of employment and curfews in the boardinghouses. The regulations, however, could not dictate what factory girls did in their free hours, for some girls a time of many temptations. Courtesy of the New Hampshire Historical Society.

Thais had mastered this more complex weaving assignment and routinely averaged eighty cents per day. One month Thais earned an average of ninety-nine cents per day. In nearly two years of continuous labor at the Amoskeag Mill, Thais Caswell earned just over four hundred dollars.[45]

The Caswell sisters worked hard during the day, staying clear of the physical dangers textile production presented. For Berengera, the evening hours presented the more dangerous times. The Caswell sisters worked with several Brompton friends, including a young machinist named Oates Tyler.[46] In the machine shop, Tyler likely worked with William Long, a laborer originally from Biddeford, Maine. After their long workday, the young men and women spent time together walking, shopping, and choosing among the varied activities Manchester had to offer. Some evenings the Caswell sisters may have spent in their boardinghouse, sewing, knitting, reading, or writing letters. Most nights, though, they likely went walking with friends or attending church meetings or lectures by well-known personalities such as phrenologist O. S. Fowler. They may have visited the Manchester Museum and Gallery of Fine Arts to view shells, fossils, curiosities, and the "entire skeleton of the Greenland . . . whale."[47] Other nights the activities may have been more entertaining than educational: visits to a circus, a lady's fair, or a fortune-teller.[48] For seventy-five cents, a daguerreotypist would take their photograph and enclose it in a silk case, recording for posterity their young and vibrant lives. Mill girls enjoyed shopping; Berengera may have treated herself to jewelry, the latest hat, scarf, or fancy fabric seductively advertised in the city papers. We have no firsthand account of how the Caswell sisters spent their free time, but we do know that William and Berengera developed an intimate tie over the summer of 1849, culminating in "unlawful relations." Berengera, by mid-nineteenth-century standards, had taken that first step toward vice.

Prescriptive literature of the nineteenth century asserted that once a woman began to turn away from virtue, there was no escape from ruin. And the autumn would bring a change in Long and Caswell's relationship—and new challenges for Berengera. In September, William was fired from his position "for not giving satisfaction to his employers," and he planned to return to Biddeford to look for a new job.[49] He saw Berengera around September 15 and left Manchester on Monday, the seventeenth. A week later, Berengera left her job at the mill. She picked up her last paycheck (seven dollars) and spent two or three days sewing and packing, giving Thais scraps of fabric from her dresses to remember her by. Berengera bid her sister good-bye and headed to Salem, Massachusetts, perhaps to work in the Naumkeag Steam Cotton Company or to enjoy the seaside air. But whatever the reason for her move, within a few weeks Berengera probably noticed some physical changes. Although factory work was routinely tiring, in Salem Berengera may have noticed she was much more tired than usual, exhausted really. She might have felt queasy but assumed she had eaten bad food. She might have noticed difficulty in concentrating and felt a new soreness in her breasts. By November, she may have realized a slight gain in weight as her body changed shape, and two months after leaving Manchester, perhaps she recalled she had missed two, maybe three, menstrual periods. Toward the end of November Berengera packed her trunks and moved once again, leaving Salem and traveling to Biddeford; she suspected she was pregnant.

Meanwhile, William was working at the Saco Water Power Company as a machinist. In an enormous machine shop, 275 feet long and 46 feet wide, William spent his day making the machines and equipment that kept the area mills turning out fabric. From his boardinghouse on Gooch Island, perched in the middle of the Saco River, he could look north to Saco and south to Biddeford. On November 26, 1849, a few days before Thanksgiving, Berengera arrived in Maine and took a room at Mrs. Sarah Means's boardinghouse in Biddeford. She was traveling with a Brompton friend, Rosalie Quimby Burt, who had a child with her. They told Mrs. Means they planned to go into the mills, and they did go to the counting room of the Water Power Company. The counting room served as the factory office where employees received their pay and new workers were hired. It would also be the ideal place to locate the address of an old friend. Despite what the women told Mrs. Means, it is doubtful they sought jobs. Their very plausible story, however, gave them a reason for walking around mill property as they tried to find William. They were successful; while the women were in the counting room, William appeared. At noon, Berengera, William, and Rosalie dined together at William's boardinghouse. Berengera and William had plenty to talk about, but she did not disclose her secret during the well-attended noon meal. That afternoon Berengera met privately with William, and they met again in the evening. What exactly the two young people said to each other is unknown, but marriage was not the outcome of their difficult conversation.

Abortion was an option for Berengera. In legal arenas in the first decades of the nineteenth century, abortion was understood to be a health issue. Early laws against abortion grew out of concerns of accidental poisoning from dangerous medicinal preparations. If a woman aborted prior to quickening—the moment at which a woman can feel the fetus move (approximately sixteen weeks)—there was no social stigma or legal prohibition; this permissiveness concerning early-term abortion was supported by fifteen hundred years of Christian doctrine that asserted that before quickening the fetus had not yet developed a soul. (Without a soul, a fetus was not life.) Since at the time there was no definitive medical test for pregnancy, prior to quickening a woman could have missed her periods (or claimed to) for any number of reasons—including a blocked menstrual flow, which put the bodily system out of balance, necessitating medicinal "regulators" as a corrective. A woman's authority to define whether she was pregnant or simply blocked put a lot of power over reproduction firmly in her own hands. By midcentury, though, the concept of quickening as the defining moment within pregnancy was losing potency, especially among scientists and regular physicians whose knowledge about reproduction was growing. Botanic physicians, like Smith, did not share this view and continued to provide abortions while allopathic physicians increasingly did not. In the coming decades, the Christian church, too, would rethink its position and change its philosophy to a belief in life beginning at conception.[50] The legal system would follow suit, and abortion law would become increasingly restrictive. In 1849, however, although abortion was not openly discussed in polite company, the practice was widely commercialized and available. Berengera and William would have been familiar with the procedure, although as a young and inexperienced couple without financial means they may not have known how to go about procuring one.

Berengera and William could have turned to the newspaper for insight. In the 1840s, abortion was very much visible in the press. Abortifacients, euphemistically called "menstrual regulators," were advertised in the newspaper and could be purchased from physicians or apothecaries. In previous generations, the knowledge of these herbal preparations would have been passed woman to woman, but in the mobile world of the 1840s, commercial products had replaced personal knowledge. Saco newspapers carried advertisements for these preparations, including "Dr. Marchisi's Uterine Catholicon for female complaints including suppressed menstruation."[51] These preparations carried stern warnings stating that if you suspected a pregnancy, you should absolutely not ingest these powerful medicines; of course, this was a selling point for women who were pregnant and did not wish to be so. A host of widely available medical guides designed for women's use also offered advice on regulating one's bodily systems. One popular recipe to stimulate a "blocked" menstruation combined extract of juniper, gin, honey, and cayenne pepper.[52]

Berengera could have chosen from a variety of abortion providers. In New York City, Madame Restell ran an infamous abortion business, providing a service that, as with medicinal preparations, previously was obtained through knowledge passed woman to woman.[53] That woman-to-woman network still existed in the rural areas of Maine, carried on by midwives and housewives. But Berengera had no ties to Maine women and had to look elsewhere for assistance. Established botanic or Thompsonian physicians may have provided abortions, but changing public sentiment and increasingly strict Maine laws made it unwise to advertise openly in the growing, but still close, community. For allopathic physicians, reliance on the Hippocratic Oath as the guideline for professional behavior prohibited involvement in both abortion and birth control.[54] An itinerant practitioner was a possibility and Maine newspapers carried advertisements for Madame C. Amy, an "independent clairvoyant and Botanic Doctoress," who advertised her presence in Biddeford, offering private rooms and discreet appointments. "Ladies in delicate health may be assured that Madame Amy is able to give them information which will be invaluable, and, to such as desire it, will reveal secrets worth knowing." On the one hand Madame Amy may have represented the legacy of the woman-centered practice of past generations; on the other, clairvoyance and fortune-telling were often used as a code for an abortionist. In the 1840s the previously private acts of women became public acts in the commercialized newspaper industry where the abortion trade, and ads for it, were highly profitable.[55] Girls like Berengera, away from home and out of the protection of their mothers, older sisters, and aunts, became disconnected from a realm of reproductive knowledge women had shared and used for centuries. Although factory girls replaced the family-centered community with a community of coworkers, these women were young, unmarried, and sexually inexperienced, if not downright ignorant.[56] Berengera had little hope of practical advice from her coworkers. Further, "good" girls would avoid "bad" girls, lest their own virtuous reputations be sullied by association—enforcing a social ostracism.[57] Boardinghouse keepers were of little help either, as their job was to uphold the sexual purity and virtue of the young women in their charge. Abortion providers like Madame Restell, and perhaps Smith, offered a service that mobility and independence had made possible, needed, and desired.

Without female connections and apparently without money, Berengera turned to William, who asked Mr. Blake, his supervisor, for advice. For Blake, this was a familiar scene, and before long a meeting was arranged in the tavern of the Saco House. Blake introduced William to Dr. James Smith, who told Long that for ten dollars up front, he would take care of the problem. William lacked money, but Blake had already offered to make the payment, probably with the understanding that Long would work off the debt in the mill. When Smith complained of his own dearth of funds, William graciously bought him a cigar and the three men concluded their arrangement with a smoke. When asked if the doctor wanted to know the name of his new patient, Smith laughingly said, "No," and gave his new boarder an alias, Mary Bean. Unbeknownst to William, this name was an inside joke between Smith and Henry Wentworth, about hidden identities. Perhaps Smith chose this name as a smug signal that as with Henry Wentworth's dodge, Smith's "Mary Bean" disguise would help him escape public notice, too.[58]

Until this moment, Berengera had made her own decisions, traveled as she pleased, and earned her own wages. But now, alone, ashamed, and desperate, she placed herself in the hands of men: her lover, Long; Blake, who paid the fee; and Smith, whom she trusted was a doctor. She needed William for marriage and respectability; and if that was not possible, to avoid the social shame of unwed motherhood, she needed Smith. And Berengera needed Blake to help her navigate the unfamiliar landscape of abortion. After Saturday tea, her traveling companion took her child and left Mrs. Means's boardinghouse, apparently for good. It would appear that she had come along for moral support, keeping Berengera company until a solution to the pregnancy dilemma was found. After dinner that evening, William and Berengera left Mrs. Means's and went to Dr. Smith's residence on Storer Street, just two blocks from the Saco River. As court testimony later revealed, Berengera, who had an extensive wardrobe, wore a red dress with green spots and a white straw bonnet with wreath and black veil and carried a blue cashmere shawl. She said nothing to Mrs. Means about her departure. She left her traveling trunks behind; clearly Berengera expected to return soon. Mrs. Means later reported to the court, with a nod to a popular formula of mysteries, that she "never saw her again." Two days after Berengera arrived at Smith's Blake called at the boardinghouse and retrieved a small wooden trunk. Berengera had wanted her other one—a leather trunk containing her clothing. But no matter, she likely thought, her stay at the Smiths' would be short. Caswell was evidently not the first young woman to reside with Smith. Elizabeth Elden, who shared the multifamily house with her father, noted later that she thought she saw Mary Bean at Smith's in the fall but couldn't be certain as "there were so many girls" who came and went as patients of Dr. Smith. At the Smiths', "Berengera" disappeared. While there, she was known to the Smith family, visitors, and neighbors only as Mary as she sewed, did light housework, and sold milk from Smith's dairy cow. Shortly after her arrival, "Mary Bean" began Smith's treatment.

If we believe the allegations in the newspapers, Smith was not an experienced physician. He was called a fraud, a quack practitioner, and, in reference to his abortion services, "one of the greatest nuisances any community can be cursed with."[59] The *Maine Democrat* questioned his medical training, noting that he was "generally called Dr. Smith but we do not know that he has ever received a medical education or a diploma."[60] The *Union* reported that "Smith for some years has been engaged in such practices as he now stands charged with, and which in one, if not more instances, has resulted in death."[61] Yet we must remember that he carried on a practice in a period where training was neither highly regulated nor required. Some physicians, especially the allopaths, attended medical schools. Others, including Thompsonian and botanic physicians, learned their skills from attending lectures, reading books, or taking correspondence courses. Some physicians were self-taught. All could call themselves physicians or use the honorific "doctor." At any rate, there is no evidence surviving to indicate how (or whether) Smith was trained as a botanic physician. We do, however, know the treatment he prescribed for Berengera Caswell to induce an abortion.

Smith began with herbal preparations. As a botanic physician, Smith would favor the use of herbs or plant medicines over mineral or chemical substances like the frequently prescribed calomel (a derivative of mercury). An ad for a Manchester, New Hampshire, botanic physician neatly summarized this philosophy: "Rejecting all known poisons and strictly adhering to the principle that poisons cannot be medicine."[62] Several plants provided components for abortifacients, including oil of tansy, rue, and ergot. For Berengera, Smith chose extracts from the juniper bush, which he chopped up, mixed with water, and gave to her to drink. This substance, savin, was a well-known abortifacient in use for centuries. An emmenagogue, savin would stimulate uterine contractions. The 1847 *Family Flora and Materia Medica Botanica* praised the efficacy of savin while also warning of its danger: Savin "is one of the most valuable, important and universal articles of the Materia Medica, and is already very generally introduced into practice. Few medical plants require to be administered with greater care or skill. None but experienced physicians should prescribe them, or they may prove dangerous."[63] Because of savin's ability to stimulate uterine contractions, *Family Flora* author Peter Good particularly cautioned "women enceinte" (pregnant) in the uses of this potentially dangerous substance. Good added a commentary on its popularity, in effect advertising savin as an abortifacient: "The power which this plant possesses in opening uterine obstructions is considered so great that it has been frequently employed, and with considerable success, for purposes the most infamous and unnatural."[64] Berengera took the preparation of savin at the end of November and again in early December, but it failed to produce the desired effect. She did not abort, nor did her period return. If there had been any doubt earlier, by now, nearly a month after leaving Salem, Berengera must have been certain she was pregnant.

On December 15, 1849, Berengera Caswell consented to a more drastic and dangerous approach to end her pregnancy. Using a wire instrument, eight inches in length, with a hook on the end, Smith performed an abortion. Berengera was fifteen to eighteen weeks pregnant. As Smith inserted the instrument through her vagina and into her womb, Berengera's uterus produced painful and intense contractions as the body resisted the foreign object's intrusion. With his wire tool, and without anesthesia, Smith attempted to puncture the amniotic sack and scrape loose the pregnancy. While Berengera did abort, during the course of the operation Smith perforated Berengera's uterus, damaging adjacent organs and leaving a gash 1/4 inch in diameter and four inches long, which quickly turned septic. In intense pain from the procedure itself, her mangled organs, and the spreading infection with its fetid, metallic smell, Caswell languished for a week, beset by fevers and chills. In an era without antibiotics, antiseptics, or analgesics, Smith would have had very little to offer her for relief. Two sticking plasters were placed on her back, a bit like giving an amputee an aspirin. Smith may not have realized the extent of her internal injuries, but even if he had, there was nothing he could have done. Late on Saturday evening, a week after the abortion, James and Sarah Smith retired for the night, fully clothed, in a nearby parlor; they knew Berengera's life was coming to an end. Berengera lay alone in the front room. On December 22, 1849, she died.

"STARTLING OUTRAGES EXPOSED TO THE LIGHT"

Smith was in quite a bit of trouble. His abortion practice was situated in a gray area in between the increasingly restrictive law and more accepting social custom. Abortion was first mentioned specifically in Maine law in 1841, among the state's regulations on "offences against chastity, morality and decency." In common law, the concept of quickening still held power, but in Maine statutory law that distinction no longer mattered. The statute forbid "every person" from administering "any medicine, drug, or substance whatever" and prohibited the use of any instruments "with the intent to destroy such child" and "with intent to procure [a] miscarriage" whether the woman was quick with child or not. The provider of the procedure could be punished, but the patient-recipient could not. The goal was to control medical practice, not outlaw abortion per se. This was still very much a debate about the safe practice of medicine rather than a moral issue. The punishment for succeeding at abortion was not more than five years in the state prison, or a maximum fine of one thousand dollars plus one year in the county jail. Yet in order for a physician to be punished, the court needed to show that the woman was pregnant, and not simply blocked, which without proving quickening was all but impossible to do. Further, the court had to demonstrate the physician's "intent" to produce an abortion (as opposed to some other intent), a position equally challenging to prove.[65]

Given a large population of young women in the mills and the lack of effective birth control for single and married women alike, abortion services were sought in Saco—and Smith appeared to have an active practice. Although the newspapers, the prosecution, and later fiction would portray him as a criminal, Smith's practice was not conducted in the stereotypical back alley. He took Berengera into his home for almost one month. He did try medicinal preparations first and turned to his instruments only when those attempts failed. Perhaps Berengera, in desperation, begged him for the procedure. Perhaps he saw himself as sympathetic to an unhappily pregnant woman's plight and as providing a service that helped women in difficulty. Or perhaps he simply sought a lucrative trade. At Berengera's Amoskeag rate of pay, as for most factory girls, his ten-dollar fee was more than two months' wages.

Even when giving his motivation the benefit of the doubt, it is not hard to imagine that Smith felt a great sense of urgency to cover up this death. When the patient died during the course of an abortion, the provider could be charged with murder, regardless that he clearly had no intention of killing her. A large wedding was scheduled to be held on December 26 in the parlor of the multifamily dwelling where Berengera had died. Fearing detection and unwanted attention to his abortion practice, it appears Smith took a board from his stable, tied Berengera's body to it, and placed her in Woodbury Brook, which ran near his home. It seems likely that someone helped Smith carry the six-foot-long board with Berengera's body to the water, but whoever that might have been is unknown. The brook funneled into a drain, passed between two dwelling houses, and then crossed under Storer Street. Where the brook crossed under the road beneath a stone covering, the culvert was four feet wide and six feet deep. The brook emptied into the Saco River two blocks away; the river, in turn, passed by the textile mills, powering the looms, and headed to the Atlantic.

After Smith returned to his home, Berengera's body began its journey to the sea, but it didn't get far. Unbeknownst to Smith, under the wide road, the path of the brook made several sharp turns. Berengera's body became wedged at the first of these, out of sight under the culvert walkway. There she stayed, partially submerged and buried under snow, ice, and accumulating debris from late December until April 13, 1850, when the first sunny day of the season urged neighbors to do some spring cleaning. News of the body's discovery traveled rapidly around Saco and no doubt reached the Smith household quickly. When Smith learned the gruesome news, he muttered, "Ah, they have found Mary." And the young Ann Coveny overheard. Testimony in the later murder trial revealed what happened next. Smith got to work removing the remaining evidence. In the four months since Berengera's death, Smith had given away, and in some cases attempted to sell, her clothing. A month after her death, Smith approached William Long, looking for money and asking about Berengera's other trunk, still at Mrs. Means's boardinghouse. Smith suggested that Long retrieve it, but he refused. Smith feigned indifference but took a sleigh and Henry Wentworth's light gray horse, Little Mouse, and went to the Means's residence himself, collecting the trunk. When Mrs. Means asked about Berengera's unpaid bill, Smith quibbled over the amount but eventually paid the long overdue charge of one dollar for a week's worth of room and board. He told Mrs. Means, who was concerned by her lengthy absence, that Berengera had left quickly to take care of family in the east and was only now calling for her trunk as she headed west. The story satisfied her, and as the winter months went by, no one, it appears, missed Mary Bean.

With public memory of Mary Bean fading, Smith had almost escaped detection. That is, until that April Saturday when Berengera's body unexpectedly reappeared and Smith once again feared discovery. On Sunday, Smith worked quickly to erase the remnants of his boarder's presence in his home. He burned the leather trunk with her identifying initials tapped out in brass buttons on its end. He scrawled his own name in pencil on her wooden trunk, as if it were his all along. He then took his black medical satchel down from its resting place in the hall closet and removed his wire instruments. He broke them into pieces and threw the bits into his airtight parlor stove. His efforts were futile. The next day, Monday, April 15, Constable Lane searched Smith's house and uncovered the curious contents of his stove, retrieving nails, hairpins, bits of metal buttons, and broken wires. Two days later, Smith was arrested and charged with the death of Mary Bean.

Newspapers struggled to keep on top of new developments. On Monday, April 15, the Portland *Eastern Argus* was one of the first newspapers to publish news of the "Dead Body Found!" Stimulating shock and mystery, the paper described the victim: "She was *enceinte* and *her hands were tied!*"[66] Because the Saco and Biddeford papers were weeklies, they were often out of sync with the fast-moving case. To address this discontinuity, the *Maine Democrat, Saco Union* and the *Biddeford Advertiser* printed one-page daily "extras" so readers could know the latest news. "Our purpose," stated the editor of the *Democrat*, "is to give our readers the earliest information of all the important facts of the case."[67] The extras were sent by train and stage to newspaper editors in Portland, Lowell, Boston, and elsewhere, facilitating the spread of this story. In Saco, the extras were sold to customers very willing to pay six cents for the latest information quite literally hot off the press. The *Maine Democrat* leapt at the chance to publish the daily testimony. The nameplate of the April 23 extra reflects the feeling of urgency—the "M" in Maine was printed upside down, this typographic error never corrected in the haste to publish.[68]

Murder was not an unusual topic for local papers. In the newspapers and in hundreds of pamphlets, crime reports, and works of sensational fiction, it was examined, explored, and explained. Murder had long been considered an appropriate literary subject: in the seventeenth and eighteenth centuries, execution sermons replayed the details of crime to remind colonists that all humans were innately evil, warning—in oral

THE MAINE DEMOCRAT.
EXTRA.
The Smith Trial.
FOR THE MURDER OF MARY BEAN, AT SACO.
Saco, Monday, afternoon, April 22, 1850.

MONDAY, p. m. April 22. The examination of Dr. Smith was expected to commence this morning at nine o'clock, when it was hoped Judge Greene would be able to be present. But his health not being sufficiently restored to make it prudent for him to be exposed in the present rainy weather, a consultation of the counsel took place, when it was agreed to go on with the examination in the afternoon before such Recorder as the Judge should appoint.

Notwithstanding the rain, a large crowd of persons had assembled in front of the hall before the hour named for the opening. The doors were opened about a quarter past two, and the hall was immediately filled. The seats will accommodate six hundred persons, and they were all occupied. In the concourse we noticed many people from neighboring towns, called together by the unusual occurrence of a trial of

twenty second day of December now last past, at Saco aforesaid, in the county aforesaid, did suffer and languish, and languishing did live, on which said twenty second day of said December, at Saco aforesaid, in the county aforesaid, she the said Mary Bean of the wound aforesaid, died—and so the complainant aforesaid, upon his oath aforesaid, does say that the said James H. Smith her the said Mary Bean, in manner and form aforesaid, then and there, feloniously, wilfully, and of his malice aforethought, did kill and murder, against the peace of said State, and contrary to the form of the statute in such case made and provided.

And the said James J. Wiggin, on his oath aforesaid, further complains that the said James H. Smith of Saco aforesaid, in the county aforesaid, yeoman, on the fifteenth day of December now last past, at Saco aforesaid, in the county aforesaid, in and upon a certain woman called and known by the name of Mary Bean.

The *Maine Democrat Extra*, April 22, 1850. The shocking news of the discovery of Caswell's body was broadcast in single sheet "extras," sold for six cents. The printer of this edition was in such haste he set the letter "M" in Maine upside down. From the collection of the Dyer Library/Saco Museum, Saco, Maine.

and later printed form—that anyone could commit sin unless he or she diligently adhered to the path of righteousness. By the first quarter of the nineteenth century, crime literature and ideas about inborn evil were changing. Evil was no longer understood to be embedded in all members of society; rather, it came forth only in aberrant individuals who could be stimulated to commit crime by forces such as lacking religion, overindulging in alcohol, or reading the wrong books. In the 1830s stories of murder found a comfortable home in the penny press, newspapers sold by the single issue rather than by annual subscription. Editors quickly discovered that featuring stories about the latest murder boosted newspaper sales. So popular a topic was crime that in the 1840s the *National Police Gazette* was created to feature news about it. City newspapers often dedicated entire columns to crime or court reports, feeding both the interest in and the anxiety about criminal activity. Crimes reported in the newspapers, especially the high-profile cases that covered several days in court, were often subsequently reprinted in pamphlet form, further enhancing their profit-making potential. For publishers, crime, in fact, did pay.[69]

Saco readers had seen a steady stream of murder stories in local papers. In the weeks surrounding the Mary Bean case, the *Maine Democrat* reported on several New England crimes, including Daniel Pearson's "horrid murder" of his wife and twin four-year-old daughters near Andover, Massachusetts.[70] Pearson's trial, conviction, and request for commutation of his death sentence made for exciting reading throughout the spring and summer. Pearson, who had killed his estranged family with an ax, was hung for his crime. Newspaper reports about the poisoning of the Gillingham family gave readers a reason to reflect on their own household help when the culprit was revealed to be the Gillingham's thirteen-year-old servant, Ann Tinker. And readers eagerly followed developments in the infamous "Harvard Murder of 1849." Sixty thousand people would view the trial of medical college professor John Webster for the murder of Dr. George Parkman, whose disarticulated remains were found in a sewerage vault among the waste from dissected corpses.[71] Thousands more would read the details in newspapers. Murder was entertainment: life-size statues of Webster and Parkman were exhibited in Portland's Union Hall; tickets were twelve and a half cents. Similarly, the details of the Mary Bean case filled the newspaper. The editor of the *Maine Democrat* apologized for how much space this topic took but noted its "importance" and how "general desire" justified the stream of information.[72] Not everyone approved of such an unseemly matter discussed in the public papers: the *Portland Transcript* observed, "This depraved taste for murderous reading is a great evil in society, and is shamefully pandered to by many sheets whose conductors rather than disappoint their patrons of their daily stimulus, do not hesitate to manufacture a few 'mysterious occurrences' and 'horrible developments.'"[73] The *Saco Union* refused to publish such tawdry news, but the intense interest in the Mary Bean case led to a revised editorial policy. Alpheus A. Hanscom, editor of the *Maine Democrat*, took great glee in pointing out this change, noticing how *Union* editor Louis O. Cowan was now "gratifying the populace and filling his pockets with pennies."[74]

The coroner's inquest jury's verdict was printed in the Saturday papers, and the town was abuzz with the news. A ghastly death, an unChristian burial—what was this town coming to? Some newspapers printed the findings verbatim, others merely stated that she had been "enceinte," for decorum's sake not using the English word "pregnant," let alone mentioning the abortion. Readers could no doubt fill in the blanks. The coroner gave the inquest findings to the constable, who then approached the local municipal judge, Frederick Greene, to lodge a formal complaint against the alleged perpetrator, James Smith. Since this was considered murder, Constable Wiggin lodged the complaint on behalf of the state of Maine. Judge Greene convened a municipal court hearing to determine whether the complaint had merit. Attorneys would be present to argue or refute the evidence. If Judge Greene found substance to the complaint, he had the authority to order Smith held for trial. The hearing was scheduled to begin on Friday, April 19, but the judge's sudden illness forced a postponement until the following Monday. Between gossip and the newspaper extras, information was plentiful and "groups of persons [were] seen in the streets at almost every hour in the day discussing the tragical affair."[75]

Curiosity, intrigue, and newspaper coverage brought hundreds of people from well beyond Saco to hear more details of this "horrid murder." As the proceedings began, "[Cutts] Hall was thronged with spectators" as over six hundred people jammed into the largest meeting room in Saco, located on Cutts Island near the factories that had provided work and the stores, public squares, and libraries that were venues for other entertainment.[76] The curious pressed the interior capacity to its limits and hundreds more lingered outside in the rain. Although the room was packed, women were few and far between, one reporter seeing only Elizabeth Elden, who had been summoned to testify, and one other woman. The audience was filled with anticipation, but Judge Greene remained ill, and the hearing was delayed yet again, testing the patience of the crowd. In Greene's place, Saco attorney John Goodwin would record the evidence and relay the information to the housebound judge. By 2:00 p.m. the court was finally ready to proceed. Smith stood and listened calmly as the handwritten complaint, many pages in length, was read. The *Maine Democrat* recorded that the audience listened in "profound silence."[77] Smith was accused of causing Bean's death by one or more of five methods: strangulation, administration of savin, a mortal wound with a wire instrument, a mortal wound with an unknown instrument, or by some manner as yet unknown. In effect, the multiple causes, mocked by the editor of the *Portland Pleasure Boat*, who lambasted Constable Wiggin for swearing one man could kill one woman five ways over seven days, covered the prosecution's bases.[78] Smith had killed Caswell—of this the coroner's jury, Constable Wiggin, and the prosecuting attorneys were sure. Exactly which action ultimately killed her, the prosecution left open.

The hearing was a drama, being played out very much like a play on a stage. Audiences in Cutts Hall were used to seeing performances in this venue, and although this was a legal hearing, many of the same elements of more familiar entertainment were present: drama, mystery, a beautiful victim, and a cold-hearted villain. Alpheus Hanscom, reporting for the *Democrat*, set the scene, providing his readers with a detailed description of the principal players and setting. Three long tables on top of a raised platform faced the assembled crowd. At the center table, the key individuals sat: recorder John Goodwin, the prosecuting attorneys, the defense attorneys, and James Smith, a man of "prepossessing appearance."[79] Goodwin sat at the center, and to his right was Smith, flanked by his attorneys Lorenzo D. Wilkinson and Rufus Tapley, both of Saco. To Goodwin's left were the prosecutors Thomas Hayes and Joseph W. Leland, who lived on Storer Street just a short distance from where the body was found. The remaining two tables provided seats to reporters (on a first-come basis) and local authorities—including coroner Tufts, Constables Lane and Wiggin, and Saco and Biddeford justices. Witnesses sat throughout the hall; when called, each would approach and sit facing this stage. This made it hard to hear, and when a particularly long-winded or low-voiced witness droned on, the crowd grew restless. But one stern look from Constable Lane silenced any chatter. Despite the serious nature of the alleged crime, Smith, a short, stocky man of middling size with light eyes, coarse features, and a complexion "as ruddy as a summer's morning," was calm, even jovial, "and at times was quite jocose in his remarks."[80] He joked with the reporters about his "devilishly pretty" wife, and at one point, while waiting for the day's proceedings to begin, sat and read the newspaper reports of his own case. Newspapers often printed detailed accounts of trials, especially the more salacious cases. Afterward, printed pamphlets captured and replayed the crime from start to finish, reprinting trial testimony for a wider audience and unfolding the crime with great drama and mystery. In effect, newspaper coverage and true-crime pamphlets provided a familiar script for those watching the trial. With the abundance of crime literature available by 1850, the Saco audience and the attorneys were already well acquainted with this type of performance—in the same way that many Americans today imagine judicial procedures from their experience with television shows from *Law & Order* to *The People's Court*.[81]

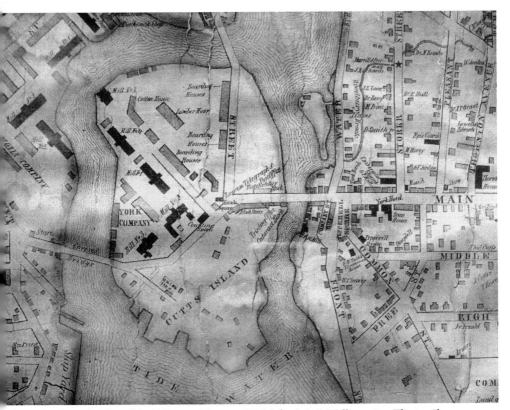

Portion of a Map of the Villages of Saco and Biddeford, A. F. Walling, 1851. The textile factories and mill worker boardinghouses were located on Cutts and Gooch Islands in the Saco River between Biddeford (left) and Saco (right). Woodbury Brook enters this image from the upper right, crosses Storer Street, and continues to the river. The star on Storer Street marks the approximate location of Berengera Caswell's body. Dr. James Smith lived nearby. From the collection of the Dyer Library/Saco Museum, Saco, Maine.

The examination began with a lengthy opening statement. Prosecutor Thomas M. Hayes spoke for an hour and a half. He decried this murder of citizen by citizen, the first, he claimed, in Saco's history. He noted the large crowd as evidence of community outrage and a demand for justice for the young woman still known only as Mary Bean, downplaying the morbid curiosity of the capacity audience well-schooled in murder mysteries and crime news. Hayes attempted to keep the spectators focused on the crime committed and the laws broken, rather than the titillating exposé the hearing promised, asserting, and perhaps warning, "this scene is not to them one of tragic and romantic interest alone."[82] He spoke of the town's duty to the victim and to protect its own members by punishing the transgressor. He argued "the very name of murder, as it falls upon the ear, startles and alarms. [It] excites in us feelings of horror and indignation. But the murder of a young and beautiful woman . . . under circumstances the most revolting to humanity, may well excite an interest amounting almost to agony."[83] To that end, he pointed out facts of law in the definition of murder and malice aforethought, setting the stage for a later battle over words and intent. The drawn-out legal definitions and slow pace of the hearing frustrated the crowd of curious onlookers, who anxiously awaited the sordid details and the twists and turns like those found in sensational fiction. But still, lawyers knew the hallmarks of crime literature, too, and with great drama, Hayes hinted that there was new information, shocking information learned just a few hours ago that would be revealed in due course. This electrified the crowd, who murmured and speculated about just what this could be.

The onlookers found they had more time for speculation and gossip. After ninety minutes of opening remarks, Osgood Stevens was called to the stand, but before he could testify, the court officers left Cutts Hall to examine the culvert where the body was found. Many in the audience had already visited Berengera's icy resting place, now quite the tourist destination much to the dismay of Smith's neighbors. When the court officers returned, finally, the examination got under way. On this first day, testimony included Osgood Stevens's description of how he discovered the body in the brook. Theodore Stevens, Samuel Brooks, and Daniel Brooks confirmed the details of discovery, the physical appearance of the corpse, and the process of moving the body from the brook to the barn. The court adjourned for the day with little revealed but with tantalizing new information promised.

On Tuesday, April 23, the bad weather continued and the testimony turned grisly. Despite the rain and cold a large crowd gathered, drawn by the hints that Hayes had dropped Monday afternoon and a rumor that "new facts had come to the knowledge of the government, which would disclose for certainty who the deceased woman was."[84] This long day of testimony began at nine, broke for lunch at noon, resumed at two, and continued all afternoon. Thomas Tufts and James Wiggin spoke about the evidence discovered in Smith's home as well as the telltale plank. Dr. Hall read a graphic autopsy account, detailing the extent of the victim's inflammation and internal infection. His language was scientific and precise. "During the entire cross-examination, which was very minute, he showed a most thorough and exact knowledge of the matters to which he testified."[85] Some newspapers refused to carry the detailed account of ripped organs; black fluid; and acrid, metallic stench. The *Union*, explaining its decision to condense the doctors' testimony, reported how "it contains allusions to the human system and to the appearances of parts of the body in this case, which although necessary to be presented in court, are not necessary to be made public."[86] Doctors Goodwin and Fessenden spoke in support of Hall's conclusion, stating that typhoid (Smith's defense) was not at all in evidence in Mary Bean's body. The physicians affirmed the multiple medical examinations had been "very critical and accurate" and "so thorough as to preclude the idea that she died of [typhoid] fever."[87] The postmortem indicated that Bean had "enjoyed a good degree of health . . . [with] an unusually healthy state of the lungs [and] the absence of nearly all evidence of disease" and concluded that she "would not miscarry from any natural cause."[88] In response to the defense attorney's question, Hall remarked that this had been her only pregnancy. Hall then described the use of savin and other abortifacients and gave a chilling description of abortion instruments, including a cannula with a retractable knifelike stylet. He emphasized the extreme skill needed to operate these tools, skill few trained regular physicians had, let alone, Hall clearly implied, an unschooled botanic physician.

The medical testimony indicated how she died, but how did this victim come into Smith's hands? Prosecuting attorneys now attempted to place Mary Bean at Smith's residence. Several of Smith's neighbors saw her at Smith's house in November and December 1849. Ten-year-old George Lane remembered buying milk from a woman he described as "fleshy and large."[89] The common transaction was etched in his mind because she wore large "knob and drop" earrings, clearly visible, with her hair bound up in a white kerchief. Changes in hairstyles in the 1840s led the wearing of earrings to fall out of fashion; Bean's earrings were so novel a sight to George that he ran home and told his mother what he had seen.[90] Critically, the young boy had also seen Smith prepare some sort of medicine and give it to Mary to drink. Smith and Bean's relationship, this suggested, was one of doctor and patient.

Mary Bean had been Smith's patient, but for what purpose? Typhoid, as Dr. Smith claimed, or abortion, as Dr. Hall contended? Perhaps she simply went to Smith to relieve her obstructed menstrual flow. In this hearing, it was up to women to provide the evidence that Mary Bean had indeed been pregnant and not simply blocked, a critical distinction for the prosecution's case. Bridget Ash, a Storer Street laundress, offered specific and pungent details. She washed twice for Smith, the first time around December 15, the date of the abortion. In the laundry, Mrs. Ash found skirts and linen with familiar stains and the distinctive odor of amniotic fluid—sweet, musky, and sharp—that came from one "confined." She noted similar blots and smells on the female clothing and linens she washed a little more than a week later, the day after Mary's death. Smith's attorneys questioned her as to whom the linens likely belonged, and she identified Mary Bean. The defense suggested that the clothes belonged to Smith's wife, Sarah, who may have soiled the linens with menstrual fluid, but Ash defended her observation despite the attorney's doubt of her olfactory knowledge. Further, Ash testified that she had seen Mary at the Smiths' and by her appearance knew that she was pregnant. Harriet Brown and Sarah Hooper, Biddeford factory girls with whom Caswell briefly lived at Mrs. Means's boardinghouse, said that "from her appearance, [each] thought her pregnant." Sarah Bryant, a neighbor to Smith, also recognized Berengera's pregnancy. When the defense attorney challenged this conclusion, doubtful of her visual knowledge, Bryant shot back that at sixty-seven years old she "ought to be able to tell when a woman is pregnant."[91] While the examination plodded along in meticulous fashion, local gossip was moving at a rapid pace. The rumor circulated that Mary Bean was not who she appeared to be. In fact, she was not from somewhere in Eastern Maine as previous news reports had stated: she was from Canada and was really a young woman named Berengera Caswell. Berengera's story, masked by the assigned persona of Mary Bean, was coming back to life.

On Wednesday morning, the third day of Smith's examination, the skies finally cleared. It was a typical Maine spring day with a bright blue sky and bracing air. It seems that gossip and the daily extras were more intriguing than sitting in stuffy Cutts Hall—only two hundred people appeared to hear what turned out to be the last day of testimony. But this day offered important information proving that James Smith was an abortionist and linking the young woman known in Saco as Mary Bean to the Canadian factory girl Berengera Caswell. James Tuttle and Rebecca Pike recalled conversations they had had with Smith in the fall of 1849. He had chatted with Tuttle at the Saco House about a pregnant woman at his home and the tools and methods he used for abortion. Tuttle recalled Smith's detailed description, providing evidence that he had owned the tools of the trade. Here again the newspaper edited the testimony, reporting that "a portion of the testimony [was omitted] on account of its grossness."[92] Rebecca Pike told how Smith had approached her to take on the boarding of a pregnant woman whom he had been "doctoring" longer than he had intended and how she had turned him down. Together, Pike's and Tuttle's testimony placed Smith in the abortion business.

The star of the day, though, was the young Irish immigrant Ann Coveny, whose testimony placed into Smith's hands the tools and a pregnant girl she knew as Mary Bean. When first summoned during the coroner's inquest, she ran away to her brothers in Biddeford, afraid of Smith and scared to speak before Saco officials. But Ann had confessed what she knew to her sister and in turn, her brothers, who convinced her to do what was right, or at least to keep the immigrant family out of trouble, and she came forward with her testimony. Ann had lived with the Smiths for nearly eighteen months, and she had seen much. Coveny described how Smith alone would use the black bag from the hall closet and how he would take girls into his parlor behind closed doors. No one else ever touched the bag or entered the parlor when Smith was in it. She recalled Bean's November 1849 arrival, remembering the long earrings that "fell down below her ear."[93] Coveny told how Mary got sick after December 15, taking to her bed. Ann revealed that while she had never been heard to utter a word of complaint during her first few weeks at the Smiths, following the abortion, she cried out in pain. Ann recalled the last night of the woman she'd known as Mary Bean. On Saturday evening, December 22, Ann approached her, lying alone in the front parlor, and asked if she could get her anything. All Berengera could manage was to look at her, too ill to speak.

Coveny continued her damning testimony. Ann identified William Long as the young man who repeatedly and dutifully visited Mary. She remembered him because he wore the same outfit on each visit: green pants, a black frock coat, and a hat. On December 23, Long appeared for his usual Sunday visit. Smith told Ann to take his two young children upstairs while he led Long into the parlor. When Ann came back to the kitchen fifteen minutes later, Long hurried out of the parlor, grabbed his cap, and left. She never saw him again. The reason for Coveny's fear of Smith became clear as she continued her testimony. On that day, Smith brought Ann into the parlor to view Mary's sheet-covered body, told her that Mary had succumbed to typhoid, and swore her to confidence. In exchange for her silence, Smith gave Coveny an apron, one Mary had worn. When Caswell's body reappeared in April, Smith reminded Ann of her vow, threatening to kill her and causing her terrified flight to her brothers' protection. Smith's wife, Sarah, the *Portland Advertiser* alleged, had also tormented Coveny, telling the frightened girl that if Smith went to prison, his family would be left alone and poor and Coveny would be put out on the street.[94] Sarah Smith later gave Ann stockings and shoes from Bean's trunk "and [Sarah] thought it no harm to take them."[95] Coveny's testimony was devastating, but she knew the deceased only as Mary Bean. Long claimed the victim was actually named Berengera Caswell, but the complaint charged Smith with the murder of Mary Bean. It was up to William Long to make the connection between Bean and Caswell and seal Smith's fate.

William Long took the court through his story, beginning with how he met Berengera in Manchester around the end of June or early July 1849 and began to keep her company. William admitted how he "was on terms of unlawful intimacy," revealing in public his private relations.[96] He described how he left Manchester in September and next saw Berengera two months later in November at the counting room of the Water Power Company. Hayes asked what everyone present wanted to know: When did Berengera tell him she was pregnant? Did she want the abortion? Did she tell William what Smith had done to her? The *New Hampshire Patriot* reported that Berengera told William that Smith used a wire instrument, but the defense attorneys objected to this statement.[97] At this point, the lawyers engaged in a protracted argument about testimony from a dead person. Unfortunately for us, the judge ruled that Berengera's declarations were hearsay and thus inadmissible, leaving the substance of the young lovers' conversations a mystery and Berengera without a voice, even one mediated by William Long.[98] Still, Long was able to describe the tavern meeting and his financial arrangement with Smith: ten dollars in advance and no names. He also reported that when he checked on Berengera that last Sunday in December, Smith told him that she had died from typhoid. Long, showing himself to be a responsible, even thoughtful young man, told Smith that he would see to having the body buried but Smith dismissed him and told Long he had "partly made arrangements for that myself."[99] It was at this point that Long left the Smith house, passing Ann Coveny in the kitchen as he hurried away. Long continued this sad tale. He described how Smith came to him in January, seeking more money and the other traveling trunk. When Long had no money to offer and no interest in retrieving his dead girlfriend's possessions, Smith, angry, told him that Mary had not died from typhoid. Cruelly, he informed Long that she had died in childbirth and that she had delivered a son as big as Smith's fist.[100] Long asked where Smith had buried Berengera, but he dodged the question, telling Long he would reveal that information some other time. In his final testimony of the day, Long confirmed that the woman he knew as Berengera Caswell and the woman Smith called Mary Bean were one and the same. The prosecution rested. The defense had nothing to say.

News traveled fast, and the next morning the hall was once again filled to capacity with a crowd anxious to hear the judge's verdict. The medical evidence against Smith was considerable. The evidence that Smith placed Caswell in the stream was deemed circumstantial, but taken together, Smith lying about typhoid, burning Caswell's trunk, and misleading investigators "formed a chain of great importance."[101] Goodwin had taken his transcripts to Judge Greene, still recuperating from his illness. Both judges were in agreement: the evidence convinced the court that Smith had likely committed murder. Goodwin relayed the decision to the assembled crowd in a statement that lasted an hour and a half. He reviewed the evidence provided by Tuttle, Coveny, and Long and spoke of duty to the residents of Saco. Key points of evidence included the plank from Smith's barn and Caswell's clothing in his possession. Goodwin praised the physicians' detailed examination of the body, stating how their evidence had "great weight" from such "scientific men," an indication of the growing recognition of "expert" testimony in nineteenth-century court cases.[102] No mention was made of the women's contributions to the debate over Caswell's reproductive state. Smith would be charged with murder and would face that charge at the fall session of the Supreme Judicial Court. No bail was possible. Although he had remained lighthearted during the examination, Smith became emotional as he bid his family good-bye. From Saco's municipal court, the case moved on to the Maine attorney general, Henry Tallman, who would draw up the papers seeking an indictment. Smith was taken to the York County jail, in the village of Alfred, to await his September trial. Assuming that Long had seduced Caswell (and not the other way around), some felt William deserved to be punished alongside Smith: "The seducer of the girl who is equally guilty, is not only permitted to run at large, but is received in court as an evidence against Smith! Strange concerns are these courts of justice!"[103] Long was ordered to put up $1,000 surety to make certain he would appear at the trial; Ann Coveny and James Tuttle were charged $200 each to guarantee their appearances. Although the

Saco Union "supposed [Long] would find difficulty in procuring bail" the *Maine Democrat* reported that all the principle witnesses did so.[104]

Newspapers across New England, including those in Manchester, New Hampshire, had carried the news of Smith's arrest for the murder of Mary Bean. While the examination began in Saco, Thais Caswell, still hard at work in the Amoskeag Mill and living at Mrs. E. B. McFarland's boardinghouse on Elm Street, read of the shocking discovery of the Saco body and very shortly learned that Mary Bean was, in fact, the sister whom she had not seen since September 1849. With great trepidation, Thais sought assistance from the Manchester city marshal, who helped her send a letter to his counterpart in Saco, T. K. Lane. Unlike the many other letters the constable had received, Thais's letter contained key details that rang true with the constable, including information about clothing Berengera had owned and that Lane recalled seeing at the Smith residence. Lane invited her to Saco; she arrived on Monday, April 29. He served as her chaperone, guiding her around town and providing Thais a room in his own home. Lane took her to Sarah Means's boardinghouse, where some of Berengera's clothing, overlooked by Smith in his haste to remove her trunk, still hung in a closet. At Smith's Storer Street home Thais identified her sister's black shawl and the remaining traveling trunk (despite Smith's added signature). In her letter to Lane, Thais had described her sister's unusually shaped bead purse in which she had "been in the practice of hoarding up bright five cent pieces out of fancy."[105] The purse, with thirty shiny nickels and a gold dollar, was at the house. Sarah Smith claimed the black shawl and purse were hers, gifts given by her husband the previous fall.

Thais's identification of her sister's possessions would prove invaluable in the coming murder trial, but her reason for the journey was more personal. She wanted to take Berengera's body home for burial. Constable Lane, moved by the sad situation, solicited donations from Saco residents. The mill agent, in charge of the day-to-day operations of the mill, was particularly generous, donating fifty dollars. With the money raised, somewhere between seventy-five and one hundred dollars, Berengera was disinterred one final time.[106] On May 1, Thais placed Berengera in a walnut coffin and began the journey home. The railroad carried her without charge. Maine and New Hampshire newspapers reported that Thais planned to take Berengera to Canada, but Caswell family history places Berengera's grave in Manchester, New Hampshire.[107] Although Thais had enough funds for the journey home, a Manchester cemetery makes sense.

The lack of trains to Brompton, the hot summer weather, and the absence of embalming technology supported a New Hampshire burial. There is no way to know, but perhaps her family did not want a hometown funeral, with too painful and shameful an episode to make so public. Or perhaps Thais wished to spare her parents any additional grief. It is possible she never told her parents the real circumstances of her sister's death, although with newspapers covering this story so intensely, it is probable that someone from the Brompton area, perhaps reading the coverage in Manchester or Lowell, sent word, and newspaper clippings, home. Whether by way of expediency or emotion, a Manchester plot was available for Berengera's coffin. Ruth Caswell's soon-to-be second husband, William Reynolds, had just purchased a family burial site in the new Valley Street cemetery, not far from the Amoskeag mills where Berengera once worked. Her sisters laid her to rest in early May. Later in the century, her name was added to a family monument in Quebec in the Greenlay Protestant Cemetery, which holds the remains of her parents and two siblings who had died as children, Stephen Abiel (died 1846 at age thirteen) and Tabitha Almira (died 1845, age ten). Interestingly, her middle name is misspelled on the monument—Dolcon instead of Dalton—the passage of time blurring the memory of her life and death.[108]

Throughout the summer, Smith's attorneys prepared his defense while state attorney general Tallman and the attorney for York County, Ira T. Drew of Waterboro, prepared the case against him. The indictment condensed to four the five possible causes of death in the original complaint, omitting the charge that Smith had strangled Caswell. In September, the grand jury reviewed the indictment and listened to twenty-four witnesses for the prosecution (each of whom was paid one dollar a day plus four cents a mile for their service), returning a true bill, a finding that kept Smith in jail awaiting his Supreme Court trial. Smith pleaded not guilty and placed himself on the mercy of the court, claiming poverty and requesting a court-appointed lawyer. Nathan Clifford became Smith's lead attorney, a very fortunate turn of events for Smith. Clifford had been a member of the U.S. Congress, was appointed U.S. attorney general by President Polk, and had just returned to Maine to reestablish his law practice. A talented attorney, Clifford would be appointed to the U.S. Supreme Court within the decade, but in 1850 he was living in an elegant home in Portland. Clifford asked for a postponement in order to prepare his argument. Since the fall court schedule was tightly booked with numerous cases, the court readily agreed to move Smith's murder

Nathan Clifford, ca. 1855. Clifford provided James Smith's defense during the January 1851 murder trial. Library of Congress.

trial (likely to be time consuming) to a special January term. Meanwhile, Smith remained at the county jail in Alfred, the York County seat.

The trial began in January 1851. Despite the cold winter weather, crowds flocked to the county courthouse in Alfred, fifteen miles west and a bit south of Saco. Alfred residents were long familiar with big trials and the publicity and crowds they brought, a boon to the village's boardinghouses and hotels, which were filled to capacity with lawyers, jurors, witnesses, and the curious who flocked to the small village to watch the Smith trial.[109] Nathan Clifford enjoyed trials in Alfred. As his biographer noted and photographs of the rotund attorney document, "during the sessions of court, the ladies of Alfred kept open house. Judges and attorneys often met in friendly relaxation over dishes prepared by the proud housewife herself in honor of the expected guests. Many stories are told of these feasts in which Mr. Clifford's love for the good things of the table is shown."[110]

The trial began with jury selection, which Smith and his attorneys turned into a protracted procedure. During the 1850 hearing, Smith had been content to sit back and observe, often joking with reporters. Perhaps he did not expect to be committed to jail. But several months in the York County jail had a physical effect and Smith's attitude had changed as well. He looked pale "and appear[ed] not quite so robust as before his confinement."[111] Nonetheless, during the trial Smith took an active role, seeming "composed but very attentive to the proceedings" especially in employing his right to challenge potential jurors.[112] Smith and his attorneys objected to numerous jurors, many on the basis that they had previously read about the case in the newspapers and would have already formed an opinion about Smith's guilt. Fifty-seven men had been called as possible jurors, three were regularly summoned, and the rest were selected as "talesmen," plucked for duty from among the bystanders. Ten men were dismissed on peremptory challenges, and thirty-five were disqualified on the grounds of already having formed an opinion from reading the newspaper coverage. Not surprisingly, editors of the local papers took issue with dismissing readers, their customers, and opined that it would be far worse to have a jury of illiterate country rubes. The *Biddeford Mercantile Advertiser* editor argued, "A man who does not take or read a newspaper should never be drawn as a juror, and this we judged was the case of some of the persons called."[113] The local citizens took issue with this insult, and in the following week's editorial, the editor apologized and indicated the dig was directed at Smith, once described as a man who does not appear to "possess intellect above mediocrity."[114] After a day of challenges and legal maneuvers, the jury was at last seated and the trial began in earnest.[115]

Reporters from Maine and the rest of New England attended the trial but newspapers published much less detail than they had in the coverage of the previous year's examination. The newspapers reported only new information, as the previous revelations, just as Smith's attorneys had argued, were well known. As the evidence against Smith was over-whelming, in many ways the trial was "old news." The trial began much like the previous year's examination, with Osgood Stevens's discovery of the body and the clues that led to James Smith's arrest. Witnesses noted Berengera's arrival and departure from Mrs. Means's boardinghouse as well as her visits with William Long prior to her fateful stay at Smith's.

Although James Smith was on trial for murder, the newspaper ac-counts of the testimony make clear that the behavior of young men and women was keenly under review. The two witnesses who knew Berengera best, William Long and Thais Caswell, provided key testi-mony and both found themselves scrutinized by the attorneys. In addi-tion, the physicians' testimony, although medical in nature, revealed a cultural and community anxiety about the consequences of what was seen as inappropriate social and moral behavior. Troubling for those in the court and beyond, Berengera's story portrayed two personas: a naive girl and a knowing woman. Her body mirrored these dichotomous images, displaying evidence of a growing separation between sexuality and reproduction that troubled mid-nineteenth-century society and pervaded literature of the 1840s.[116]

During the second day of testimony, the physicians gave "a minute account of the appearance of the several parts of the body," detailed information on the state of Berengera's physical being.[117] Internally the body spoke of sexual activity and the awful consequences of the unskilled attempt to end that pregnancy. In sickening detail physicians related the physical state of putrefaction and sepsis. So unsettling was the testimony that more than one paper declared that the information was simply "too gross" to be printed. Yet, the coroner's report and the newspaper coverage of it in both the preliminary hearing and the murder trial had an erotic element, with lingering descriptions of Berengera's breasts (strangely described as the right size for a virgin), fulsome thighs, and finely tapered legs. And although discussion of a uterus was regarded as "too gross," there was little difficulty printing the gory details of her rat-gnawed face and neck, a vicarious horror show as readers visualized the desecration of Caswell's body. Berengera's body presented a troubling image of female youth. She was virginal in appearance, yet had been pregnant. It was acceptable to linger on the details of the exterior body, lurid as those details may have been, yet to expose the consequences of acting on sexual stimuli was out of bounds. The autopsy report led the reader to contemplate Caswell's internal physiology, an image of sexual activity that countered the stereotype of the naive passive victim.[118] Thais Caswell's testimony continued the troubling imagery, unintentionally painting a portrait of a young woman too independent for her own, or society's, good.

The younger Caswell's testimony was covered in great detail in the newspapers, as she had not testified during the April 1850 hearing. She recounted their personal history as factory girls, traveling from their rural home in Canada with their sister Ruth and leaving behind their parents, sisters, and brothers. The attorneys and newspapers made a point of describing in detail the number of Caswell siblings, drawing a picture of the domestic sphere Berengera had left behind. A year before the murder trial, in May 1850, newspaper readers learned how the dutiful younger sister had arrived in Saco. Under the watchful eye and protection of Constable T. K. Lane, Thais had identified Berengera's clothing and, thanks to the generosity of Saco's citizens, accompanied her victim-sister's body home for burial. This was one portrait of Berengera, the unfortunate victim of a cruel seducer. The court now began to imagine a second picture, as Thais described how the Caswell sisters worked first in Lowell, then in Manchester. They, like many factory girls of the period, were independent agents, moving from mill to mill in search of new experiences or better pay and working conditions. They chose when to visit home and when to return to the mills. In this portrayal, they did not need the protection of the local constable or a collection of money—it was a frightening picture of women refusing and denying male authority and economic dominance. These women were in charge of themselves and of their own money. And in her travels around New England, and with her own money, Berengera Caswell obtained clothing. The prosecuting attorneys gave great attention to Berengera's personal belongings, displaying each item in court, while Thais identified her sister's possessions, so many things that she required two trunks when traveling.

Berengera's clothing testified on her behalf. She owned dresses of calico and alpaca, a brown cotton skirt, and a long red crepe scarf; she had a lace veil, an old veil, and a straw bonnet called "Birds Eye [sic] Florence." She owned jewelry, too, including a bosom pin of glass set in gold and knob and drop earrings—both the smaller pair displayed in court and a pair with long drops that hung below her ears.[119] The newspaper reporters were both interested in and bored with this sartorial questioning. While on the one hand, the clothing placed Berengera at Smith's house and confirmed once again that Mary Bean and Berengera Caswell were one and the same, on the other there was apparently a limit to how long one could listen attentively to testimony about women's dresses. At first, the reporter records the clothing in great—and for the historian, helpful—detail noting the fabric, colors, and pattern. By the end of the long afternoon, the reporter simply records repeatedly: "one other calico dress identified." Yet Thais continued to provide detail, despite a restless audience: the pattern of knots Berengera created in her shawl as a means of identification among the many girls' shawls at the mill, "marks and other peculiarities" by which Thais recognized Berengera's clothing. To many of those present in the courtroom, the evidence being displayed was simply a pile of women's dresses. But to Thais, these items told the story of her sister's life. Thais had kept scraps of fabric from Berengera's dresses, a keepsake connection between textile-producing sisters. Thais pointed out which items Berengera had obtained in Manchester and which she had purchased previously, perhaps in Lowell, posthumous remembrances of the places her sister had worked. Thais indicated which of Berengera's items (including a wool skirt and a towel) their mother had woven herself, a touching connection between mother and daughter, both working with textile production, although with different technologies. Although the expected model in such a murder case was an isolated victim, Thais's testimony indicated just how connected Berengera was to a world of women linked by textiles.

While clothing, at least to a degree, was a necessity of living, the accessories were deemed "frippery" and "gewgaws" by the critics of factory girls. The *Maine Democrat*, in an article titled "Woman's Proper Sphere," chided young women "whose precious time is lavished only upon dress and gaiety . . . who wear the bright apparel of the butterfly and are as light and graceful and useless, too. . . . [and] whose conversation finds no higher or more improving subject than . . . the never-failing topic—dress."[120] Attorneys questioned Thais about Berengera's accessories such as hats, scarves, and jewelry. Constable Lane called these possessions "trinkets" and noted that Berengera had sufficient quantities to "fill a two foot trunk."[121] A Biddeford poem entitled "The Factory Girl" scolded young women who spent their "hard earned money, foolishly, for any worthless thing, as many oft do most needlessly."[122] For those opposed to women as wage laborers, factory girls' fondness for these items was taken as evidence of their inability to use money wisely. But for the factory girls, these items were the just rewards of their labor, things they could buy and display with pride. It spoke of their independence and ability to provide for themselves, forgoing the need of men to provide them with necessities or extras. The different fabrics and patterns reflected Berengera's concept of self, her economic abilities, and her connections to other women—her coworkers, sisters, and mother among others—information that women likely noted and understood. To the men, however, the details Thais provided were meaningless. The message to them was quite plain: she owned a lot of clothes and vanities. Too many. In addition, Berengera owned a calling-card rack and the court took note of a card with a man's name imprinted, H. W. Prescott. Thais stated her sister received the card from Prescott in Manchester, but the reporter recorded no other information about him.

Clearly a behavior judgment was being made. While fellow factory girls saw an economic message about the products and rewards of labor, the court viewed a moral lesson, that Berengera was in part, the line of questioning implied, responsible for her fate. Newspapers had already opined that she was said to be the most beautiful of her sex, "her character excepted."[123] The drop earrings, repeatedly noticed by witnesses, were items not usually worn by respectable women of this era, and each mention carried with it an assumed understanding of her morals, where a particular style of dress indicated an invitation to certain behaviors. Her abundant clothing, assumed extravagant spending, and supposed association with multiple Manchester men painted a far different picture than that of the poor, friendless victim pulled from Woodbury Brook. Thais's description of Berengera's clothing had in part made the victim a party to her own death in a murder trial that also reviewed and disciplined women's behavior.[124]

While Berengera's behavior was examined posthumously, William Long's actions were scrutinized in a grueling afternoon of testimony. Attorneys for both the prosecution and the defense grilled Long about meeting and courting Berengera. Long spoke with "much feeling and apparent sincerity, often shedding tears."[125] The questions became intensely personal: Did he have sexual relations with Berengera? How many times? When was the last time? Attorneys reviewed his barroom meeting with Blake and the arrangements made with Smith. The defense painted him as an arch seducer who was little more than abetting prostitution in using and then abandoning Berengera and perhaps others. Although Smith performed the abortion, the defense worked to cast doubt on Long's character to make him a party to this tragic event. Smith's attorneys produced witnesses to show that Blake was ill in November and thus Long himself delivered Berengera into Smith's hands. Defense witnesses testified that Long's reputation for "truth and veracity" was bad, at least in the barrooms of public houses.[126] The alcohol-centered locale of these allegations suggested Long had led a life of dissipation and associated with disreputable individuals. Although he had left the area in 1842, witnesses recalled that as a ten- to twelve-year-old boy he already had a bad reputation, building a case that as a boy and a young man he was not a model citizen; as the New Hampshire papers phrased it, he was "an illiterate low-lived fellow" and "machine shop rowdy."[127] Long was raked over the coals as his personality and sexual life were made very public. If this experience were not humiliating enough, the prosecution took its turn, countering the defense's portrait of William as a fiend and carefully plotting cad. Instead, the prosecution placed blame squarely on Smith; after all, they argued, Long was far too naive and too much of a rube to be able to mastermind a seduction plot and then walk into court and admit to it. So, he was either a heartless cad or too dumb to plan a seduction. As had happened in the previous year's examination, this interrogation was "extremely crushing and scathing to the witness."[128] Neither the defense nor the prosecution painted a flattering portrait, rather one that served as a warning to young men contemplating a similar lifestyle as that described as Long's.

Despite the aspersions cast on William Long and the deceased Berengera Caswell, the issue at hand was Smith's guilt or innocence of the charge of murder. Witnesses testified about Smith's attempts to sell Berengera's clothing and to board out a pregnant girl. Ann Coveny took the stand for four long hours, repeating her important information on Smith's practice. Despite her gender, youth, and ethnicity, the reporter surmised, Coveny "appears to be a very intelligent, modest girl" who "sustained herself" in the "searching cross-examination," much to the evident surprise and "admiration of all present."[129] Although the $200 surety guaranteed that James Tuttle appeared before the court, it did not guarantee his memory. Strangely, or conveniently for Smith, Tuttle could not recall the conversation in which he and Smith discussed medical instruments used for abortion; "The lapse of time or some other cause appeared to have obliterated the facts from the mind of the witness."[130] But even without Tuttle's testimony, there was considerable evidence against Smith. Defense attorney Nathan Clifford's "argument was ingenious and forcibly presented but he labored under the embarrassment of having the law and evidence against him."[131] It took the jury two hours to reach a verdict: Smith was convicted of second-degree murder and sent to the Maine state prison for life. The outcome of the trial surprised few, and newspapers reported the verdict matter-of-factly.

Smith, one of four murderers among the eighty-seven inmates (and the only one convicted of murder in the second degree), worked in the prison's shoe shop, and prison life seemed to agree with him. He gained twenty pounds and was described as "fat and hearty." He even made himself useful when a prisoner attempted suicide by hanging. With the prison doctor absent, Smith stepped in and helped revive the near-dead man. Perhaps Smith had some medical skill after all.[132]

While Smith embarked on what one newspaper called "his dreary task," his attorneys were making themselves quite useful. It would have been pointless for Nathan Clifford to argue that Smith was innocent of killing Caswell, yet he could argue about the legal meaning of that death. Clifford's appeal offered an alternative storyline to this case. Instead of showing Berengera as the quiet victim of Smith's crooked wire, a manslaughter charge painted a different view—a horrible accident, a bungled procedure, a culpable doctor, but a portrait that suggested Berengera was there by choice. The jury, Clifford suggested in filing this writ, should have considered another possibility: manslaughter. Prior to the trial, he had challenged the accusation of murder, arguing that manslaughter was the appropriate charge. The court set aside his challenge and the trial went ahead as a murder trial. Clifford did not give up. On March 20, 1851, he filed a writ of error—an earlier form of what today we call an appeal—claiming that there were errors in the indictment that have led "to grievous damage of the said James Smith."[133] In this writ, Smith's attorneys identified twenty-two points of contention. The Maine Supreme Court examined the argument and considered it for nearly a year, focusing on three of the causes for reversal.

The crux of the appeal rested on the third count in Smith's indictment and the clash between Maine common law (abortion was permitted prior to quickening; after quickening it was punishable) and Maine statute (abortion at any point was illegal). Had Smith committed a misdemeanor under common law, or a felony under the statute? Which understanding of abortion set the stage for Smith and Caswell's interaction? A charge of murder better fit the public expectation, borne of decades of true-crime writings and more recent sensational fiction, of a passive, and passionless, victim. A charge of manslaughter, on the other hand, returned to Berengera some agency in placing herself in Smith's (bungling) hands, willingly soliciting an abortion. Clifford's redefinition of Berengera's death suggested yet another story about "Mary Bean." The change from murder to manslaughter paralleled the changing image of the Woodbury Brook body from a victim Saco residents found worthy of sympathy to one less so. The more active a role Berengera was imagined to have played in the seduction and securing an abortion, the less "guilty" of murder Smith appeared to be.[134]

But although no one believed that Smith intended to kill Caswell, when she died as a consequence of him committing another crime (the abortion), her death became part of *that* crime. By Maine law, if the initial crime was a felony, then the subsequent death was considered murder, regardless of intent. A felony was defined as a crime punishable in the state prison. It was a bit circular for the crime to be defined according to its punishment, but because the penalty for abortion was time in the state prison, Berengera's death was a felony, and thus Smith was charged with murder. However, the statute on abortion gave *two* possible punishments: state prison or a fine plus time in the county jail. A crime punishable by a fine and county jail indicated a misdemeanor, and, therefore, a death in committing a misdemeanor would be considered manslaughter. Clifford saw two possible scenarios in the law, and when he reviewed the attorney general's indictment, he found that it had been worded to assume that abortion was a felony and punishable only by prison time. Henry Tallman had seen and prosecuted this case through the lens of murder; Clifford imagined a different scenario.

Smith's intent proved key to this appeal. The statute punished those who had intent to destroy the child with which a woman may be pregnant, whether quick or not. The indictment against Smith charged an "intent to cause and procure the said Berengera to miscarry and to bring forth the said child."[135] After a lengthy argument, the court determined that the word "miscarry" did not assume any intent to cause the child's death. That, in fact, and especially since Berengera was quick with child (and therefore along in her pregnancy), a "miscarriage" (as the term was used in law) could produce a viable, live infant. Without proving Smith's intent to destroy Berengera's child and without alleging that intention in the indictment, the court found that "the indictment, not containing an allegation of a design, which is an essential ingredient in the offence first charged . . . to make it a felony [according to Maine statute], the subsequent and principal accusation is that of manslaughter only."[136] After more than a year of considering Clifford's detailed argument, in

April 1852 Supreme Court justice Ether Shepley announced his decision: Smith had been improperly charged. His conviction for murder was overturned, and since he had already served more than enough time for a manslaughter charge, he was free to go.

Smith returned to Saco and was reunited with his wife and children. The *Biddeford Mercantile Advertiser* was aghast at this turn of events and castigated the "carelessness or ignorance of the Attorney General who managed the case for the government." Because of a "gross blunder, the cruel death of a young female is unavenged, justice is set aside, . . . and a man convicted of murder goes unpunished."[137] The newspaper editor politely suggested that Smith reside somewhere other than Saco or Biddeford. Smith stayed in Saco, but he would not be there for long; he had contracted tuberculosis, likely in prison, and died in 1855.[138]

There were many lessons learned in the Smith trial, stories residents could tell themselves about the dangers of life at the midpoint of the nineteenth century. In 1850, the extensive newspaper coverage of the discovery of Berengera Caswell's body, its examination, and the ensuing trial provided the reading public with a peek into the darker shadows of their bright city—where they saw "such startling outrages exposed to the light."[139] James Smith, having appeared twice in the public papers for two different murders, revealed to area residents that their city was harboring a class of criminals—potential thieves, murderers, counterfeiters—who during the day passed among them as citizens, yet at night and in dark places like taverns and woods engaged in "nefarious crimes." An editorial in the *Maine Democrat* was blunt: the recent case resulted from "a state of things existing among us which has been gradually but surely poisoning the fountains of virtue, and lowering the standard of morality." Further, the editor chided the citizenry for its ambivalence toward "vice and immorality" and asked how long "the sluggish indifference which has heretofore been manifested in our community to the idleness, intemperance, profanity and Sabbath-breaking which abounds is to continue."[140] Abortionists and "quack physicians" with their "pestiferous influences" were warned against shady practices, a preview of the increasing antipathy toward abortion and its practitioners that would come to define the founding of the American Medical Association (AMA) and the battle between regular physicians and their so-called irregular competitors.[141] The *Mercantile Advertiser* was blunt on this point: Smith, who took "upon himself the garb of a physician . . . trifled with the lives of his fellow beings, and his ignorance of the healing has at last brought upon him a most just and deserved award. We hope the example which has been made of Smith will have the desired effect and put a check upon the gross and frequent quackery of the present age."[142]

Smith's practice and the death of his patient encapsulated the growing tensions between medical professionals at midcentury. In the 1840s, the abortion business boomed, and Smith, moving into a mill town, took advantage of the commercial visibility and common-law practice that sustained his trade. Yet his trial, with its condemnation of untrained physicians, reflected the growing tension around abortion as a political, legal, and medical issue. In 1857, the American Medical Association (founded in 1847 by regular physicians) initiated a powerful campaign to make all abortions illegal. This quest was driven by a desire to control the medical profession and limit competition from midwives, botanics, and other competing medical philosophies.[143] Among the upper classes, the antiabortion movement gained momentum in response to the perceived threat presented by the growing number of white elite single and married women procuring abortions. The Maine Medical Association reported that "the most remarkable and appalling feature of [abortion] is that it prevails chiefly amongst married and otherwise respectable women."[144] Women who solicited abortions were now punished along with the practitioners, and increasingly these women were seen as immoral, unwomanly, and unpatriotic, a reflection of the fear that without the offspring of the elite, the country would soon be populated by immigrants and Catholics.[145] The antiabortion campaign targeted the concept of quickening, and in rejecting its validity and insisting that only trained physicians—not women—could determine a state of pregnancy, women's knowledge of and power over their own bodies were dismissed and diminished, as Bridget Ash, Sarah Bryant, and others had experienced in Smith's trial.[146]

Smith's ineptitude had killed Berengera, but the doctor was not the only one punished in this trial. Just as new, stricter abortion laws and strong antiabortion rhetoric would work to circumscribe the behavior of middle-class white women, newspaper reports of the Smith trial enforced moral standards.[147] Young men and young women learned very clearly that there were boundaries to acceptable behavior and consequences for those who transgressed them. We see this in a change in the media coverage of Berengera. When first found she was described as an "unfortunate girl."[148] But by the end of the trial, the unknown mystery girl became a woman of mystery. The media attention in this case and others concerning abortion deaths warned girls that sex without marriage, and pregnancy without motherhood, would bring public condemnation and even death. Novels, trial reports, and crime columns in newspapers all used abortion stories as a scare tactic to reiterate the cultural ideals of virginity and beliefs that proper women did not evince sexual passion.[149] Moreover, the itemizing of Berengera's possessions and the allusions to her immorality enforced a social prescription of behavior. And women who survived abortions risked enduring a police investigation with its personal questions; fear of the possibility of the private made public enforced a social punishment that humiliated the patient and frightened other women.[150] The printed word, public trials, and other official proceedings could thus coerce and shape women's private behavior in explicit laws and implicit social punishments.

Similarly, William Long—cad, rube, arch seducer, or just a twenty-year-old boy—received his own social punishment. The editor of the *Portland Pleasure Boat*, J. Hacker, was explicit in his condemnation, noting on Smith's conviction that "the villain who seduced the victim and then placed her in the doctor's hands is permitted to go at large without reproof! Such is law!"[151] But the editor was not entirely correct. Long's grueling testimony on the most intimate facets of his life was humiliating; he learned his lesson. In the summer between the initial examination and the murder trial, he married Mary Ann Carter, a Saco factory girl.[152] Publishing the details of abortion cases in newspapers worked to enforce standards of morality and behavior for young men, and, especially, women. The great irony for Berengera and William was that while they tried to hide their activity and its result by seeking an abortion, her death actually revealed every sordid detail.

Did Berengera want the abortion? On the one hand, her decision not to give birth reflects that important connection between a woman's ability to control reproduction and her ability to be in the workforce. There are numerous nineteenth-century true-crime–inspired narratives that tell a story similar to Caswell's, of how young, independent working girls engaged in sex and ended up dead. Sarah Cornell's death challenged mill agents' claims that factory life was safe for the first generation of factory girls. The ghastly murder of Helen Jewett, for whom sex was her work, epitomized the dangerous consequences of "illicit sexuality."[153] Mary Rogers sold cigars in a New York City tobacco shop before her battered body was found floating in the Hudson River in 1841; Pearl Bryant, at the end of the nineteenth century, sold shoes in Kentucky before the discovery of her beheaded corpse shocked midwestern readers. Like Caswell, Rogers and Bryant (and many other young women) had died after abortions, and their stories became fodder for numerous narratives that afforded prurient views into the lives of single women while simultaneously critiquing the industrialized society that made those lives possible.[154] It was, after all, the industrial world that gave women their ability to make and sell the commodities (including sex) that undergirded America's growth, and it was commercialism that sold their stories when they died. True-crime–inspired literature asked readers to look inward at individual moral virtues while also looking outward at broader social concerns. The prevalence of abortion stories and the hostility toward working women were linked in wider social misgivings about independent women and unregulated sexual activity.[155] The subtle court condemnation of Berengera Caswell was of her behavior, but behavior born of her employment history. Cases like Berengera Caswell's raised twofold social anxiety: a nervousness toward both women's economic independence *and* women's sexual and reproductive independence. A wage-earning, sexually active single mill girl (or sales girl, or even a prostitute) embodied the perceived threat to domesticity and marriage that so worried midcentury middle-class society. As newspapers, trials, and novels suggested, the solution to the problem of free-roaming women, sexually aggressive seducers, and ill-trained physicians was strong moral fiber and greater public scrutiny and regulation. The court of public humiliation, the cautionary tales of dead women, and the regulations of the AMA would secure the public safety.

Yet Berengera Caswell was not the worrisome antiwoman a nervous middle class feared. More likely, when she traveled to Saco Berengera was set on marriage. If she had desired an abortion, she did not need to travel to Maine or see William Long to obtain it. In September 1849 Long and Caswell had apparently gone their separate ways—he to Biddeford, she to Salem. They reunited only when Berengera learned she was pregnant. Marriage would prevent public shame. But for reasons that are not clear, Long arranged the abortion. If he refused to marry her, perhaps Berengera was willing to undertake the treatment. Perhaps she had stopped working and did need his financial assistance, though in reality he had none to offer. In November, she was still well within the pre-quickening period and, at least initially, was under the impression the treatment would be by way of medicine. For unmarried women like Berengera, it was far more shameful to have lost their virtue and give evidence of that through pregnancy than to undertake an abortion. A

"Winter—A Skating Scene," *Harper's Weekly*, March 6, 1858. The gruesome circumstance of Berengera Caswell's death faded from family memory and over time was replaced by a story of a skating accident during a holiday party in Canada. From the author's collection.

Maine medical journal described the effect of a young woman's loss of virtue, a "scene of sin and sorrow—of a young life forever blasted, of disgrace a thousand times worse than death entering an honorable family; of fathers, mothers, sisters, brothers . . . ready to sink under the burden of grief and shame that has fallen upon them like a thunder-bolt from a cloudless sky."[156]

In this light, it is not surprising that Berengera's surviving family forgot the story of her death and replaced a story of shame and horror with a sweet tale of innocence. As Caswell descendants tell the story today, in December 1849 Berengera, nicknamed Berry, attended a holiday party in Canada, where guests enjoyed skating on the Saint Francis River. Happiness turned to horror when she fell through the ice and her body was swept away in the rapid current, only to reemerge months later and hundreds of miles away in Maine. In effect, the family buried the story of a mangled body tossed into a river by an abortionist and instead passed along the tale of a young girl's heartbreaking accident. Berengera's life of independence and labor in the textile factories was erased and replaced with the memory of Berry in the heart of her domestic circle, a passive, and innocent, victim once more.

The last people who saw Berengera Caswell alive did not even know her real name and the story of her tragic death in Saco was quickly forgotten as new murders and new events took over everyday life. The details became blurred over time. Saco librarian John Haley's 1913 notes on the history of Saco relegated the story to "dust and d—d oblivion" but provided an outline for history's sake. In what he understood to have happened, Haley made Smith (whom he identified as using the alias James Dewey) and William Long (whom Haley called Green H. Long, perhaps a reference to his trademark green pants) partners in the crime. Berengera, whom Haley referred to only as "a young lady, who was unfortunate enough to get snarled up with one of Dewey's pals," found herself in "a delicate condition" and was brought to Smith's house, where Smith tried to "relieve her by ways that were dark," resulting in her death. In Haley's retelling, Long assisted Smith in tying the body to the plank and together they pushed her into the brook. Haley condensed the time until discovery of the body from nearly four months to just a few days, when "her presence became known by a smell that aroused the whole vicinity." Smith received his just punishment for his crime in this version: in prison, "his health failed so fast that he was pardoned that he might come home to die. He died soon in Bacon's Court in the most abject poverty."[157] Rewritten by her family and misremembered in Saco, Berengera Caswell's brief life faded into history. Yet, the story of this sad death was not entirely lost. An enterprising publisher saw a lesson to be learned and a profit to be made and resurrected the story of Mary Bean.

"FOUNDED ON RECENT EVENTS"

James Smith had just settled into his cell in the York County jail in May 1850 when the *Maine Democrat* carried an enticing advertisement. For just twelve and a half cents, eager readers could once again dive into the details of the story of Berengera Caswell. As advertised, "just published and complete in one number," the Boston firm of Hotchkiss and Company offered *Mary Bean, The Factory Girl; or The Victim of Seduction*.[158] Borrowing Caswell's assigned alias, the title left little doubt as to the storyline of this short sensational novel authored by "Miss J.A.B, a resident of Manchester." Two years later, in 1852, the "Reverend Mr. Miller" provided *A Full and Complete Confession of the Horrid Transaction in the Life of George Hamilton,*

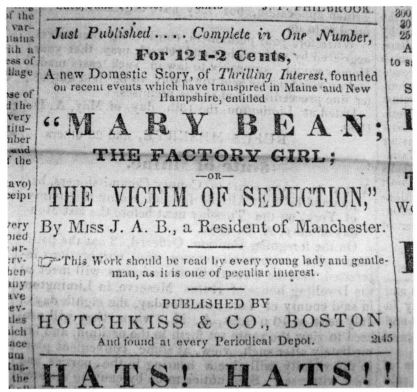

Just Published . . . . Complete in One Number,

For 12 1-2 Cents,

A new Domestic Story, of *Thrilling Interest*, founded on recent events which have transpired in Maine and New Hampshire, entitled

"MARY BEAN;

THE FACTORY GIRL;

—OR—

THE VICTIM OF SEDUCTION,"

By Miss J. A. B., a Resident of Manchester.

☞ This Work should be read by every young lady and gentleman, as it is one of peculiar interest.

PUBLISHED BY

HOTCHKISS & CO., BOSTON,

And found at every Periodical Depot.   2145

HATS! HATS!!!

Advertisement from the *Maine Democrat*, June 1850. James Smith had yet to come to trial for Caswell's death when her story appeared as a work of sensational fiction. From the collection of the Dyer Library/Saco Museum, Saco, Maine.

the Murderer of Mary Bean, the Factory Girl, described as "Part the Second and Last of Mary Bean." This tale focused on Bean's fictional murderer, the "vile scoundrel and ultimate seducer" George Hamilton. Although these tales were advertised as "founded on recent events," the authors used great creative license in crafting them. Berengera Caswell's name was abandoned in favor of the more familiar and mellifluous Mary Bean, and her life became nothing but a mine for details to create the fictional story. George Hamilton was a composite character, a formulaic seducer drawn not from William Long's life, but rather from cultural and literary models as well as from incidents revealed during Smith's hearing and trial. As sensational novels, as city-mysteries, and as true-crime accounts these two tales blurred the distinction between fact and fiction and continued to feed an audience hungry for the details of murder.[159] They are published here for the first time together and for the first time since 1852.

The authors of these novels had at hand newspaper accounts of Smith's April 1850 hearing and 1851 later murder trial as well as newspaper reports from the reexamination of the Wentworth brothers, arrested again in May 1850 for the murder of Jonas Parker. Once more the Saco papers were filled with news of murder as the second arrest "coming as it did immediately after the close of the exciting trial of Dr. Smith, and his detention for a similar crime, . . . created some excitement here."[160] For this newsworthy event, the *Union* and the *Democrat* joined forces "for greater convenience in getting out the reports." This money-saving strategy did not erase entirely the competitive spirit of the press. Although the Saco papers were united, they were certain to publish their reports the first thing each morning "before it is possible for the place to be supplied with reports from other sources."[161] But many papers carried news of the Wentworths' investigation. The *New Hampshire Farmers' Cabinet* declared that Dr. Smith was implicated in the crime. The *Eastern Argus*, on the other hand, suggested that the new evidence just come to light had been provided by Dr. James Smith, presenting an intriguing connection between these two apparently isolated crimes.[162] The Wentworths were extradited to New Hampshire. Their hearing began in May and ran several weeks. Like Smith, the Wentworths had very good luck with legal counsel: their court-appointed attorney was Franklin Pierce, future U.S. president and at the top of his legal game in 1850. The Wentworths were indicted for murder, but Pierce had raised considerable reasonable doubt during the proceedings and the court eventually dismissed the case. Once again the Wentworths escaped jail. A later writer derided Smith's connection to the Parker murder, noting how Smith "got himself connected with the Parker case by pretending to know a great many things about it, and making statements which were afterwards easily shown to be false."[163] This did not prevent the authors of fiction from connecting the Caswell and Parker deaths. With the help of the extensive newspaper coverage, "Miss J.A.B." and the "Reverend Mr. Miller" turned these two real-life crimes, tenuously intersecting in Saco, into the story of the fictional Mary Bean and her seducer-murderer George Hamilton.

Where the real-life case presented numerous shades of gray, the fiction was black and white, with victims and villains clearly drawn. Smith's murder trial had raised questions and concerns about Berengera Caswell's agency and the independent lives factory girls led. In the fiction, there is no ambiguity. Mary Bean is a virtuous victim, easily falling prey to a master scoundrel. Her fatal flaw, her overly generous and trusting

Portrait of MARY BEAN, the Factory Girl.   Portrait of GEORGE HAMILTON.

Portraits of Mary Bean and George Hamilton from *Life of George Hamilton*, 1852. This image of Mary Bean also appeared on the cover of all three editions of *Mary Bean, The Factory Girl*. Interestingly, the portrait of George Hamilton does not match his physical description in *The Factory Girl*, where Hamilton was described as a man who wore "whiskers and a mustache." From the author's collection.

nature, was really an overabundant virtue. These novels dealt firmly with villains as well. Although Smith escaped a life sentence and Long moved on with his own life, the fiction provided a more satisfying resolution to the dilemma of a dead factory girl and a murdered tax collector: all the criminals died, went to jail, became insane, or committed suicide. In Saco, some saw Caswell's death as "unavenged" and the inability to prosecute Long or convict Smith of murder as a failure of the justice system. As readers found in many works of sensational fiction, the Mary Bean novels righted those perceived wrongs.

With a rise in literacy and new printing technologies, the penny-daily papers and stories about murder could be relayed to a wider audience faster than ever before. Innovations in printing between 1825 and 1850 made production of pamphlets and short, paper-bound novels quick and inexpensive. The flatbed press and the cylinder press allowed for very rapid printing with thousands of impressions per hour. In addition, the rise of the railroad system created an efficient means of distribution as well as an audience for a portable, cheap read to pass the time during trips by train. As the advertisement for *Mary Bean, The Factory Girl*

The Murder of Mr. Parsons in the woods, near Manchester, N. H.

"The Murder of Mr. Parsons," from the *Life of George Hamilton*. The 1845 murder of Jonas Parker was re-created in fiction as the murder of Mr. Parsons. In this scene, Hamilton and his associates, Wenton and Bowen (a reference to the real-life Wentworth brothers), dispatch the tax collector. From the author's collection.

promised, the latest works of sensational literature were "found at every periodical depot," conveniently located near train stations, factories, and other places where potential customers gathered.[164]

Sensational literature captured a new openness in American culture in examining sexuality, while at the same time decrying it. Growing in tandem with the literature of reform, sensational literature moved beyond the desire to correct aberrant behavior and explored in explicit detail the very action proper individuals should avoid. While these sensational texts often espoused a sense of duty, morality, and traditional gender roles, they did so with lingering descriptions of the acts and types of individuals who would lure young women, and men, away from cultural ideals. Sexual crimes—including abortion, rape, seduction, and incest—were particularly featured. From the merely suggestive to the outright pornographic, sensational tales found an eager audience willing to transgress, if only vicariously, approved boundaries of behavior.

"What was to be done! the body must be secreted! the mill-stream was a favorable place!
It was done!" Page —

Illustration from the *Life of George Hamilton*. Taking his cue from Dr. James Smith,
the fictional George Hamilton attempted to hide Mary Bean's body in a mill stream.
From the author's collection.

As works of sensational fiction, *Mary Bean, The Factory Girl* and the *Life of George Hamilton* drew on a number of key attributes of the genre. Mary Bean was the quintessential fallen woman, described as a "deluded," "helpless," and "unsuspecting girl."[165] She was a naive victim of seduction whose fall from grace provided a means to explore the seducer's criminal mind. In the 1840s and 1850s, readers were intensely curious to understand how criminals operated, further propelling the popularity of crime literature. The *Life of George Hamilton* purports to be a criminal biography of sorts, another very popular nineteenth-century form, supposedly written by Hamilton as part confession and part explanation of his life of crime. True-crime accounts and criminal biographies attempted to answer the questions of how and why aberrant individuals engaged in crime, although in the hands of sensationalist authors, the emphasis was not so much on discovering the key to criminal reform as it was on the lurid details of their lives.

Both novels addressed the uncertainty and fear that came with rapid population growth. Touching on the genre of city-mysteries, Mary Bean and George Hamilton invited readers to look at the darker side of city life from the safety of readers' homes. With titles like *New York by Gas-Light* and *City Crimes*, city-mysteries revealed what happened in the dark alleys, hidden taverns, and mysterious buildings that comprised the city.[166] As one would find in novels set in the big cities of New York or Philadelphia, in the Mary Bean tales, Saco is shown to have its share of hidden alleys, dark taverns, and mysterious labyrinthine buildings. City-mysteries portrayed a calm and orderly urban life by day, but by night that facade was pulled aside to reveal a turbulent underclass that defied control. During Smith's murder trial Saco residents were shocked to learn that abortionists, counterfeiters, and cross-dressers lived in their midst; the novels, too, revealed an assortment of master plotters, unsavory criminals, and disinterested citizens who inhabited the city but did little to stop the growing crime around them.

Mary Bean, The Factory Girl drew on all of these popular genres. The cover of the paper-bound, pamphlet-like novel was printed on a cream paper with eye-catching green and red ink. Later editions would use the bright yellow paper covers that signaled a sensational read. For nineteenth-century readers, the cover portrait of Mary Bean suggested her coming disgrace and readers could, and were encouraged to, imagine how such attractive women would fall prey. In this engraved rendering (an artist's generic creation), Mary sits gazing off to the reader's left, absentmindedly,

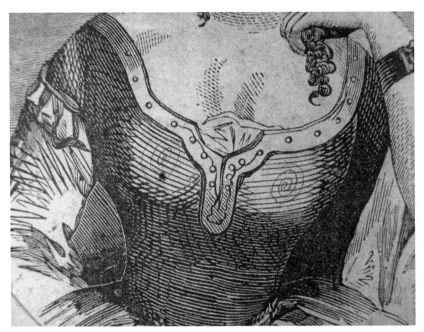

A section of the portrait of Mary Bean from the cover of *Thrilling and Exciting Account of the Murder of Mary Bean* (Rulison, 1852). This reader's doodle on Bean's bosom captures the salacious and sexual overtones such works of sensational fiction contained. Courtesy of the Borowitz Crime Collection, Department of Special Collections and Archives, Kent State University Libraries and Media Services.

or coyly, playing with styled, curled hair. She wears a low-cut dress and one raised arm is bared to the elbow, revealing her ornate bracelet. She seems unaware of her own beauty, and therefore of the danger that beauty can bring upon her. Here is the irony of the young woman's situation. Her unself-conscious concept of her own virtuous purity, the cultural ideal for which a young woman strove, was what attracted scoundrels set on her ruin. The intention here was to put readers on that narrow edge between virtue and vice, to see on which side of the line they would walk. A copy of this work now in the Borowitz Crime Collection at Kent State University illustrates this point. One nineteenth-century reader, apparently thinking more of vice than virtue, drew two small spirals on Bean's cover portrait, carefully locating his doodles on top of her imagined nipples. As publishers had no doubt hoped, this reader viewed this text and its subject as salacious, sensational, and sexual.

Readers, in fact, knew Mary Bean's story before even opening the book. Its title page highlighted the novel's connections to both sentimental and sensational fiction. The title page emphasized that this work was a "domestic story, illustrative of the trials and temptations of factory life," informing readers that a young woman was about to yield to inappropriate desires. With stories of dead, seduced, or abandoned factory girls frequently in the newspapers and novels, the phrase "factory girl" alone provided a key to the events that would unfold. That the story was "founded on recent events" provided an authentication to assure readers that they would not be wasting their time or money on fiction (a counterfeit story); they would read fact, a true crime to bring them as close to real experience as possible without experiencing personal danger.[167] The title-page epigraph, quoting from *Romeo and Juliet*, revealed the plot of this tale: "Her form was faultless, and her mind, untainted yet by art, was noble, just, humane and kind; And virtue warmed her heart: But ah! The cruel spoiler came." This same epigraph is found on the title page of *Charlotte Temple*, one of the best-selling sentimental novels of the nineteenth century and itself a dramatic and heart-wrenching tale of seduction, abandonment, and death.[168] The bold, colorful cover and the clue-laden title page made clear to readers what their twelve and a half cents would buy.

Hotchkiss published at least four editions of *Mary Bean, The Factory Girl*. In 1851, Boston publisher J. Merone released an edition under a new title, *A Thrilling and Exciting Account of the Horrible Murder of Mary Bean, the Factory Girl*. In this endeavor, the text was repackaged to appeal to a wider audience.[169] The title page of this edition downplayed the "domestic story" and instead emphasized the sensational murder and attendant mystery. In addition, it promised information on the murder of Mr. Parsons (the fictionalized Jonas Parker), George Hamilton's connections with other criminals (the recrafted Wentworth brothers), and, with an embedded double entendre, "a thrilling narrative of his intercourse with Mary Bean." In case the real-life events had grown dim in the reader's mind, the publisher reminded his potential customer of the "betrayal of the beautiful, but unfortunate girl, whose body was found floating in a mill stream in Saco, near Boston," this latter phrase suggesting that this text was being sold in areas more distant from Northern New England, where potential readers were less likely to know Maine geography but were nonetheless eager to read about Maine murders.[170]

The story of Mary Bean continued to move across the country. In 1852 H. M. Rulison's Queen City Publishing offered a version identical to the Merone edition. Rulison, a Cincinnati publisher, specialized in sensational stories, crime literature, and city-mysteries. Miss J.A.B.'s *Mary Bean, The Factory Girl* was in good company, listed in Rulison's catalogs alongside such works as *Miss Jane Clark: Buried Alive* and *Adalaska; or, The Strange and Mysterious Family of the Cave of Genreva,* and numerous works with the words "thrilling narrative" in the title. Rulison continued to offer *The Factory Girl* well into the 1850s, although its price rose from twelve and a half cents to fifteen to twenty.[171]

Some commentators saw works like *The Factory Girl* as an example of "the miserable trash which is inundating every community and enervating and dissipating the minds of youth."[172] To defend against such views, Miss J.A.B. took great pains to establish her work as factual and worthy of a wide readership. Arguing that parents, young women, and young men would all learn from this tale, the author established a "moral pretext" to dive into the salacious story.[173] She told readers what they would find and learn in this work: "The virtuous and the pure minded need not fear to read the narrative, lest they should find something that would mantle the cheek of modesty with a blush. . . . The sensualist must seek elsewhere for material to gratify his depraved taste; but if he would find his own character depicted, and see its deformity, and has one faint desire to reform, we invite him to read, in the hope that he may be stimulated to virtue."[174] Miss J.A.B. of Manchester was herself a fiction, a publisher's creation to suggest to readers that this female, factory-town confidante was an appropriate guide for young female readers.[175] In the preface "Miss J.A.B." claimed she published out of a sense of duty: "Its object is a pure one, being merely to warn the inexperienced female," but the rationale behind these texts was profit.[176] Murder sold.

Mary Bean, The Factory Girl covered Mary's life from her home in Canada to her fateful meeting with the arch seducer George Hamilton, who took her to Manchester, seduced and abandoned her. Like Berengera Caswell, who journeyed from Salem to Biddeford, the fictional, intrepid Mary follows George to Saco, then to Boston, then back to Maine where Hamilton introduced her to Dr. Savin, to whose home she traveled and *"never was seen to come from."*[177] This novel was written in May and early June of 1850, before Smith came to trial for Caswell's death and before William Long married another factory girl and enhanced his respectability. Thus, its storylines mirrored the real-life events of 1850 and as such remained unresolved at novel's end: "Thus have the guilty been enabled to escape justice and community is cursed by a new accession to the number of desperadoes which infest it."[178]

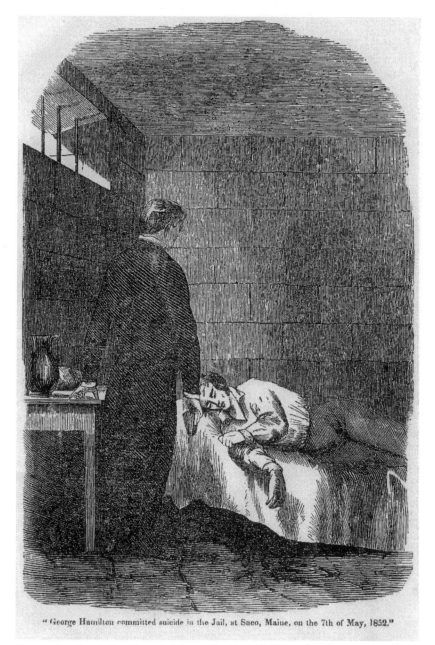

" George Hamilton committed suicide in the Jail, at Saco, Maine, on the 7th of May, 1852."

George Hamilton's Suicide, *Life of George Hamilton*. Dr. James Smith narrowly avoided life in prison for Berengera Caswell's death, but the fictional George Hamilton paid for the murder of Mary Bean with his own life. Before committing suicide, Hamilton penned his autobiography, later discovered and published by the Reverend Mr. Miller (seen here with Hamilton's body), as a lesson to youth. From the author's collection.

To address this lack of resolution, J. Merone (who published the 1851 edition of *Mary Bean*) in 1852 offered readers the *Narrative of the Life of George Hamilton*. Bean's presence in this story is brief. The tale began with the discovery of Bean's body in the Saco stream. This rest of the forty-one-page text focused on the life of George Hamilton: seducer, murderer, and thief. Where the fictional Mary Bean reflected details from Berengera Caswell's life, the fictional George Hamilton bore little resemblance to the real William Long, other than playing the role of the paramour. The character of George Hamilton reflected what Smith's defense attorneys had attempted to portray, unsuccessfully, William Long to be. Long's uncertain real-life character—cad or kid—in fiction becomes definitive: cold-hearted cad and con man. And because seduction alone was not a crime, the fictional Long-turned-Hamilton also becomes a criminal. There was no escaping punishment in this story of Mary Bean.

The fiction rewrote the independent life and unsettling death of Berengera Caswell and brought it into alignment with the cultural formula of murdered-girl narratives so popular at midcentury. In this case, life was made to imitate art. The novels provided the resolution to the act of seduction and the crime of murder that society expected and deemed appropriate. Putting fact into fiction helped readers see clearly and make sense of the kind of troubling situations that so worried residents of Saco and other burgeoning cities.[179] The fiction erased the ambiguity of Smith's trial and in its place created a world of clarity where, eventually, justice prevailed and everyone got what they deserved. Both texts were sensational, lurid, loosely based on fact, and didactic. Each espoused a clear message to its audience; *Mary Bean* addressed young women and *George Hamilton* advised young men.

Mary Bean, The Factory Girl posited that the best place for young women was home, close to the hearth and family and away from those trials and temptations that factory life, the city, and the world of commerce and labor increasingly made available to young women. Here again we see expressed the fear of the link between women's economic and reproductive independence. Temptations included the desire to spend money on frivolous things. During the trial, the court scrutinized Berengera's purchases; in the novel, Prosperity Jones, a peddler, offered Mary Bean and her fellow factory operatives "a notion or two" including "anything, from a horn comb to a gold ring."[180] The defense attorneys portrayed William Long as the seducer, tempting Berengera away from her mill duties, her sister, and her better judgment. In the novel, George Hamilton's flattering words and promises of city excitement tempted Mary Bean away from her rural home. Neither storyline is entirely fact nor entirely fiction.

The nineteenth-century reader, well familiar with sensational fiction, knew Mary Bean would not succeed. The author reminded readers along the way of her dilemma in the same coded speech some Maine newspapers used to describe Caswell and her pregnancy. In the novel, Mary visited a Boston fortune-teller who foresaw that Bean would die by violence. Although Mary did not know her fate, her nineteenth-century readers did. When Hamilton and Bean returned to Saco, Miss J.A.B. spelled out the scenario, in case the reader had missed the clues so far: "The true condition of Mary Bean could no longer be concealed; she was disgraced, and would soon become *a mother*," the result of her transgression italicized as if spit out in disgust.[181] A final clue to Mary's fate was offered: in this text, Dr. James Smith became Dr. Savin, and savvy readers knew the surname referred to the abortifacient, in this context, a fatal remedy. Audiences imagined the story's conclusion as easily as they would today for a novel that featured a Dr. Cyanide.

Mary Bean, The Factory Girl urged girls to remain at home and embark on a life of duty to family. The *Life of George Hamilton*, however, assumed young men would leave their parents' homes for the fast-paced urban world. Where the pseudonymous Miss J.A.B. played the role of counselor to young women, in the *Life of George Hamilton*, the equally fictional author Reverend Mr. Miller offered advice to his male readers, a not uncommon role for nineteenth-century ministers who authored numerous life guides for men. The *Life of George Hamilton* offered a warning to young men: beware of your friends. Where *Mary Bean* touched on the consequences of women in the workforce, out of the protective domestic realm, *George Hamilton* addressed fears of population growth, mobility, and the inability to really know who anyone was.

The *Life of George Hamilton* illustrated the dangers of the city. Confidence men could be mistaken for gentlemen, while upright citizens appeared murderers. "Hamilton was one of those kind of men who had rigidly schooled his outward demeanor, and by the aid of a respectable looking suit of clothes, would be able to commit almost any depredation without being suspected of any impropriety."[182] This was a story of mistaken identity and dishonor among criminals. Just as James Smith's background and training were suspect, mobility presented the opportunity to reinvent one's identity. To prove one's veracity to one's neighbors and business associates, a complicated cult of sincerity developed among the rising middle class. Elaborate standards of dress and detailed etiquette to cover every conceivable social situation gave midcentury participants a security blanket. Etiquette books, advice guides, and periodicals all detailed this system and provided anxious consumers with more printed material. Yet, if a worthy individual could read such a guide (or a sensational novel) to check one's own behavior, what would prevent a pretend "friend" from doing the same and acting the part? It was these pretend friends and false urban mentors that young men were cautioned to avoid. George Hamilton was such a confidence man well-practiced in the art of deception: he "had schooled himself for his part, and he acted it with great skill."[183]

Mary Bean, The Factory Girl and the *Life of George Hamilton* served as guides to the dangers of strangers and the ways of the city. Increased literacy in the nineteenth century intersected with the lack of a female support network when young girls moved into the workforce. Texts like *Mary Bean, The Factory Girl* counseled their readers on what not to do while simultaneously suggesting the excitement of what one might do. Similarly, women's medical and health guides, sensational fiction, and the carefully worded newspaper ads for clairvoyants and menstrual regulators informed girls (and boys) about possible courses of action if they did follow in Mary Bean's steps. Although the two Mary Bean novels attracted readers with their depictions of the temptations of city life and racy insight into seduction and the world of criminals, both books ultimately reassured their worried readers that protection could be found in the literature of true crime, where one would learn the ways of the confidence men and thus take steps to avoid falling into their traps. By eschewing dark places, alcohol, strangers, and impetuous decisions, one would be safe. The effect of not following the advice offered by these cautionary tales was made quite clear: young women would be shamed and die, young men would be drawn into a world of crime and punishment they would not likely escape. In works part titillating exposé and part cultural critique, stories drawing on the genres of city-mysteries, true crime, and sensational fiction provided a guidepost and sense of stability in a world where sexual and economic independence brought dangers real and imagined to both women and men.

Similarly, the newspaper accounts of the examination and murder trial of James Smith revealed that behind the facade of Saco and Biddeford's staggering economic growth lurked a criminal underclass that threatened local safety. As trial testimony revealed, in addition to murder, "respectable" town residents were involved in abortion, counterfeiting, robbery, and cross-dressing. When even the victim had been reinvented, Saco residents came to understand that they had paid a price for their success. An editorial chastised Saco residents for their "indifference . . . this feeling no sense of individual responsibility commonly shared, which strengthens vice and gives crime its boldness."[184] Yet, despite these disturbing revelations, the newspaper accounts of the hearing and trial, like the fiction based on Caswell's life and death, presented a similar directive to behavior. The gruesome details of the discovery and autopsy of Berengera Caswell's body portrayed the consequences of straying from accepted behavior and from home. The excoriation of William Long and the careful detailing of Caswell's clothing reminded readers of the boundaries of that accepted behavior and warned young men and women of the public humiliation they, too, would face should they dare to transgress.

The printed word, both factual and fictional, in local newspapers and nationally distributed novels, provided the salacious reading and the safety precautions that would help residents navigate this new landscape of modernity. Osgood Stevens's discovery of the body in Woodbury Brook that bright day in April 1850 thus revealed more than just the sad conclusion to Berengera Caswell's life. His discovery opened a window through which readers could confront the fears attendant to change, mobility, and identity in the urban setting. In newspapers and novels, readers could vicariously explore and experience the lives of men and women who were tempted. From the safety of their armchairs, readers of sensational fiction and true crime could avoid those vice-filled paths, remind themselves of virtue, and await the next thrilling narrative to test their moral progress.

PART TWO

THE

MURDER

OF

MARY BEAN

NOTE ON THE TEXTS

Mary Bean, The Factory Girl is transcribed from the Rulison 1852 edition found in the Borowitz Crime Collection, Department of Special Collections and Archives, Kent State University Libraries and Media Services. *Life of George Hamilton* is transcribed from the 1852 edition published by J. Merone, also in the Borowitz Crime Collection. In both texts, obvious typographical errors have been silently corrected. Nineteenth-century spelling and punctuation have been left as originally published except in cases where meaning is obscured.

MARY BEAN:

OR, THE

MYSTERIOUS MURDER.

Portrait of Mary Bean, the Factory Girl.

BOSTON:
J. MERONE & CO.,
1851.

MARY BEAN, THE FACTORY GIRL

A
Thrilling and Exciting Account
of the
Horrible Murder
of
Mary Bean, The Factory Girl;
Together with an
Authentic Statement of George Hamilton,
The Notorious Burglar and Murderer, and an Account of the
Murder and Robbery of Mr. Parsons, of Manchester, New
Hampshire, and Perpetrated By Hamilton and His Coadjutors in
Crime, Bowen and Wenton;
A Thrilling Narrative of His Intercourse with
Mary Bean,
And His Betrayal of the Beautiful But Unfortunate Girl, Whose
Body was Found
Floating in a Mill Stream in Saco, Near Boston.

Founded on Recent Events.
'Her form was faultless, and her mind,
Untainted yet by art,
Was noble, just, humane and kind;
And virtue warmed her heart:
But ah! The cruel spoiler came!'—

By Miss J.A.B., of Manchester.
Cincinnati:
H.M. Rulison
1852

Facing page: Cover of the 1851 Boston Merone edition of *Thrilling and Exciting Account of the Murder of Mary Bean.* Three different publishers produced editions of Mary Bean's story. There were variations in the cover and titles of the works, but Bean's portrait and the text of the novel remained identical in each. Courtesy of the New Hampshire Historical Society.

PREFACE.

Novel writing, and novel reading, are now become so common, that one can scarcely muster courage sufficient to detail facts, in the form of a story, without laying themselves open to the charge of writing fiction. Still the charge is not a very grave one, and the author can see no reason why a good and wholesome moral may not be imparted in the form of a story, especially when we consider that a story is often seized upon with avidity by those who would throw aside a newspaper article, whose object might be to inculcate a moral equally as pure.

The writer of the following narrative lays no claim to literary merit in its production; hence it will afford no food for the critic; neither is it offered to those who may deem it worthy of a perusal, as a specimen of proficiency in the ordinary story telling of the day. There has been no effort made for effect, by a relation of improbabilities, or by the picturing of scenes which could only have transpired in the powerful imaginings of an accomplished descriptive writer. It claims only to be a brief story, devoid of prolixity and unnecessary detail. Its object is a pure one, being merely to warn the inexperienced female, by a relation of events in which an amiable young lady became deeply interested, and whose fortunes and fate are developed from chapter to chapter.

Many who read the story may be able to recall to mind some who may have been placed in similar circumstances, and who may have met with a death equally premature and lamentable.

It is certain that no parent can, without emotion, peruse these details, especially if they be the guardian of daughters, where youth, beauty and inexperience, all tend to induce them to listen to the voice of the deceiver, who, by his protestations of love and devotion, is secretly and inhumanly laying the plot which shall ultimately prove their ruin. The virtuous and pure minded need not fear to read the narrative, lest they should find something that would mantle the cheek of modesty with a blush; nothing of that character is to be found in these pages. The sensualist must seek elsewhere for material to gratify his depraved taste; but if he would find his own character depicted, and see its deformity, and has one faint desire to reform, we invite him to read, in the hope that he may be stimulated to virtue.

Should this brief narrative and sequel be the means of reclaiming even one who may now be indulging in her first departure from virtue, and save her from the toils of the villainous seducer, it will have accomplished a good object, and the writer will feel that the time used in committing it to paper, will have been profitably expended.

With a desire to do good, which motive it is hoped will appear upon every page, this eventful story is presented for perusal, in the humble hope that it may effect its desired object.
The Author.

CHAPTER I.

In a somewhat populous village within the limits of one of the Canadas, was located an antique looking farm-house, whose every external appearance indicated thrift, and also bespoke order and neatness on the part of its occupants.

The green-sward, in the yard at the front of the dwelling was closely cut—the door of the house was newly painted—the creeping vines about the windows were neatly trimmed, and due care having been bestowed upon the various appurtenances of this happy home, gave it such an inviting air, that the traveller was almost involuntarily compelled to tarry a moment without, either to survey the general neatness displayed, or to enter, that he might become acquainted with those whose labors without, gave such promise of economy and comfort within.

At the window of a room in the north-west corner of this antique mansion, were seated two females; one was two years the senior of the other; the eldest was of form and feature such as we picture to our minds when we would image forth the nearest approach to perfection; in connection with these, an amiable disposition, and universal affability, made the lady a center of attraction in her native village, at whose shrine of beauty and loveliness many an amorous swain ardently desired to offer up his heartfelt devotions.

Such a female as we have described, was Mary Bean.

Ellen, her sister, who was her companion at the window, though not so attractive in person, was no less amiable in her disposition; she was affectionately devoted to her sister Mary, and so bound up did she appear to be in her happiness and prosperity, that their two lives seemed blended in one.

It was on a delightful morning in early spring, that we find these two young ladies seated at the window as we have already described. But a short distance from them might be seen the low-roofed school-house, wherein they spent their earlier days, in acquiring the elementary principles of education, upon this school-house they often gazed from that very window, and recalled to mind those happy scenes and sports of childhood, "long since passed away." Mary sat with her head resting upon her hand, whilst her eyes were directed towards a spot a little beyond, and at the right of the school-house, upon which she seemed intently gazing. Ellen observed the fixedness of her sister's look, and watched her until she saw a tear stealing down her cheek, which dropped upon the window seat.

"Dear sister," said Ellen, "why do you weep?"

"'Tis nothing, Ellen; I was merely gazing upon the stones in yonder grave yard," said Mary, "and somehow a feeling of melancholy stole over me that I could not resist; but it is over now; but tell me, sister," said Mary, "why are you so troubled about me? You seem to watch my every word and act, and almost to read the very secrets of my heart."

"I know not why I am," said Ellen, "unless it be the promptings of my earnest affection for you; to see you happy is my joy; to see you otherwise, would constitute my misery." With this remark, Ellen threw her arms about her sister's neck, which act was reciprocated by Mary, and the impress of a kiss from each, gave token of the continuance of their mutual love.

"Look at this, sister," said Mary, as she drew from her bosom a neatly folded billet; "here is a note of invitation from Col. Chase; he gives a select party at his house this evening, and invites us to make two among the number. I received it this morning by the hand of his serving man, who left it just before breakfast. What say? Shall we go?"

"If you go," replied Ellen, "I should be most happy to accept the invitation."

"I think we had better," added Mary, "for this is the first time we have received an invitation to Col. Chase's house, he might feel offended if we did not answer in person a summons so pressing and courteous."

"Well, then," replied Ellen, "let us go."

"So be it then," responded Mary, "and now let us away to our domestic duties."

Both of the ladies now arose to depart, when, Ellen accidentally looking once more from the window, discovered in the distance a gentleman approaching the house. "See, sister," said Ellen, pointing in the direction of her vision, "who is that coming this way?"

"Really I cannot imagine," said Mary, following the direction of Ellen's finger; "he is so far off I cannot make out who it is; the branches of the trees, and the stone wall, so hide his form, and I am unable to decide; wait a minute, till he gets around the bend of the road, then we can tell."

"There," exclaimed Ellen, "I see him; I know who it is; it is William Churchill."

At the sound of this name, Mary's face was crimson.

"Nay, sister," said Ellen, "you have no occasion to blush at the name of so worthy a young man as William Churchill, if he is your lover."

"Why sister," replied Mary, in a seemingly pettish mood, "I am not blushing; beside if I were,—why—one that one *respects*,—coming so *suddenly* upon one,—why,"—

"Ah, Mary," said Ellen, laughing, "you would make a poor lawyer if you had to vindicate *yourself* in this *suit;* so come, come, say no more; let us go down and receive him, for he is almost at the door."

At this juncture both ladies retired from the window, and went down to receive the lover of Mary, and the friend of Ellen.

To describe William Churchill, will require but a few words. He was one of those few, who are free from the practice of any of those vices which disgrace the character of so many of the young men of the present age, and the lady, who should become the object of the love and devotion of such a man as William Churchill, might in truth consider herself fortunate indeed, when, in such an age as this, the obtaining of a good husband is like drawing a prize in a lottery, where all the tickets but one are blanks, or the obtaining of truly good wives, which, like the visitations of angels, are "few and far between."

The author does not fear the censure of any lady or gentleman reader, who may be accustomed to survey, and to reflect upon, the various matrimonial alliances around them, for such persons, she feels assured, will coincide with her in the sentiment and truth of the above remark.

But to go on with our description of William Churchill. He was an upright and truly moral young man, possessing the confidence and esteem of all who knew him. He was most devotedly attached to Mary Bean, and most vividly did he portray the attachment. Not by those sickening protestations of undying love and devotion, which too often lay the foundation of a female's ruin, while at the same time they serve to blind the eyes of the deluded girl, and thus effectually to cover the design which the villain has proposed in his heart, to effect upon the virtue of his victim.

No such person was William Churchill; in conduct he was upright; in heart pure; in his intentions, honorable; and in his love virtuous.

The object of his call upon Mary Bean at this early hour in the forenoon was to see if she designed visiting the mansion of Col. Chase in the evening, as he had received an invitation for himself and her, and likewise knew that a similar one had been sent to Mary and her sister Ellen.

We will not portray the ceremonies of his reception by the two sisters, or set before our reader the subjects of their conversation, but leave them to the enjoyment of their *tête-à-tête,* while we turn our attention to another important personage connected with our story.

At the time when Mary and Ellen were seated at the window, an individual might have been seen in a thicket of trees some little distance from the house, surveying them for a moment through a glass, as if to assure himself that *this* was really the residence of Mary Bean, and also which of the twain at the window, if either, was Mary Bean herself.

Having satisfied himself with regard to these two, to him, important facts, he might also have been seen to put up his glass, and to thread his way unseen among the trees, and by pursuing a circuitous route, he at length entered a sort of bower, or summer house nearly under the window, where he overheard all the conversation that passed between the sisters.

This man was George Hamilton, a vile scoundrel, and ultimate seducer. He was formerly acquainted with Mary Bean; he was for several years a resident of the village in which Mary lived; he knew she was pretty three years ago, when he left the town to reside in Manchester, N.H.; he had heard much of her beauty and loveliness during the three years of his absence; he was resolved to return to the place of Mary's nativity, and spend a few days, and obtain an interview with her whom he had resolved to ruin. Consequently he decked his person in as rich a manner as the fruits of gambling would allow him (in the tricks and deception of which he was an adept), and sought the place of his former residence, for the purposes which have already been described.

He met many of his former acquaintances who appeared happy to see him, to whom he related various conflicting stories as to his wealth, and to whom he gave various reasons for the brief visit he designed to pay the town of which he was formerly an inhabitant.

After entering the summer house near the window where the two sisters were seated, he became, as we have observed, an auditor to their conversation. Having learned that Mary designed visiting Col. Chase's mansion that evening, he determined to make one of that party, as thus a favorable opportunity would be presented for an interview with her, and for the furtherance of that villainous design which he had concocted, and of which poor Mary Bean was to be the victim.

"Yes," said he, as he stole out of the summer home, and retraced his steps by the same route to the woods, "yes, I am resolved to visit Col. Chase's mansion to-night, and make one of that joyous party. She cannot escape me; she is mine! mine!"

"True she is young, inexperienced, and artless, hence she will become the easier prey to my plot. What have I to fear, or why should I stop in the pursuit of my object? I have nothing to lose, whereas if I succeed in moulding her to my wishes, I have gained the object of my yearning heart. Down then, busy conscience, I heed you not; my object *shall* be accomplished. It is a dangerous game to play, I know, but I am a skillful player, hence my success is certain. To-night then, at the mansion of Col. Chase, I will instill into the ears of the unsuspecting Mary Bean, the first poison that shall ultimately make her mine.—Yes, Mary Bean, with thee the die is cast; though art mine! mine! I am resolved!"

CHAPTER II.

Let us turn from the heart sickening scene just described, to one, in some respects, more pleasant. The day was rapidly drawing to a close, and Mary Bean and her sister Ellen were preparing themselves for the contemplated visit to the hospitable dwelling of the wealthy and aris-tocratic Col. Chase.

In the more densely populated portion of the village in which Mary lived, and on one of its principal streets, was located the lofty mansion of Col. Chase. It was one of those unique buildings of ancient architecture, almost entirely unlike any of the present day. Its unlikeness to houses of modern date was mostly visible in its interior arrangement. On entering the wide, old fashioned door, you find yourself in a spacious entry, with a broad, magnificent stairway, containing in its ascent several niches in the wall, each one of which was filled with the bust of some distinguished military officer. On entering the right or left door from the hall or entry, you were ushered into a large and splendid parlor on either side, which were hung with pictures illustrative of scenes in ancient and modern wars, both on sea and land. The windows were clad in heavy tapestry, and the mantels were loaded with small busts, interspersed with various curious specimens of minerals and shells.

This ancient edifice descended to Col. Chase from his father, who was a distinguished British officer, and it was now occupied by Col. Chase, who was himself a retired officer of the English army, though still subject to be called to duty.

Col. Chase was a gentleman of talent and great respectability, and much esteemed in community. He was a widower, having no household or family, save a man servant and a cook, both of whom, being husband and wife, resided in one wing of the mansion. Miss Gordon, a niece of Col. Chase, usually made him a visit once a year, on which occasion the Colonel always gave a party, and invited a few of his acquaintances, to add to the pleasure of his niece's visit.

It was on the occasion of one of Miss Gordon's visits that the party was given to which Mary Bean and her sister Ellen were invited.

It was about seven o'clock in the evening when the parlors of Col. Chase's mansion were thrown open for the reception of the invited guests, soon after which the company assembled. In true English style, the visitors were announced by name, by the man servant, and as each came in, Col. Chase with his niece arose to greet them, and bid them welcome to his dwelling.

Quite a large company had arrived when the serving man announced "the Misses Mary and Ellen Bean."

Col. Chase arose and extended to them his hand, and at the same time introduced to them his niece, who had never met with the sisters before. The sisters were accompanied, of course, by William Churchill, who was an acquaintance of Col. Chase's, but unacquainted with Miss Gordon.

The serving man again appeared and announced Mr. George Hamilton, who was also received by the Colonel in the same courteous manner as others had been. Hamilton bowed gracefully to the ladies and gentlemen, who rose to receive him when he was announced, while the Colonel conducted him to a seat near himself. The company now being generally engaged in conversation, either standing around or sitting, in little cliques or squads, as is often observable in gatherings of this kind, George Hamilton took from a table near him a small folio of engravings, and under pretence of examining *them*, was, in fact, scrutinizing the company. He saw Mary Bean sitting at the opposite side of the room, in conversation with her sister, another lady, and William Churchill. Never had he seen so much loveliness combined in one female as was portrayed in the person of Mary Bean. Several times he was just on the point of going to her and disclosing himself; but he would as often check himself by saying,

"No! not yet! a more favorable opportunity may yet offer."

Who can describe the feelings rankling in the heart of George Hamilton, as he beheld Mary Bean smiling upon William Churchill, as he occasionally made some remark to her, or bore part in the conversation in which the four were engaged.

Mysterious as it may be, Mary's eyes would occasionally stray to the opposite side of the room, and rest for a moment upon the fine form of George Hamilton, advantageously set off, as it was, with a splendid suit of black of the most approved fashion. Soon this little company of four separated; the lady engaging in conversation with a gentleman a few steps from her, and Ellen, desiring to inspect the paintings around the room, took the arm of William Churchill, for that purpose. Mary Bean was for a moment left alone.

"Now," said Hamilton to himself, "now is the auspicious moment." He arose, and passing carelessly over to that part of the room where Mary sat, approached her with the most profound respect.

"I think," said Hamilton, "I have the honor of addressing Miss Mary Bean."

Mary slightly bowed her head, and replied, "yes, sir, my name is Mary Bean, but I must confess I do not recognize you."

"Is it possible that three years absence has wrought so great a change in me that you do not remember George Hamilton?"

Mary started with surprise as she recognized one with whom she had been formerly acquainted, at the same time smiled as she extended her hand to grasp that of his which was also presented to her.

"Why, really, Mr. Hamilton," said Mary, as a most bewitching smile illuminated her beautiful countenance, "I should not have imagined that three years could have altered one so much."

"It is not surprising, in fact, Mary," said Hamilton, "that you should not have known me, for whiskers and a moustache do alter one prodigiously."

"In truth," replied Mary, "they have so altered you that I think you might have passed as a stranger without being discovered on my part."

"Tell me, Mary," said Hamilton, "is that young lady leaning upon that gentleman's arm yonder, your sister Ellen?"

"It is," replied Mary.

"And the gentleman," said Hamilton, in a manner somewhat sarcastic, "is her lover, I suppose."

Mary made no reply, but looking up, discovered that they were approaching. "Mr. Hamilton," said Mary, "my sister and friend are coming this way, shall I introduce them to you?"

"I should be most happy," replied Hamilton, "to make their acquaintance; perhaps your sister Ellen may recognize me."

"Oh no, she never will, depend on that," said Mary, laughing.

The two had now approached, when Mary said, "Ellen, do you recognize this gentleman?"

"I do not, indeed," said Ellen.

"Nor do you, Mr. Churchill," added Mary.

"I must confess with Ellen," replied William Churchill, "that I am equally at a loss in recognition."

"Well, then," replied Mary, "allow me to introduce to you a former acquaintance, Mr. George Hamilton."

No small surprise was expressed both by William Churchill and Ellen, that they did not recognize a former acquaintance, yet the great change which three years had effected in the personal appearance of Mr. Hamilton was the cause. Conversation was at length interrupted by the serving man, who announced refreshments.

Col. Chase and his niece preceded the company in their passage to a spacious room in the rear of one of the parlors, where a splendid repast was served up, of which all were invited to partake.

In passing out of the parlors, Mr. Hamilton offered his arm to Mary Bean, which she accepted, and passed with him to the supper room, while William Churchill escorted her sister Ellen.

At the supper table, Mr. Hamilton paid the most assiduous attentions to Mary, which she received, with all the courtesy which they were apparently proffered.

While the company were busily engaged in laughing and joking, and at a moment when he was unobserved, Hamilton took from his vest pocket a card, upon which he hurriedly wrote a request that Mary would meet him in the entry after supper was over. This card he placed upon a plate and covered it with a piece of cake and passed it to her. On discovering the card, she cautiously slipped it from her plate and secreted it in her handkerchief, having first hastily read it, as she removed the cake.

Hamilton saw her take the card and secrete it, and as she did so, she looked over to Hamilton, who was seated on the opposite side of the table as was each gentleman opposite the lady whom he escorted; their eyes met; he smiled and bowed slightly; she did the same, and the company observed nothing. The party having partaken sufficiently of the dainties provided for them, Col. Chase and his niece arose, and desired them to proceed to the parlors, when each gentleman reconducted his lady to the room which they had previously occupied.

In this remark, we must except Mr. Hamilton and Mary, who contrived to become the *last couple* in the procession, and who remained behind in the entry, unmissed by the company.

"Mary," said Hamilton, "our present interview must be brief. I have something to impart to you which I am anxious you should hear, but I cannot do it now; it is impossible to do so under the present circumstances."

"Indeed, Mr. Hamilton," said Mary, "what can it be?"

"I cannot even intimate what it is *now*, Mary," said Hamilton, "but meet me to-morrow morning in the thicket near the burying ground, and I will tell you. There we shall be unnoticed and undisturbed. Say, will you do it, and let us join the company, for we shall be missed."

Urged beyond her better judgment by the hypocritical protestations of Hamilton, Mary consented to meet him on the following morning at ten o'clock, at the place specified, and each of them glided into the room unperceived. Mary joined the company of Wm. Churchill and her sister, who entered into a general conversation; still Mary's eyes would wander to that part of the room where Hamilton might be, and several times William Churchill had observed it, which tended greatly to diminish his enjoyments. He became somewhat serious, and talked but little.

"What is the matter, William," said Mary, "you don't seem to talk much?"

"Do you wish to hear me talk?" inquired Churchill.

"Why, yes, certainly," said Mary, "what a strange question."

"Come then this way, you and Ellen," said Churchill, "I have something to say to both."

The sisters retired apart from the company, where Wm. Churchill expressed to Mary what he had already said to Ellen:

"Come, William," said Mary, "what is it you are about to say?"

"Well, Mary," replied Churchill, "it is simply this: I wish to ask you what you think of George Hamilton?"

"What do I think of him," echoed Mary, and at the same time blushing at the remembrance of the card at the supper table, the meeting in the entry, and appointment for the morning—"why, he seems to me to be a very pleasant young man, and a gentleman. Don't you think so, William?"

"In truth, Mary," replied William, "my mind misgives me. I think him a *dangerous* man."

"For shame, William," said Mary, "you are jealous of him because of the little attentions he has shown me this evening."

"Not so, Mary; not so; but enough of this; I'll say no more. Some of the company are going, and let us retire."

William Churchill, Mary, and Ellen, now began their preparations for departure, and as they were passing towards the front door, to gain the street, Hamilton came up and offered his hand to Churchill, and bade him good evening. Churchill took his hand in rather a cool manner, and said "good evening." Hamilton also shook hands with the two sisters, and bade them good night. As he took the hand of Mary, he whispered in her ear, unperceived by Churchill or Ellen, "*Remember the appointment in the woods,*" and the parties separated.

"*Remember the appointment in the woods.*" These words rung in the ears of Mary Bean, and could she have but foreseen that they were to prove the death knell of all her earthly hopes, how fortunate would it have been for her. But no, Hamilton had, as it were, cast a spell upon her; she was fascinated with his person, and her woman's curiosity was all on tiptoe, for the revelation which he had proposed to make to her, at their contemplated meeting in the woods. It was getting late, and Mary retired to rest. She lay thinking of the singular meeting between herself and Hamilton, till she fell into a sort of dreamy reverie, and "*remember the appointment in the woods,*" died on her lips as she dropped to sleep.

CHAPTER III.

Mary Bean awoke early in the morning and made preparations for the meeting which she had pledged to Hamilton. It was a glorious morning; not a cloud appeared in the blue expanse; all nature seemed glad, and the surrounding trees were vocal with the songs of the happy birds. Yes, all were happy; but little did Mary think what was in reserve for her, as she was busily preparing to meet the man who was plotting her ruin.

Breakfast over, and the usual morning's work having been accomplished, Mary threw on a light bonnet, and glided unperceived out of the house, and pursued her course toward the thicket.

Hamilton had been sometime there, and had become quite impatient, notwithstanding he was in advance of the time appointed. At length he discovered the fair form of Mary Bean as she entered the wood, and quickly rising, went forward to meet her.

"Dear Mary," said Hamilton, as he took her gently by the hand, "I was fearful you would disappoint me; but you are here; thanks, a thousand thanks for the precious opportunity you have afforded me of imparting to you that which I alluded last evening. Come, let us go a little farther into the wood." Thus saying, he urged her still further onward until they came to the trunk of a prostrate tree; "here Mary, let us sit together and I will tell you all I have to say."

Mary sat down beside the arch seducer, to listen to the conversation which was to prove her ruin.

"Dear Mary," said Hamilton, "I have planned this meeting for the purpose of expressing to you the *love I have for you.*"

Mary started from her seat, and exclaimed, "Mr. Hamilton, you must not speak to me of that, for I am an affianced bride."

"But sit quietly, dear Mary," said Hamilton, as he gently drew her back to the seat, "sit quietly, Mary, and listen to me, and then I will hear your objections."

Mary was again seated, and again within the coil of the serpent.

"You know, Mary, that I left this village three years ago, and went to Manchester; during that space of time I have been in business there, and have been prosperous; I am wealthy; I have long been desirous of forming an alliance with some one that I could devotedly and truly love; one who would be worthy of the distinguished circles in which I move. I have looked in vain for such an one; my thoughts at length have turned to this village; I thought of you; I knew your worth, your virtues and your accomplishments. I resolved to see you, and having declared my *honest* love, to throw myself and fortune at your feet."—With this rhapsody of nonsense, Hamilton placed his arm about the waist of Mary, who was so overcome with the passionate speech of Hamilton, that she scarcely noticed it, nor even offered resistance. At this Hamilton took courage. Mary heaved a sigh, which too plainly told the conflict in her heart.

"Come, dearest Mary," said Hamilton, "speak to me; bid me at least to hope!"

"Mr. Hamilton," said Mary, "how can I listen to such protestations as these, when I am already pledged to William Churchill? What would the world think to find me even here now, listening to the declarations of a rival lover?"

"Nay, nay, Mary," urged Hamilton, "I am no rival lover; I am a *true admirer, adorer* of yourself; I love you for yourself alone.—Churchill is in no way adapted to you; nay, I know, if you will speak the honest sentiments of your heart that you do not feel that love and regard for him that you ought to feel if you would become his wife."

The poison was beginning to take effect; Mary contrasted in her mind the difference between the two in regard to intellectual attainments, respectability and wealth. She weighed with a partial scale; her predilections were in favor of Hamilton; she remembered that she had given her heart to Churchill at his first solicitation; there had been no strife for it; there were no competitors for her affections, when Churchill won her; now there was a strife; she listened to the rhapsodies of Hamilton; his protestations of love; his oath of unchangeable fidelity; her heart was affected; the citadel had been powerfully attacked; she thought,—reflected,—*consented*. Alas! poor Mary!

"Come, dearest Mary," anxiously exclaimed Hamilton, "do no longer remain silent; speak to me; my course is plain before me; if you yield to my wishes, I am the happiest of men; if you refuse me, *I will not long survive the shock!*"

The last exclamation being given with true *melo-dramatic* emphasis, roused Mary from her reverie.

"Mr. Hamilton, every one would censure me for this act, and how can I yield my heart when I know I shall be despised of the world, and rejected by my friends?"

"Dearest Mary," said Hamilton, "what is the world to you or me? Happiness is the great end of existence; to enjoy the greatest amount of happiness is the true object that Heaven sent us into this world to effect. How can it be better effected than by correcting the mistakes we have fallen into, as soon as the mistakes are discovered? If in the moments of youthful indiscretion, before, perhaps, your mind was sufficiently matured to decide and choose for yourself, you have unwisely given your affections to one, who, though he may be externally moral, yet is entirely incapable of appreciating or reciprocating your love, is it not the part of wisdom, nay, Mary, is it not a duty that you owe yourself, and the Being that made you, to withdraw those affections which he has given you, from an unworthy object, and place them where they shall be truly valued and appreciated, and honestly reciprocated by a *faithful heart?* I need not appeal to your education, to your intellect, for confirmation of this truth, for I know that your heart approves it, and answers *yes.*"

Alas for Mary! she was now fully secured within the toils of the spoiler, for she could not withstand *such a display of heartfelt* eloquence, or *such an appeal to her vanity and intellect.*

"Alas! Mr. Hamilton," said Mary, "how can I escape the scorn and derision of my friends and acquaintances did I yield to you my heart?"

"Easily, Mary, easily," earnestly replied Hamilton. "Let us leave this place instantly, and go to Manchester, where I reside, and when there we will have the marriage ceremony performed. As for Churchill, he will soon get over it, for his love is not *very deep* I'll warrant you, and your friends will speedily overlook your course when they find that you have formed an honorable and lucrative alliance, and as for the community, why, with them it will be but a nine days wonder, and soon will be forgotten."

The remainder of the interview between the black-hearted scoundrel and deluded girl, was spent in arranging for the proposed departure, and in forming plans of future action.

They separated; Hamilton exulting in the success which had attended his efforts, and Mary with a mind filled with doubts and misgivings; yet, as she reflected upon the arguments adduced by Hamilton she endeavored to persuade herself that the end justified the means, and finally settled down in a confirmed resolution to adopt the course which her *lover* had so ingeniously marked out.

Not for a moment in the day was the subject out of her mind, and often, during the process of making her preparations for departure, would her imagination paint to her in most glowing colors, the scenes of happiness and delight which Hamilton had so cunningly portrayed.

CHAPTER IV.

Brief was the period of sleep that Mary enjoyed on the night succeeding her interview; her head was busy in planning future schemes, although at times she felt misgivings in leaving the home of her nativity. Her sister Ellen had portrayed the endearments of home, and had also made use of all available arguments that she could think of to dissuade her from going, yet to no purpose.

Mary was headstrong; although the possessor of great beauty, still she was not without faults. Accustomed to being petted and indulged, she could not brook restraint. On the afternoon of the day on which she met Hamilton in the woods, Mr. Churchill became accidentally acquainted of Mary's intention to leave for Manchester, and immediately addressed her a note.

"Dear Mary:

"I have heard from your sister Ellen, that you intend leaving this place in company with the Mr. Hamilton whom we met at the party at Col. Chase's.

"I write to know if it can be possible that you can contemplate such an act?

"Is it possible that you can disregard your vows to one who *truly loves you*, and consent by such an act to wound the feelings of a devoted sister, and to bring upon yourself the suspicions of your friends? I will not attempt, dear Mary, to portray the emotions of my heart at this intelligence, for if you appreciate my love, you can appreciate these feelings. I cannot persuade myself, nor will I believe, that it is true that you intend to depart.

"Affectionately, your devoted Churchill"

"P.S.—I will call on you in an hour."

Mary, in reply, informed him that it was true, and gave him, as well as her sister Ellen, what *she* considered satisfactory reasons for so doing, although they were by no means the *true* ones. At nine o'clock Mary was at the stage office; Hamilton joined her by appointment, at a designated place on her way from home, and but a few moments elapsed before the stage coach was at the office door.

Mary Bean and George Hamilton took their seats in the coach, and while Hamilton was perusing a morning paper, Mary took a survey of her native village, and of the various familiar objects, as the coach rolled out of town.—Little did the infatuated Mary Bean think that she saw her native village for the last, *last* time.

As she looked upon the neat village church standing upon its carpet of green, and thought of the times that she had been called there, in company with others, at the sound of the Sabbath bell, a feeling of melancholy stole over her spirit. As she gazed through the trees and saw the smoke rising from the kitchen chimney of Col. Chase's mansion, where she had so recently spent a happy evening, and recalled to her mind the *possibility* that she might never behold her native village again, she sighed in spirit, and an unbidden tear forced a passage down her cheek. To portray all the feelings of poor Mary's heart, would be an almost endless task, so we will leave her to her reflections, and turn to other incidents of travel.

According to proposal, William Churchill called to see Mary at her sister's, but found that she had gone. Anticipating that he might not see her, he had written and despatched a letter to the stage office, with directions that it should be presented to her on her departure.

When Mary arrived at the office, she found that a letter had been left there for her, which the gentleman who kept the stage office was desired to give her on her arrival. This letter she concealed about her person, intending to read it the first favorable opportunity. No opportunity had yet occurred, as passengers had been getting into the coach at intervals, and now the number consisted of eight persons.—Three elderly gentlemen sat upon the back seat; Mr. Hamilton, and a young gentleman, apparently a stranger in the place, occupied the middle seat, and the forward one was occupied by Mary and two old ladies. As yet no conversation had been begun, and thus far they had rode on in silence.

Having now arrived at the station where they were to change horses, the passengers alighted and stepped into the hotel, and waited until the coach was prepared to proceed.

While waiting in a room of the hotel, Mary found a good opportunity to read her letter; she accordingly broke the seal and opened it. It was from William Churchill, the man she had deserted, but who, of all others, she had most reason to love. The letter contained no upbraidings, but breathed an honest and ardent devotion couched in the mildest and most respectful language:

"Dear Mary,—for such you will ever be to me—it would be impossible for you to conceive, as it would be for me to express, the anguish that now wrings my heart. If leaving your native village, and those who fondly love you, was calculated to increase the sum of your happiness, I would freely give you up; tho' hard indeed would be the sacrifice, for none love you with a deeper devotion than I do.—But when I reflect that you are deceived and deluded by one, whom I believe unworthy of the smallest favor that you can bestow,—when I reflect that you are led astray by false statements and falser prospects, can you be surprised that my heart should be torn with anguish? Ah, dearest Mary! I pity you, from my heart I pity you, but I will not upbraid you. When you have proved the falsity of this man's love, then you will think of what I have here written. I know not from whence I receive the impression, unless it be from Heaven, but I fear it, I feel it, nay, I would almost say, I know it—*that man will deceive you and desert you. I warn you, beware!* Wm. Churchill."

Mary had just finished her letter, as the driver shouted, "all aboard." The passengers were once more seated in the coach, and again it moved forward at a rapid pace.

Mary's heart was full, for the letter had very much troubled her, still she managed to disguise her feelings, and entered into a conversation with Hamilton, which served to banish for the time all recollections of home and the letter.

Our travellers were now interrupted in their progress by the stopping of the coach to receive an additional passenger, which would make up their complement, as nine only could be seated in the coach. This last individual who was about stepping into the stage, was no less a personage than a genuine Yankee pedlar, who wouldn't foot it any further no how.

"Well, I reck'n you're about as thick as three in a bed inside here; but I say, can't you kinder pucker up a leetle and wedge me in somehow? I'm nation tired."

All this was said while the pedlar stood upon the step, just ready to enter the coach.

Finding that they were to have a rather pleasant addition to their number, the passengers made room sufficient to accommodate the pedlar, and once more the stage was on its way. No one being much disposed to talk, our Yankee thought it would be a good opportunity to say something. Accordingly he pulled a razor out of his pocket, and opened the conversation.

"I say, I spose there ain't none o' you that knows who I am. Well, that ain't no matter no how, but I just as live you'd know my name as not. My name is Prosperity Jones, and I was raised up in Connecticut, and I reck'n I'm a pretty tall specimen of domestic manufacter from that ere State, for I'm six foot without any stockins on. Say wouldn't some o' you like to buy a razor? Well, p'raps you wouldn't."

"Mr. Jones, are you a married man?" inquired one of the passengers, more perhaps for the purpose of hearing the pedlar talk, than from any real curiosity as to the matter.

"Well, kinder yes, and then agin, kinder no! I'm sorter engaged; I'm going to be hitched when I git home. The good book says it ain't good for man to be alone, no how, so I thought I'd git married. But yet I do believe there is a time when it's better for a man to be alone."

"When is that, Mr. Jones?"

"Well, when there aint dinner enough only for one."

"Well, certainly, Mr. Jones," responded the gentleman, "that is a very philosophical remark, and we must all admit the truth of it."

"Yes!—well,"—said the pedlar, "I reck'n it's putty near the truth. I seed it 'lustrated yesterday."

"In what way, Mr. Jones?"

"Waal, I'll tell yer: you see I went into a grocery store and bought ten cents worth o' gingerbread and a cent's worth o' cheese for my dinner, and when I cum out o' the store I went along till I cum to a stone, and down I sot kerchunk, and thought I'd eat my dinner; well, I hadn't tuk but jest one bite when 'long cum an old woman, dress'd awful shabby; her face was all pucker'd up jest like a piece o' scorched sole leether; well, you see, she kept first eyeing me, and then my gingerbread; finally, says I, look here old critter, what on airth are you staring at me so fur, ha? Well, you see, she gin a most orful groan, and said she was hungry; well, I guess I didn't drop that cake and cheese quick nor nothing. Here old woman, says I, take this, what there is on't, and I'll wait till supper time; so off I started and left the old critter laying in the eatables. So you see from that circumstance that when the good book says, it ain't good for man to be alone, I concluded that it hadn't the slightest allusion no how, to dinner time, when there aint only dinner enough for one."

The company joined in a hearty laugh at this recital, and applauded the countryman's generosity.

The Yankee pedlar served a good purpose, in relieving the tedium of the journey, by his wit and stories, and kept the company of travellers in most excellent humor.

The journey in due course of time, was accomplished without accident, and three of the passengers, Mary, Hamilton, and the pedlar stopped at Manchester; the others left at intervals before reaching this town, which was the end of the stage route.

CHAPTER V.

Mary was much pleased with Manchester; it opened to her new scenes, and, forming new acquaintances diverted her mind from home and its associations. Hamilton was assiduous in his attentions to her, and embraced every opportunity to display Mary to the best advantage. He took her to the factories, and showed her the various machines used in the manufacture of the goods, and introduced her to several of the pretty factory girls.

Hamilton boarded Mary at one of the factory boarding houses, where, by special agreement, she was accommodated with a furnished room, not only for her own convenience, but also to accommodate Hamilton, who visited her regularly every evening.

Mary's mind was ill at ease, for Hamilton had of late said nothing to her about the marriage ceremony which was to have taken place soon after their arrival in Manchester; and often, when he had visited her, Mary discovered that he was somewhat under the influence of stimulus, which made him less respectful in his deportment towards her. She greatly feared that all was not as it should be, and intimated something to that effect to one of the girls who boarded in the house, but received nothing in reply that was in any degree satisfactory.

One evening Hamilton left Mary in considerable agitation of mind in consequence of a base proposal he had made to her. So great an impression did it make upon her mind, that even sleep could not efface it. She dreamed that she was deserted by Hamilton, and that he was implicated in causing the death of an individual, for which he was to be hung.

Poor Mary experienced in her dream all the anguish of reality, and awoke with the anguish still filling her heart. She related her dream to some of the factory girls, who interpreted it upon the ground of "dreams going by contraries," and assured her that it was ominous of her prosperity and success.

Just after dinner, on the day following her dream, Mary stood in the front yard of her boarding house, in company with one or two of the operatives, when they were startled by a voice exclaiming:

"Well, gals, how do you dew? I couldn't sell you nothing, no how, could I?"

Mary turned quickly round, and sure enough, there stood the identical pedlar, that self-same Prosperity Jones who formed one of the party in the stage coach.

"Well, I swan to man," said the pedlar, "I'd eenmost swear right out that I've seen you afore; it strikes me I kinder recollect o' seeing that smiling face o' your'n in some other place afore this?"

"Yes," said Mary, "we have met before; you were a fellow passenger with me in the stage coach when I came to Manchester a short time since."

"Yes, so I was," exclaimed Jones; "I van, I know'd it; well, I'm glad to see you. Couldn't I sell you a notion or two to-day? I've got eenamost anything, from a horn comb to a gold ring."

"Well," said one of the girls, "we will look at your articles and see what you have."

The pedlar opened his packs for their inspection, and then turned to Mary and invited her "to examine the articles."

"It won't be of any use, Mr. Jones, as I don't wish to buy anything."

"Lord bless your pooty little mouth," said the pedlar, "you ain't forgot my name, have you."

"O, no," said Mary, "I shall never forget your face or your name, as long as I remember the story you told in the stage."

"Story?" said the pedlar, "I don't recollect any story, miss."

"Why," said Mary, "the story about the poor woman, and the gingerbread you gave her."

"Well, I van," said the pedlar, "I believe I did tell that story."

"Ah, Mr. Jones, it was kind in you to do that, it manifested a benevolent heart," said Mary.

"Well, I thank you for that compliment, miss," said the pedlar, "and may you never see the time when you shall want for food or friends."

Mary heaved a deep sigh as the past and the present were before her mind's eye, and thought it not entirely impossible that she *might* see the time when she might need *both*.

The pedlar succeeded in selling the young women a few small articles, and bidding them a "good day," jogged onward, previously telling them, however, that he was going to be round in "these ere parts for a spell or so," and if they should happen to want anything in his line, he should be happy to supply them.

The factory bell now tolled for the operatives to go to work, and the young women separated.

On the morning of this day on which the pedlar and the girls had the interview, Hamilton took his gun and went into Manchester woods on a shooting excursion. This was an amusement he was exceedingly fond of, and one in which he frequently indulged.

Having traversed the woods in pursuit of game until he had become somewhat fatigued he sat down upon a log to rest himself, and to partake of some luncheon with which he had provided himself. As he sat enjoying his repast, he heard the crack of a rifle not very far from him, and immediately the scattering of shot rather too near him for comfort or safety. He sprang to his feet, and looking in the direction from whence the noise of the rifle had appeared to come, he saw a man advancing, clad in a hunting dress, who appeared to be out for the same purpose as himself.

As the man approached, Hamilton instantly recognized Wenton, an old associate, and his equal in crime. These two persons were soon seated together engaged in close conversation.

"Where have you been along back?" inquired Wenton; "I have not seen or heard anything about you; up to your old tricks, eh?"

"Well, as to that," replied Hamilton, "I haven't been idle altogether; I've taken a short trip to Canada since I saw you."

"Have you, though?" inquired Wenton—"Well, how go matters and things in those regions? Any chance to do anything by which a fellow can enrich himself in an *honorable* way?"

"Why, as to that," replied Hamilton, "I can't answer for *your* success, but *mine* has been complete."

"Ah! has it?" observed his friend, "how so? tell us about it."

"You must know then," remarked Hamilton, "that I brought away with me as pretty a girl as ever you laid your two eyes upon."

"No! and who is she?"

"Well, Mary Bean."

"Tell me, Hamilton, are you going to make a *wife* of her?"

"As to that, I *rayther* think I shan't right off; nevertheless, I've promised to marry, and I shall do so."

"And when will that *happy* day come?" inquired Wenton, sarcastically.

"I hardly think it will take place until two Sundays happen in the same week, and when they do, I shall marry her on *one* of them."

"I understand," replied Wenton, "you design to have her a wife without going through the ceremony."

"Well," replied Hamilton, "you've guessed it pretty tolerable near; in fact, you have come so near to it, that it does not require any further explanation."

"Well, well, enough on that matter;" said Wenton; "I've got something to propose if you are up for a bit of a raise in the money line. It is a great chance and if well planned can be carried through, and something handsome made all round. What say, are you ripe?"

"For anything," replied Hamilton, "that will put me in funds, for I'm about drained out—the last suit of clothes I *purchased* for my visit to Canada hasn't been paid for yet, and what's more, I don't think it will be unless I make a raise in some quarter."

"There's no trouble about the money," added Wenton, "if you are up for a time there'll be money enough when the work is accomplished."

"Well, proceed Wenton, let me hear the plot," demanded Hamilton.

"Well, then, to business! You've heard of Mr. Parsons, I suppose, who lives here in Manchester?"

"What, the tax gatherer?"

"The same!"

"O, yes, I've not only heard of him, but I know him, and what's more my Mary knows him; she's been down to his house several times."

"That's well," replied Wenton, "for *that* will materially assist us in our plans. You know Bowen too, don't you?"

"Well, I reckon I do; he's one of us."

"He is so, and wide awake for a spree," replied Wenton, "but listen to the plan; you know this Parsons generally has in his possession large amounts of the town's money; and if a convenient opportunity should occur it would require but a slight tap on the head to come in possession of it."

"Just so," replied Hamilton, "but the difficulty in my opinion will be to obtain this *convenient opportunity* that you speak of; for it is not likely that he carries his money about with him wherever he goes."

"That's true," observed Wenton, "but we must seek to draw him from his home in an unexpected manner, and that too *very soon*, as he is now in funds, having collected large amounts of money within a few days."

"True; it must be so," replied Hamilton; "but tell me, Wenton, what about Bowen?"

"O, he and I have talked the matter all over, and he is prepared for the undertaking. I shall leave here to-night, and return to-morrow; meanwhile I shall see Bowen, and when we are ready to commence operations, we shall send you a letter, and of course you will follow its instructions. There must be no *failure* here; the blow, when struck, must be *decisive*."

"I understand," replied Hamilton, "you can depend on me."

The matter being thus arranged between these two black hearted villains, they separated; Wenton one way, while Hamilton returned to prepare for his usual visit to Mary.

Most of the day being now spent, Hamilton arrayed himself in his best, and started, as the shades of the evening closed in, for the boarding house of the deceived Mary Bean. She was expecting him, it being near his usual hour, and rose to receive him as he gently tapped upon the door of her apartment. As they met they cordially embraced each other; the fair form of the deluded and deceived Mary was enfolded in the arms of a vile seducer who that night was determined to effect her ruin.

They both seated themselves upon the sofa, and Hamilton began his damning work of destruction.

"Dearest Mary, you know not how much it grieves me to be obliged to communicate to you intelligence of an unpleasant character; but my *love* for you will not allow me to with-hold from you that which you *must* sooner or later hear from other tongues, should I fail to retrieve my fortune."

"Speak, dear George," said the devoted girl, "let me know the worst; to lose your love and esteem would be the heaviest calamity that could befall me. It is not that?"

"Nay, Mary, not that; but I am a bankrupt in consequence of the fail-ure of a large firm in a neighboring city. I have lost all that I possessed, and poverty is staring me in the face. I would give you a maintenance becoming your situation, and one worthy the love you bear me; but while I possess the disposition I lack the means."

It will readily be perceived that this false statement being made at this time to Mary, was for the purpose of blinding her eyes and allaying any suspicions that she might indulge, on hearing of Hamilton's leaving the town for a few days, or in case he should soon return to her with replenished funds.

"Nay, dear George," said Mary, "speak not thus despondingly of your condition, for I can earn something for you and myself. There is an open-ing in the factory, where I can be employed to do a light kind of work, and I should admire to pass a few months in a factory just for the novelty of it."

This of all others, was the very thing Hamilton desired, and which he designed to propose to her, but happily for himself, the proposal came from her, to which he consented, but not without *seeming* reluctance.

"Well, dearest Mary," said Hamilton, as he impressed a kiss upon her fair cheek, "as you desire it, I will consent, though I would to heaven my necessities did not compel me to do so. To assist me thus in my misfortune and distress is kind, very kind, in you, and will ever be gratefully remembered by me."

"Nay, speak not thus, dear George; it is but doing my duty to you, and were I not willing to do so little as this, you might well suspect me of want of true attachment."

Hamilton had been foiled in his first attempts upon the virtue of Mary Bean, but tonight he was determined to succeed, and consummate her ruin.

"Mary," said Hamilton, in the blandest manners, as with his arm he encircled her waist, "business will call me to-morrow from town, for a day or two; I am going to see the firm by which I have lost my property, to ascertain if anything can be done by them in regard to making up any part of my loss; and another part of my business is to make some arrangements in view of our marriage."

"Marriage, dear George," exclaimed Mary, "shall we then be married? Then, indeed, will the eye of suspicion be turned from us. I greatly fear, dear George, that we are suffering in our reputation, and were the world to speak disrespectfully of you, it would occasion me the deepest sorrow."

It is true Mr. Hamilton bore a good character in community, for no one knew what his real character was. He usually dressed well, travelled much, and frequently visited Boston and other neighboring cities, and was supposed to be transacting some agency business, and consequently his reputation was not subjected to scrutiny.

"Fear not, Mary," said Hamilton, "we shall neither of us suffer in this respect, for it is generally known that we are to be married, and that ceremony shall take place on my return, which will be but two or three days at farthest. But, dearest Mary, why need we wait for that ceremony? We are married in heart already; heaven knows it; you know it; I know it; we mutually feel it."

Mary started at this intimation, as she feared that Hamilton was designing to act dishonorably.

"Nay, start not, dear Mary; the delay of a day or two in the mere ceremonies of our marriage can be of no importance to us."

"Ah, dear George, do not talk thus! You do not love me!"

"Not love you, Mary? Heaven hear me swear!" Here Hamilton in true tragic style dropped upon his knees, and raising his hands towards heaven, was about to utter something in confirmation on his declaration, when Mary stopped him.

"Hold, George, utter no oath for me: if you love me, your acts will speak more convincingly to me than words."

"Then do not doubt me, Mary! Do you think that I would do aught to cause one pang of grief to that fond heart? that I would cause one penitential tear to flow down that fair face? that I would do aught to sully the fair reputation of her who is my idol, the divinity I adore? Nay, wrong me not, Mary, by the thought."

It is unnecessary to detail the conversation that passed between them upon this occasion, as it will be remembered how easy Hamilton, by his sophistry, overcame the compunctions of Mary, when he desired her to leave her native village, and accompany him to Manchester. Suffice it to say that in the latter case he was equally successful, and on that fatal night accomplished the ruin and dishonor of the ill-fated Mary Bean.

* * *

In order to a complete elucidation of our story, there are three persons whom we must describe, one of which has already been described in part. These persons are Hamilton, Wenton and Bowen.

Hamilton's true character, as we have already intimated, was not known, save by those with whom he was associated in crime. The purlieus of Ann Street in Boston, where dwelt some of his companions in iniquity, of course possessed some knowledge of him, as also did those in a few other towns of less magnitude, who were likewise his partners in guilt.—Hamilton was one of those kind of men who had rigidly schooled his outward demeanor, and by the aid of a respectable looking suit of clothes, would be able to commit almost any depredation without being suspected of any impropriety. It was this display of demeanor, together with his respectable appearance, added to a degree of presumption founded upon a slight former acquaintance with Mary Bean, that enabled him so successfully to win her to his purpose, and induce her to fly with him, as it were, from the home of her nativity.

With regard to Wenton, little can be said in favor of his demeanor. He was rather rough than otherwise, yet evidently not very deeply schooled in crime. He had the ingenuity to contrive and plot, but did not possess so great a share of courage as would enable him to execute, except he were fired by stimulus, or wrought to the point of courage by the animadversions of his iniquitous associates. Still the *courage* of Wenton they could better dispense with in the matter that they had in hand, than they could do without his planning. In this he was an adept, and to his they were indebted for what success they met with in effecting their purposes.

Of Bowen, little can be said that is in any degree flattering. He was a hard-hearted, unfeeling fellow, with just enough of the devil in him to qualify him for the execution of any mission, however repulsive in its nature.

Such constituted the trio who had planned and were about to execute "a most foul and unnatural murder."

* * *

Keen were the compunctions, and painful the reflections of poor Mary Bean the morning following her *last* evening's interview with Hamilton. She was a ruined girl; far from the place of her nativity, bereft of home and all its endearments, she felt that she stood alone, unsupported, unprotected. Could she have received the consolations and caresses of her sister Ellen, these would have served to assuage her grief, and mitigate somewhat her mental sufferings. But no, her sister had never written to her during her absence, or sent her the slightest token that she still loved or thought of poor Mary. Whichever way the deluded girl might turn her eye, it could rest upon no one to whom she could look for counsel. To make her conduct known would be sure ruin to her reputation, and perhaps would incur Hamilton's everlasting displeasure. What, then, could she do? To whom, then, could she go? She believed that Hamilton loved her, and this afforded her some comfort! But *could* he love that one whose virtue was thus corruptible? This thought occurred to Mary; a doubt flitted across her mind; the thought was too painful; it would produce a phrenzy if encouraged; she would not doubt! He did, *he did love her!*

We have faintly portrayed some of the feelings which wrung the heart of poor Mary Bean after Hamilton had effected her downfall. On that fatal night, Hamilton took a most affectionate leave of Mary, informing her that it was necessary for him to leave the town for a few days on business of great importance, deeply affecting his pecuniary interests. This, as we have already observed in another place, was told Mary to allay any suspicions she might have with regard to the truth of the failure of the Boston firm, and of his loss of property. After Hamilton left Mary, he disguised his person, and on the following morning went immediately to the outskirts of the town, where he was to remain until he should receive intelligence from Wenton and Bowen.

A certain place was fixed upon in this piece of woods where the messenger should deposit the letter that was to convey to Hamilton information concerning the time, place and manner of executing the business.

Hamilton had provided himself with a little food, for he knew not how long he might be kept waiting for the letter, and in a state of anxious suspense he remained all that day in the woods.

It being as late as eight o'clock in the evening, Hamilton stole into the village, and retired hastily to his apartment unobserved by any, designing to seek the woods again at the earliest dawning of the morning light.

Having imbibed a portion of that *nectar* which villains always require to aid them in carrying on to completion their murderous designs, he threw himself upon the bed, with his clothes on, to dream of future success.

CHAPTER VI.

At early daybreak Hamilton arose, and providing himself with food sufficient for the day, pursued his course to the wood. He immediately repaired to the place designated as the repository of the letter, but found no letter there. The forenoon passed away, and no intelligence had been received. He remained in anxious suspense until about half past three o'clock in the afternoon, when, in the distance, he discovered a boy making towards the wood. Hamilton secreted himself in a favorable position to observe the movements of the boy, and beheld him enter the woods, and draw from his jacket pocket a letter, and deposit it under the trunk of a fallen tree.

As soon as the boy had disappeared, Hamilton emerged from his hiding place, and drew from its resting place the long looked for letter. He hastily broke the seal, and read as follows:

"Hamilton:—
"Meet me in the Manchester woods to-night, near the spot where the boy will deposit this letter. Bowen will be with us. We shall be there about seven o'clock. Be prompt, and success is ours.
Wenton."

Hamilton was overjoyed to receive the letter; he had long waited for it; he feared that the plan was thrown up, and all his bright prospects blighted. But not so; the letter had come; hope revived; success was placed almost beyond a question, and soon his wishes would be realized.

Hamilton remained in the woods that day until nearly dusk; but how heavily dragged the hours along. But nightfall did at last arrive, and he stole to his room; having disguised his person as much as possible, and placing a pistol of brandy in his pocket, and armed himself with a sharp knife, he again set out for the wood.

He walked to and fro, waiting with impatience the arrival of his coadjutors in crime, and while thinking intently on the business of the night, a low but shrill whistle resounded through the wood; it was answered by Hamilton; soon Bowen and Wenton were there, and the three ministers of death recognised each other.

"Come, Hamilton," said Bowen, "have you brought any *comfort* with you?"

"Take this, and see how it is," said Hamilton, as he drew from his pocket the pistol of brandy.

"Ah, this looks like it," said Bowen, as he seized the pistol, and quaffed a portion of its contents.

"I've brought some eatables," said Wenton, as he unrolled a paper containing some ham and bread. "It isn't so dark yet but that we can find the way to our mouths; come, let's take a bite all round, for it won't do to go to this business with weak hearts or empty stomachs."

The trio seated themselves on the trunk of the fallen tree near them, and partook of their repast, taking good care, by way of dessert, to empty the pistol of its last drop.

Having sufficiently refreshed themselves, and having become adequately wrought upon by their potations of brandy, they began their preparations.

"Now," said Wenton, "my plan is this; I'll go over to Parsons' house, and ascertain if he is at home; if so, I'll tell him that Mary Bean wishes to see him; I will offer to go with him to her; our course will necessarily lay by the edge of these woods; secrete yourselves near the road running by the outskirts of the wood, and when I get along to the point where you are secreted, you two must rush out upon him, gag him, and drag him into the woods; the rest we will leave to be governed by the circumstances. What think you of my plan?"

"Capital, capital!" exclaimed the two listeners, "that will work first rate."

Wenton started off upon his mission of villany, and Hamilton and Bowen secreted themselves according to directions.

A moment or two after they had gained their hiding place, a man was seen to enter the wood.

"Damnation!" exclaimed Hamilton, in a whisper, "are we to be foiled in our undertaking? Some one has just entered the wood."

"Most likely some person going home," replied Bowen; "he won't trouble us; see, he is hurrying on, and is now almost lost in the darkness."

"Lucky for us," said Hamilton, "that he is gone, for had he entered the wood at the time when Wenton should arrive with his victim, our scheme would be all knocked in the head."

While Hamilton and Bowen are awaiting the arrival of their unsuspecting victim, we will for a moment visit Mr. Parsons' house, and then return to the watchers in the wood.

* * *

Wenton had arrived at the house of Mr. Parsons; the demand at the door was answered by Mrs. Parsons.

"Good evening, madam," said Wenton, "is Mr. Parsons within?"

"He is," replied the lady, "will you walk in?"

"No, I thank you; I merely wish to see him a moment," replied Wenton, "will you ask him just to step to the door?"

Mr. Parsons immediately appeared, and inquired what the gentleman's business was.

"I think, sir," said Wenton, "you are acquainted with Mary Bean, are you not, sir?"

"I am," replied Mr. Parsons.

"She desired me to call on you, sir," said Wenton, "and request you to visit her this evening, as she wishes to see you on some business of importance."

"Will it not do in the morning, sir?" inquired Mr. Parsons. "It is rather a dark night, and I do not care about going out this evening, if I can avoid it."

"She informed me," remarked Wenton, "that she designed leaving town early in the morning, and that if she saw you, it must be to-night. Besides, sir, I am going in that direction, and will accompany you, if you desire it."

"Very well, sir," replied Mr. Parsons, "step in, and I will be ready in a moment."

Wenton excused himself from going in, and Mr. Parsons soon re-appeared with a lantern, and proceeded with Wenton.

* * *

Hamilton and Bowen are anxiously watching the arrival of Wenton and Parsons.

"Look yonder, Bowen," said Hamilton, "don't you see a light moving this way?"

"I do, just beyond the bend in the road; who in the devil can that be, I wonder? Another intruder, perhaps. See, it moves this way very fast."

"We shall know pretty quick who it is," said Hamilton, "for if it is Wenton, he will give us the signal."

The light becoming brighter, indicated the nearer approach of the person who bore it.—Soon voices were heard, and a loud "hem," from Wenton, assured the two ruffians in ambush that their victim was in their power.

They arrived opposite the spot where Hamilton and Bowen were secreted, when they both rushed out and seized Parsons.

"What means this?" exclaimed Parsons, addressing himself to Wenton. "Villain, you have deceived me!"

"To the woods,—to the woods,—quick!"—whispered Wenton.

"Nay, nay sir—no resistance," exclaimed Hamilton, as he flourished the knife before his face; "make neither noise or resistance at your peril."

Hamilton seized the lantern and dashed it to atoms against a tree, while Wenton and Bowen dragged Parsons to the woods.

Parsons made a desperate effort, and freed himself from the grasp of Wenton and Bowen, but Hamilton jumping forward seized him by the collar of his coat and jerked him to the ground.

"Not so fast, old fellow," said Hamilton, "you don't slip away quite so easy."

Meanwhile Bowen and Wenton were beside him, and Mr. Parsons found himself surrounded by a trio of base ruffians.

"Are ye fiends or men?" ejaculated Parsons. "Why do you thus assail me? what would you with me? would you murder me?"

"You have money about you, and we want it. Come, surrender!" demanded Bowen.

"The money is not mine; I cannot give what is not mine to give. If money is your object, go home with me, and I will give you any promise you require."

"Not so," replied Wenton, "we've had too much trouble to get you here, to place ourselves in jeopardy again."

"Oh, then, let me conjure you, spare my life! I am a husband and a father; I pray you spare my life."

The anguish of soul in which this appeal was made, took such hold of Wenton as almost to unnerve him, and he loosed his hold upon the unfortunate man.

Hamilton saw this, and in a fierce manner whispered to Wenton, "How now, brave man, do you falter from your purpose?"

"I cannot slay him," exclaimed Wenton.

Mr. Parsons heard this remark; "Thanks, thanks, that you have pity in your heart; would that your companions had as much."

"Cease, prating fool!" angrily exclaimed Hamilton. "Bowen, do your work at once, nor falter at this crisis."

"Mercy, mercy!" exclaimed Parsons; "spare me; I'll never reveal it to a living soul!"

Hamilton was impatient, and feared detection; his knife was in his grasp; he clenched it firmly in his hand, and with one bound he seized the unfortunate Parsons by the hair, and as he drew the fatal instrument across his throat, exclaimed:

"Be mine, then, the *glory* and the *shame!*"

Parsons fell, a bleeding, lifeless corpse at the feet of George Hamilton. Wenton stood horror-stricken at the bloody sight before him.

The two ruffians, Hamilton and Bowen, proceeded to search the pockets of the murdered man, and drew therefrom a pocket book containing sundry notes of hand, besides several bank bills of a large denomination, together with private papers, which were to them of no value.

Having extracted all the money, they proceeded to divide it among themselves, but Wenton, still standing fixed and motionless, refused the money, and appeared unconscious of the fact that Hamilton thrust his portion into his waistcoat pocket, for he was determined that Wenton should take his portion of the spoils.

As they were busily engaged in preparing to leave the woods, a rustling in the trees near by attracted Hamilton's attention. He rushed towards the spot, exclaiming, "We are betrayed! we have a witness here;" at the same time he dragged by the throat from behind a tree the man who had been a witness of the scene.

This was the man seen to enter the woods just before the arrival of Wenton and Parsons.

"Thunder and lightning, let go," exclaimed Prosperity Jones, as soon as he could get a chance to speak, "What in thunder you doin' on? why, you might a choked me to death!"

"Fool," exclaimed Hamilton, "you shall die for your presumption." Saying this, he brandished the knife above the pedlar's head.

"Why, look here, you, don't be so infernal careless with that are sharp knife; if it should happen to hit me, it might cut me pooty considerable."

Wenton here stepped forward and entreated Hamilton not to stain his hands with the blood of another fellow creature. Look on *this* murdered man, and be satisfied.

"I'm exactly of that gentleman's 'pinion. I have got a most decided objection to being sent out o' the world by the night train. I think you'd better follow his advice."

"We are not safe if this man lives," exclaimed Hamilton. "Dead men tell no tales; so let's dispatch him."

"Why, look o' here, you, don't be in such a thunderin' hurry; if you murder me, I'll be consarned if I don't expose the hull concern; but if you'll let me off with a hull skin, I'll never say nothin' nowhere to nobody, nothin' about it."

"I'll spare you," said Hamilton, "on two conditions. The first is that you'll swear and bind yourself to secrecy."

"I'll dew it; I'll dew it; I'll swear the handle right clean off of a jack knife."

"The second condition," observed Hamilton, "is that you immediately leave the country."

"What," said Prosperity, "go and live in the city all my days? By thunder, I'll dew it."

"No, fool," said Bowen, "he means that you shall leave America immediately and forever."

"Why, look here, you, I'm a pedlar, and how in fury can I get a livin' any how, if I go to England?"

"That's your affair," said Bowen, "and not ours. You can take your choice between that and death."

"Well, I'm up in a corner, and I s'pose I must come tew it, so I'll agree to what you say," replied Prosperity.

"Get up then," said Hamilton, as he urged him with a jerk of his collar; "come this way and kneel down beside this murdered man."

"No, no; now don't," exclaimed Prosperity, "I'm awful afeard o' dead folks."

"Down fool, upon your knees, as I bid you," growled out Hamilton, at the same time pulling him to the ground. "Now take that dead man's hand in yours."

"O good gracious! I daren't dew it no how," said Prosperity.

"Do that or die!" said Hamilton, brandishing the knife. "Have you the dead man by the hand?"

"Ye-ye-yes," stammered Prosperity, as he took the cold hand of Parsons, which made him shiver all over.

Hamilton laid the pedlar under a most solemn and binding obligation to keep the secret, and to immediately leave the country.

"Now go," said Hamilton to the pedlar, "and if you ever betray us by a look or a word, either written or spoken, or tell what you have this night seen and done, I'll have your life as the forfeit. Now go."

The pedlar made tracks, and has never since been seen.

The parties separated, leaving the body of Parsons in the wood, with the knife laying beside him. Hamilton went to his lodgings, cleaned the blood from his hands, drank freely of brandy, and finally overcome by its effects, sunk into a fitful sleep. Bowen betook himself in another direction to his abode, while poor, unfortunate Wenton was distressed beyond expression, at the recollection of the part he had taken in the transaction. Many a sleepless night did he pass in consequence of it, and do what he would, the form of the murdered man was continually before his eyes.

* * *

The day following, the intelligence of the mysterious disappearance of Mr. Parsons became noised abroad. Great was the excitement in the town, and various rumors were current as each one in its turn received credence.

Every effort was made to discover, if possible, where Mr. Parsons had gone. His house was thronged by anxious inquirers,—various interrogations were put to the family, but all that could be learned was, that a gentleman called at the house the evening before, near the hour of seven, and that Mr. Parsons went off with him, since which time he had not been seen.

The rivers were dragged,—every old building was searched,—inquiries were made at every place that he had been accustomed to visit, but no clue could be obtained of the whereabouts of the absent man. Days passed without receiving any intelligence, until at length search was made in the woods, and lo! the body of Mr. Parsons was found. When the announcement was made, tremendous excitement prevailed. A coroner's inquest was held upon the remains, and all the evidence that could possibly be obtained was laid before them. The decision was, "that the deceased came to his death by having his throat cut with a knife, by some person or persons to the jury unknown."

Here was a mystery—a man decoyed away from his home, robbed and murdered, and no clue could be obtained to the perpetrators of the deed. Who shall unravel the mystery of the "murdered man?"

CHAPTER VII.

Although Mary Bean was almost continually employed in the factory, still she had some leisure hours when her mind was unoccupied. Those were the times when she was most unhappy. Her thoughts would frequently turn to the home, and friends she had left; her mind often dwelt upon those scenes of enjoyment in which she had once participated, but as often as she contrasted that home, those friends, and those scenes, with her present condition, bitter were the feelings of anguish which took possession of her heart.

Often had she wished that she might for a brief period return to her native village, and gaze upon those familiar faces, and once more participate in those joyous scenes in which she had once been interested. But no; she had deserted home, friends, everything that was dear to her, and in confiding herself to one whose conduct had given the lie to his protestations, she could only look upon herself as the subject of a blasted reputation, and blighted hopes.

While Mary was thus far distant from Churchill, and perhaps seldom thought of him, he was not forgetful of her. Many were the tears that he shed over the wayward course pursued by Mary Bean, and no sacrifice would have been considered too great for him to make, could he have been assured of winning her back again to love and virtue.

One evening as Mary was returning to her boarding place, after the business of the day was over, she met a female friend who informed her that there was a letter in the post office for her. She immediately visited the office, and procured it, and on reading the post mark, found that it came from her native village. She hurried home, and having taken tea, retired to her own room to peruse the letter. It was from one who was *truly* her friend; it was the hand writing of William Churchill. Like the letter that was placed in her hand by his direction, when she left in the stage, it breathed no censure, no reproach, but, on the contrary, evinced the most tender solicitude.

"Mary:—

"Supposing that you are still at Manchester, I direct this letter to that place, hoping that it may fall into your hands, as I desire.

"The anxious solicitude that I feel, induces me again to address you, although I write under the influence of a grief-oppressed heart, and with a trembling hand. Associated as we have been,—loving as I *have* loved,—nay, more, loving as I *do still love,* I cannot forget you;—I cannot banish you from my remembrance. With *you* departed all my happiness, and I am constrained to do my own heart the justice to say that I shall never be happy again.

"A few nights since, after retiring to rest, my mind wandered to where you are, and while intently thinking of you, I fell asleep. I am not inclined to superstition, nor have I much faith in dreams; still, what I did dream, made a deep impression on my mind. The substance of it was that your husband (for such I presume he is now) had been discovered as the participator in a most fiendish murder, and that he was arrested, and that in consequence you were suffering the most bitter anguish of soul. Oh, Mary! when I awoke from that painful dream, happy indeed was I to find that it was *but a dream.*

"I know not, dear Mary, what your present condition is, but I hope you are happy. I should be cruel in the extreme did I hope or wish your condition otherwise. To know that *you* were miserable, would make my misery still deeper. Though you may forget me, and banish from your mind every remembrance of my love for you, still, living, I shall think of you, and dying, if permitted, would breathe a prayer to Heaven for your happiness. Farewell.
    William Churchill."

Mary's heart was not yet callous to every noble sentiment; she felt that Churchill's letter breathed the pure sentiments of ardent devotion. "Yes," said she, in a half audible voice, "his *is* true devotion. What tender solicitude he expresses for one so entirely unworthy of a single thought of his. Ah, how is he deceived! He thinks me married! I would to Heaven it were so; but no! no! agonizing thought, I am but—"

Here Mary's soliloquy was interrupted by a rap at the door. She rose to answer it, as Hamilton entered.

"Have you company, Mary?" said Hamilton, "I thought I heard you talking with some one."

"No," replied Mary, "no company—I was merely talking to myself."

"For the want of better company, perhaps," said Hamilton, laughing. "But tell me, what's the matter, Mary? Your eyes look red, as if you had been weeping; what is the matter?"

"Oh, Hamilton!" said Mary, bursting into tears, "I am indeed unhappy, very unhappy."

"And why should you be so, dearest? Am I not kind to you, and indulge you in all your wishes?"

"Ah, Hamilton, what have I not left for you? home, friends, relatives, all, all, I have left to follow you."

"You have, Mary, and have I not devotedly loved you? nay, do I not *now* love you?"

"But, Hamilton, have you acted honorably towards me? That vow of marriage still remains unfulfilled."

"It does, Mary; but why is it so? because I cannot maintain you as I would, and as your love deserves. But not many days shall pass before I will own you *wife* before the whole world."

Mary sighed, for well she knew that he had before promised this very same thing, and that promise had been broken.

"What have you here, a letter?" said Hamilton, as he took hold of the corner as it protruded from beneath her handkerchief; "may I read it?"

"You had better not," said Mary.

"Why not," replied Hamilton, "is it private?"

"Oh, no! I have no secrets from you, Hamilton, but if you read it, it may not please you."

"Never fear that," said Hamilton, "if that is all you fear, I'll read if you have no objections."

Hamilton read the letter, and a close observer of his countenance, while reading, might readily have perceived the workings of his mind displayed upon his face. He seemed as if at loss to know which was the most judicious course for him to take, whether to treat it seriously, or to laugh it off as a joke. At length he gave utterance to something, doubtless very unlike that which moved his heart.

"Well, Mary, your old lover takes a great deal of interest in you or me, I don't know exactly which; at all events, he does not slight either of us, for he *writes* to you, and *dreams* of me; but it is all nonsense, the whole of it; give it no heed, Mary."

"But," said Mary, "I cannot but think he feels what he says; it *seems* the language of true devotion."

"O yes," replied Hamilton, "he *plays* the lover very well, but you may depend that his principal uneasiness is occasioned by the reflection that he has lost so valuable a prize as yourself."

"I have always found him honorable," said Mary.

"True, you may," replied Hamilton, "for you had not tried him long enough to find him otherwise. But come, Mary, banish him from your thoughts, and think only of me, and of that pure devotion I entertain for you."

Having spent some hour longer with Mary, Hamilton left her; but his mind was uneasy; that dream of Churchill's troubled him; it came a little too near home, as well as a little too near the truth; but having reached his lodgings, he pursued his usual custom when thoughts oppressed him; a hearty drink from the bottle, soon drowned all remembrance of the dream.

To Mary's eyes sleep came not for many hours; she could not forget her situation; when she thought of the broken vows of Hamilton,—of the declarations of devotion and attachment set forth in Churchill's letters,—of her absence from friends and home,—how happy she doubtless would have been, had she linked her destinies with Churchill,—how miserable she might be in her connections with Hamilton,—when all these thoughts crowded upon her mind, she sunk beneath their weight, and gave vent to the agony of her heart in a flood of scalding tears, till at length nature becoming exhausted by protracted wakefulness, she fell into a disturbed sleep.

* * *

Who, that has thus far followed the unfortunate Mary Bean in her career, is not pained to witness the suffering and misery which she had thus brought upon herself? How forcibly does it illustrate, by contrast, that "the path of duty is the only path of safety." How truthfully, too, does it set forth the disposition of the female heart to take everything upon trust, without reflecting upon the rashness of acting without due consideration.

We know full well that there are hearts sufficiently steeped in villany to enable the possessor, without compunction, to coolly and deliberately plan and execute the overthrow of a virtuous female; we know, also, that there are too many females ready to lend a willing ear to the base flatteries of those who have no other object but to encompass the ruin of their victim.

The fault with Mary Bean, was a readiness to hear, a willingness to believe; and when flattering appeals were made to her heart and its native pride, she fell a victim. The moment she began to *doubt*, that moment she began to *err*. And when the conflict was going on in her heart, between home, friends, sister, and a well tried lover, on the one hand, and a comparative stranger on the other, using those arts which he, from his vicious life, knew to be most successful with woman, she should have paused—reflected—and decided according to the dictates of her better judgment. But no; she was rash and precipitate, and now she reaps the bitter fruit.

CHAPTER VIII.

Hamilton's visit to Mary was not as protracted as usual; the relation of Churchill's dream, containing, as it did, facts coming closely home, troubled Hamilton, although he endeavored to treat it with so much indifference. Mary had pressed upon his attention again, the subject of their marriage, for which he was now as unprepared as on former occasions, and the idea of leaving town for a few days suggested itself to his mind. This suggestion he followed, and on the next day left for Saco, in the State of Maine.

He departed without leaving any intimation whereby Mary could know where he had gone, consequently his failing to visit her on the following evening, excited her surprise. She felt uneasy, and on the next day went out to endeavor to ascertain, if possible, whither he had gone, or at least, to find out what had interrupted his usual visit. In her walk, she met an individual who was acquainted with Hamilton, and who had heard him say that he intended soon to go to Saco, and the fair presumption was, that he had gone there.

Having obtained this intelligence, Mary returned to her boarding house, resolved to address a letter to Hamilton, and ascertain why he had so unceremoniously left her.

"Dear Hamilton:—

"Not receiving the accustomed evening visit from you, and not having met you during the day, you cannot be surprised that I was at a loss to know the cause. I accordingly went among your acquaintance to ascertain where you were, and by the merest accident learned that you had left for Saco. Why you should have thus abruptly left me, affording me no intelligence of your intention to leave town, I am unable to answer in a manner satisfactory to my own mind.

"Why, dear George, should you neglect me thus? Have I not been, am I not still, earnestly devoted to you? Have you become wearied of me? How often have you declared me to be the object of your adoration and devotion, and how have I believed your

protestations? Have I become hateful to you, that you should thus steal from me, and endeavor to keep me in ignorance of where you are? Oh, George, pity me, for I am indeed unhappy! Flying with you, as I did, from my native village, what has it not cost me? I have sacrificed everything that is dear in life, and shall I be abandoned by you in my extremest need? Oh, George! as you value your peace in this life, and the welfare of your soul, come to me, for I am alone, wretched, and unhappy.
Mary."

When Hamilton read this letter, he felt conscious that he had done wrong, but still resolved to go immediately to Boston, without answering the letter, or even returning to Manchester, to console the heart-stricken Mary Bean.

Mary had waited two days since she sent the letter, and had received no answer, and she resolved to start for Saco, and endeavor to find Hamilton.

It did not require much reflection to bring Mary to this conclusion. She knew well her situation; she was a ruined girl—forsaken of friends, and Hamilton was the only one she felt she had a claim upon, and he, as the cause of her ruin, was bound, in pity and in honor, to protect her from suffering and want.

Mary started for Saco. It is not material that we record the various places in which she sought him, or the manner in which she found him; suffice it to say that she *did* find him, and threw herself upon his pity and protection.

Hamilton's heart was moved (for it was not yet wholly destitute of feeling), yes, his heart was moved as he gazed upon Mary Bean, the *wreck* only of what she once was. He had seen her in her joyous, happy days; he *now* saw her what his *passion* and his wicked counsel had made her.

Hamilton was overcome by her piteous appeals to his *honor* and to his mercy. He apologized to her for his unceremonious departure as well as he could, and took the unhappy girl to his heart.

They stayed but a very short time in Saco, as Hamilton intimated to Mary his intention of going to Boston *upon business,* as he said. This was a sufficient reason to blind Mary's eyes, but the *true* object of his visit was to hunt up Wenton and Bowen, who were his participants in the murder of Parsons, and to learn of them if they had any new project on foot which would result in the replenishing of his now almost exhausted funds.

On the second day after Mary's arrival, both left Saco for Boston.

*   *   *

It requires no prophet's eye to foresee, no prophet's tongue to foretell, the termination of a life the first step of which was an error. Nor does it become the reader to lavish blame upon the suffering victim of this error, until they feel assured in their own heart that they would not, or might not, have committed the same.

The steps which she had taken could not be retrieved; counsel and blame would both be equally useless. Instead of censure, the case of the unfortunate Mary calls for sympathy; and every kind and noble heart will award it to her without a murmur.

Those who do sympathize, may they never be cursed by such a result as hers, either in themselves or their friends. To those who refuse their sympathy, let me counsel you *"to look well to your own path,"* lest, while you condemn in Mary, you shall allow in yourself that which in her meets your condemnation.

Chapter IX.

On their arrival in Boston, Hamilton placed Mary in a cheap boarding house, in a remote part of the city, and then betook himself to a search after his old companions. He had learned from an associate of theirs, that Wenton and Bowen had gone to Boston, and he felt quite certain that he should ultimately succeed in ascertaining their whereabouts.

Mary was not much pleased with her stopping place, for she did not very well like the visitors who frequented the house, consequently she kept herself most of the time in her own room. As she sat perusing the morning paper, on the day after her arrival, she accidentally saw the advertisement of a famous astrologer; she was no believer in fortune telling, but she *did* believe that the *planets* had much to do in influencing a person's fortune for good or for evil, and believing also that astrology was in reality a *science*, and that in the hands of a *scientific person*, it could reveal much that was important to her with regard to her future life, she resolved to visit the gentleman, and desire him to draw her "horoscope." Without further reflection, she threw on her bonnet and shawl, and, following the directions of the advertisement, proceeded to the residence of the astrologer.

On arriving, she was shown into a room, in the centre of which was a table covered with mysterious looking books; charts of the "sidereal heavens" were hung about the room; in one part of it stood the celestial and terrestrial globes, and in another was a second table, upon which lay several finely drawn diagrams, illustrative of the course of the planets.

Mary entered the room, while her heart beat with anxiety, and took her seat on one side of the table; immediately the celebrated professor of the science appeared, and seated himself opposite his lady visiter. The professor was a fine looking man, with a most splendidly developed head, at once indicating the possession of intellect of a high order. He proceeded by ascertaining the day and hour of the birth of his visiter, and, after consulting for a moment two or three of those mysterious looking books before him, commenced drawing Mary's "horoscope," in the following language, to which she listened with almost breathless attention:

"Young lady, this city is not the place of your nativity; you was born some distance from here, in a village not far from the sea, in a westerly direction. Nothing material occurred during your period of childhood; by your family you were greatly beloved, especially by one member of it, a female; she, I should judge to be a sister; but *another* loves you—a young gentleman of real worth; but you will not marry him; miles divide you, and with him you will never meet again.

"I see another here who proffers you his love, but there is no honesty in him; he is a deceiver, and if he has not already deceived you, be sure that he soon will do so.

"There's quite a contrast between these two individuals; the first, of which I spoke as being now absent from you, I should judge, was noble, generous and just, and worthy any lady's love; but not so with the last; he is vindictive, harsh and jealous. Beware of him, young woman.

"He is not altogether free from crime, I fear, for, judging from the aspect of the planets *now, I see blood; he has, or will, shed blood!*"

Mary was agitated, and stopped the astrologer by asking a question.

"Sir, am I married?"

"No," promptly replied the astrologer; "you are not! The first young man never *promised* marriage, but *would have married you;* the last *has promised it,* but never will. Young woman, *you never will be married!*

"I can proceed no further in detail; your future looks quite dark; I see your end, but cannot tell how soon it will come; when you die, *it will be by violence.*"

Here the astrologer ceased his labors, and Mary departed. His words troubled her much, and she trembled for the future; the *past* she *knew* was true; she feared the future *might be.*

*　*　*

We have said that Hamilton went in pursuit of his comrades.

In a low, degraded portion of Ann Street, in the city of Boston, is an old dilapidated building, the lower story of which is used as a rummery, where liquors of the worst kind are sold, clandestinely, to those who are acquainted with the keeper, and the inmates, of the house. The room in the rear is used for dancing; in this miserable and filthy place, persons of the vilest character, and of different colors, congregate for purposes of drinking and dancing. It was half past ten o'clock on the evening after the arrival of Hamilton and Mary, that Hamilton might have been seen pursuing his way through this street, in search of some place of the above description of character. As he came along to the front of the house to which allusion has been made, the sound of a violin attracted his attention, and he entered this miserable den of infamy. He was immediately recognized, for he was no stranger; he had been in this place on other occasions when he had visited Boston, hence he required no introduction to its inmates.

"Yah, yah, Lord a' mercy, if dere isn't Massa Hamilton," exclaimed a burley negro with a comical looking phiz, at the same time dropping his fiddle; "why, Massa Hamilton, where de debbil you been dese tree, four, seberal weeks?"

"Well, you old son of Ham," said Hamilton, as he shook the negro's extended hand, "aint you dead yet?"

"Me dead," said the negro, "gorry, massa, no; me no tinks ob being dead, no how; no, no, dis child is alibe and kicking, jest like a crab."

All present seemed pleased at the visit of Hamilton, and welcomed him as an old customer to the house. The landlord, or rather keeper of this miserable hole, was in the front room, used as the bar room, which was separated from the dance room by two doors, an entry running between, so that when a person entered the outer door of the house, he could also enter the bar room through a door at his right hand, or keep on to the dance room without any communication with the drinking room, or even being able to see who might be in there.

"Massa Hamilton," said the negro, showing a good set of ivories, "what will you hab to drink? dis nigger will stand de treat on dis 'casion."

"Where's the landlord, Jumbo?" inquired Hamilton.

"In de s'loon, Massa Hamilton. Dis nigger'll go rite in and call de genlum rite off, 'fore soon, dis minnit."

"Well, call him; tell him I want to see him."

The negro disappeared, and opening the door of the saloon, as he called it, informed the keeper that "Massa Hamilton wanted to see him."

As soon as the negro spoke the name of Hamilton, two persons who were seated in the bar room, and the only persons there except the keeper of the house rose and went into the dance room with him. Those two persons were Bowen and Wenton. Hamilton was right glad to find his associates, and each having provided himself with a glass of spirit, sat down together and engaged in close conversation, while the negro commenced scraping his fiddle for those who were desirous of dancing.

The revelry had continued up to a late hour, it being now just upon twelve o'clock, and Hamilton, Wenton and Bowen rose to go out. Previous to their departure, a sailor came in, and making his way into the dance room, called for liquor. He was so far "over the bay," as folks sometimes say when they would describe a person who is considerably intoxicated and so boisterous and noisy withal, that, strange to say, the landlord refused him liquor, which so maddened him, that he severely threatened the keeper, and manifested a strong determination to do him personal injury. Hamilton interfered, and tried to reason with the sailor, which only served to exasperate him still more, and drawing from his breast pocket a loaded pistol, threatened to shoot Hamilton if he said another word.

Hamilton adroitly snatched the pistol from the hand of the sailor, while he directed at the same time a blow which prostrated him upon the floor. Jumping over the fallen sailor, who laid directly in the doorway; he made his way out of the house, followed by Wenton and Bowen; but before they had time to get many steps, the sailor had recovered himself, gained the street, and was pursuing them as well as he could, at the same time crying "Watch! watch! watch!" at the top of his voice. This trio of young men were soon pursued by two watchmen; they ran the length of Ann Street, and through Congress Street, the watchmen still in pursuit, when Hamilton drew the pistol which he had wrested from the sailor, and turning round presented it to the watchmen, exclaiming:

"Pursue me no further at your peril."

The watchman who was the foremost of the two in pursuit, halted, when his comrade remarked:

"Go on; don't let him bully you; rush up on him and seize him."

"If you do so," exclaimed Hamilton, "on your head be the consequences."

The watchman in the rear now urged again his companion to pursue; he started on to arrest Hamilton, while the rear watchman followed close upon his heels. *Hamilton fired;* the watchman *fell dead* into the arms of his companion. Hamilton fled, *and the assassin was never known.*

The three who had been thus hotly pursued by the watchmen, met in a saloon at the south part of the city, and while partaking of the refreshments they had ordered, talked over, in a subdued tone, the incident of the evening. The keeper of the saloon showing evident signs that he desired to close his establishment, it being nearly one o'clock, the parties left; Bowen and Wenton directing their steps to their temporary home, while Hamilton proceeded to his lodgings to prepare for his approaching departure from the city.

Early on the following morning, Hamilton and Mary Bean met, and taking the first train of cars for the East, they left Boston for Saco.

CHAPTER X.

The remainder of our story is briefly told. The true condition of Mary Bean could no longer be concealed; she was disgraced, and would soon become *a mother.* She again besought Hamilton to a fulfillment of his promise of marriage, before that ceremony would come too late to cover her shame.

Hamilton still plead for delay, and desired her to accompany him on a visit to one Dr. Savin, who was a particular friend of his, who in all probability would relieve her from all fears of her shame ever being made public. Mary refused, for her heart revolted at the idea. Hamilton reasoned with, and persuaded her, until at length she yielded to his infamous proposal.

Mary Bean entered the house of Dr. Savin, but *never was seen to come from it.* Death had done its work; *she died from violence!* How fearfully was the astrologer's prediction fulfilled!—What was to be done? The body must be secreted; the mill stream was a favorable place. It was done!

Days passed off, and Hamilton felt himself relieved of a burthen. Mary was dead, and none lived to tell the fearful story.

Shortly after the event, a body was discovered floating in the stream. It occasioned great excitement, and for a long time the manner of her death remained shrouded in mystery. Ellen Bean read the story of the mysterious death of her sister, as it appeared in the papers. At first, she was ready to question whether it could indeed be her; but the evidence was too strong to admit even of a single doubt. Her heart, her sympathies were strongly moved, and she resolved to visit the place. In company with William Churchill, she did so, and there beheld poor Mary's form laid in the cold embrace of death.

William Churchill and Ellen mingled their tears together as they stood gazing at Mary, mourning the premature departure of one who had thus fallen a victim to the wiles of a heartless seducer.

Preparations were immediately made to convey the remains of Mary Bean to her native village, and William Churchill and Ellen having received the body, enclosed in a neat coffin, proceeded on their sorrowful journey.

* * *

So great had been the excitement consequent upon the discovery of the violent death of Mr. Parsons, that the most assiduous efforts had been put forth for the purpose of ascertaining, if possible, who were the perpetrators of that horrible outrage. Many were questioned and closely scrutinized as to any knowledge that they might have of the affair, when at last Hamilton, Wenton and Bowen were suspected as being in some way implicated. They were arrested as the *supposed murderers*, and lodged in prison to await their trial.

* * *

If any reader should chance to visit, in Canada, the native village of Mary Bean, they will doubtless recognize the house where she was born, as we have described in our story. Should they find the house, by travelling a very short distance west from her birthplace, they will arrive at that neat little burying yard which is discernible from the window at which Ellen and Mary Bean sat in company, at the opening of our story. Enter this silent garden of the dead and in the northwest corner you will discover a new-made mound. Over this mound is erected a marble tablet, on which is the following inscription:

"Sacred to the memory of
MARY.
"To perpetuate that remembrance this tablet is
erected over her remains by one
who knew and loved her."

It is hardly necessary to inform the reader that this tablet was placed there by the faithful William Churchill.

'Sacred to the memory of
MARY.
To perpetuate that remembrance, this tablet is erected over her remains by one
who knew and loved her.'

The sudden departure and long absence of Mary had greatly saddened the heart of Churchill, and to that extent that a degree of melancholy had settled upon his spirit. Ellen too, had mourned her sister's absence, and now was mourning her death. Churchill and Ellen were thus enabled to sympathize with each other in a calamity so deeply affecting both.

A few months passed away, and William Churchill led Ellen Bean to the altar, and often may they be seen occupying that window where

Ellen and Mary had so frequently sat, and as they gaze out upon that grave yard, half hid from view, as it is, by intervening trees, the fate of poor Mary is their theme of converse.

Here let the curtain drop. We have told the piteous story of poor Mary. Hers was a short, but yet eventful life, and none can read it without lamenting her sad end.

Who, that has daughters, does not tremble at their fate as they look to the future? In such a world, surrounded, as they frequently are, by persons destitute of every virtuous sentiment, what father or mother is there that does not feel solicitous for his daughters? Inexperienced as they are, how apt are they to be led astray by false appearances, as well as hollow pretensions of love and friendship? Not unfrequently impatient of restraint, and indisposed to listen to the voice of counsel, the unthinking female is ensnared in the toils of the destroyer, and being insidiously led onward, step by step, she awakes from her dream of fancied happiness, but to mourn over her dishonor, and the destruction of her cherished hopes.

Such was the case with Mary Bean. Her life, her sufferings, and her death, are but a picture of the life, the sufferings, and the death of many others. Let those of her sex, then, who may chance to read these pages, be admonished in season, and not turn a deaf ear to those counsels, which, if regarded, would save them from misery and dishonor.

CHAPTER XI.

We have, in the last chapter, made an allusion to the marriage of William Churchill and Ellen Bean. Let not the reader suppose that this marriage was a precipitate affair.

For months did William Churchill mourn over the miseries and premature death of poor Mary Bean. Had she really been the wife of his youthful love, he could not have manifested more unfeigned sorrow, than was depicted in his very looks, expressions, and actions.

And poor Ellen will scarcely turn her eye to the last resting-place of her unfortunate sister, without giving vent to the deep grief of her heart in a flood of tears.

In short, both of them felt that they had indeed lost a *sister*, and they mourned over that precipitate course of conduct which had resulted in this untimely death, rather than foolishly to stigmatize her memory, by recounting her follies.

Every one in the village sympathized deeply with Ellen, and they never spoke of the unfortunate Mary but in terms of the kindest regard.

William Churchill and Ellen Bean were married, and two truer hearts were never united in the firm bonds of undissembled affection. They lived but for each other's society; but to anticipate and to execute each other's wishes. With hearts deeply devoted to each other, the whole object of their lives seemed to be, but to contribute each to the other's happiness. Of course they were happy! With such dispositions, and actuated by such motives, they could not be otherwise.

Were you to visit the residence of William Churchill, you would see the fond wife and the devoted husband occupying the once happy home of the ill-fated sister; and in the parlor of that house still hangs the portrait of Mary Bean, shrouded in crape, placed there as a signal of mourning and a test of remembrance, by the hand of the surviving sister.

None knew Mary Bean but to love her; she was kind, good, and gentle, but not so wise as she should have been, nay, not so wise as she would have been, had she followed more closely her reason and judgment, and less her impulsive and too generous nature. But she has passed away. Spring, with all its beauties and all its green foliage, may murmur its gentle breathings over the earth, making every eye beam with lustre, and, by its influence, gladdening every heart; but it cannot revive the lonely tenant of the grave. She sleeps, unheeding our animadversions upon her course of life, equally indifferent to our censures and our praises. In the beautiful language of one of nature's poets, we would say, to those who may read this narrative,

> "Speak gently of the erring:
>   Ye know not all the power
> With which the dark temptation came,
>   In some unguarded hour;
> Ye may not know how earnestly
>   *She* struggled, or how well,
> Until the hour of weakness came,
>   And sadly thus *she* fell."

*   *   *

In a previous chapter, we have mentioned that the *supposed murderers* were arrested and cast into prison, there to await a trial. They were arraigned, and pleaded *not guilty*, and were tried for the offence which it was supposed, by a large majority of people, that they actually committed. And the belief is, at this day, as general as it was on the day of their arrest. But they were acquitted, and are again at large in the community, ready for a repetition of a like offence, whenever their cupidity or vengeance may prompt them to it. It is not at all surprising, that the death of Mr. Parsons remains, to this day, *unavenged*—for who could prove them guilty? No eye saw the commission of the deed, save that of the pedlar; and though he was known to have been in the neighborhood on that day, and even until the evening when Mr. Parsons was murdered, yet he could be no where found. He had conformed to the letter and spirit of the *oath* which was *extorted* from him, and had left the country, for *parts unknown.*

Thus have the guilty been enabled to escape justice, and community is cursed by a new accession to the number of desperadoes which infest it.

And not only is the murder of Mr. Parsons unavenged, but also that of the watchman, who, in the faithful discharge of his duty, was coldly and heartlessly shot down on that memorable night, by the villanous Hamilton.

Thus it is, that justice, however strict, does oftentimes fail to reach the transgressor. But although this is true of *human* justice, it is not so of the *divine*, which will be *sure to overtake* them, sooner or later.

* * *

There is yet another whose villanous conduct richly entitles him to a post in the *penitentiary*—the famous Dr. Savin, who was the instrument in causing the death of Mary Bean.

When the body was discovered floating in the mill stream, a coroner's inquest was held upon it; but who could tell *how* the body came in the stream, or who put it there, or how it came to its evidently violent end? No one! Hamilton was far away, incarcerated within the walls of a prison; and had he been at large, he would have given no testimony, as *any* testimony that he might give would most surely implicate himself. Is it surprising, then, that the jury should render a verdict that "the person came to her death from causes to the jury unknown?" Not at all; and while this mystery enshrouds the whole transaction, the *murder* of Mary Bean is also *unavenged.*

* * *

Thus have we come to the

> "—last scene of all,
> That ends this strange, eventful history!"

Eventful, in truth, it has been; and, in as far as it may serve as a beacon light to others, in warning them of the dangers that beset them, so far is the author doing a public service. If it produce no good effect, she had better remained silent. But the hope, nay the belief, that some *will* read to be benefitted, has induced her to add the sequel, in order to finish what seemed before to require some further elucidation.

Part Second and Last of Mary Bean.

A

CONFESSION OF GEORGE HAMILTON

FOR THE

MURDER OF MARY BEAN.

Portrait of GEORGE HAMILTON.

PUBLISHED BY THE
REV. MR. MILLER.
1852.

Cover of *Life of George Hamilton* (1852). Part one of the Mary Bean story focused on the crime; in this continuation the focus was on the eventual punishment. Courtesy of the Borowitz Crime Collection, Department of Special Collections and Archives, Kent State University Libraries and Media Services.

LIFE OF GEORGE HAMILTON

A
Full and Complete Confession
Of the Horrid Transactions in the
Life of George Hamilton,
The Murderer of
Mary Bean, the Factory Girl,
Whose Lamentable Fate Has for Several Years Been Wrapt in
Mystery the Most Profound
Together with an
Authentic Narrative and Confession of Dr. Savin,
Who Was Tried at the September Term of the Criminal Court at
Saco, for His Participation
in the Murder of Mary Bean,
And a Thrilling Narrative of
Hamilton's Intercourse with a Gang of Notorious Counterfeiters;
Also Comprising a Clear and Distinct Account of the Extra-
ordinary and Highly Interesting Trial for this Shocking Murder,
and Hamilton's Conviction and Heart-rending End by Suicide,
Whilst in Jail, Previous to His Execution, in Saco, in the State of
Maine.
From the Memoir Written by Himself,
And
Edited by the Rev. Mr. Miller

Published by Rev. Mr. Miller
1852.

CHAPTER I.

With electrical rapidity the news of the murder of Mary Bean spread over the city. Every moment added to the number of the crowd, and to the powerful excitement that pervaded every heart. The ordinary business of the day was suspended, and men, in hurrying to the scene of the blood and death, looked at each other, and asked,

What has caused this heinous crime?

Upon the alarm, the police hastened to the spot, and with the greatest difficulty found their way to the murdered girl. Up and down the street, for many rods, stretched a swaying mass of human beings. The coroner was sent for at once.

Whilst they were awaiting his arrival, a handkerchief and gloves were discovered in the bosom of the murdered Mary Bean; and upon examination, a name was found written upon them. With a groan of agony, they read, "Frederick Hamilton."

The coroner at last arrived. The mob without had become impatient, and somewhat turbulent; but all commotion ceased on his arrival, as there was a prospect that they should soon have all the particulars of the horrible tragedy.

The coroner and the policemen examined the dead body; merely for form's sake, a jury of the bystanders were sworn, and some physicians examined with regard to the wounds.

All knew that a bloody murder had been committed, and so the jury declared with scarcely a moment's deliberation, merely adding, "by some person or persons to us unknown."

The result was communicated to the crowd, and at once they began to disperse.

The police, assisted by Frederick's father, commenced a search. Nothing was found, however, save the gloves and the handkerchief, and they bore the name of Frederick Hamilton, brother to George, and the youngest of the two. Humanity revolted at the idea of his being the murderer. Yet, how came the gloves and handkerchief upon the person of the girl?

His father was interrogated.

"Had Frederick Hamilton been at home on the day before, or on the evening of the murder?"

With tears in his eyes, the old man was compelled to answer, "No; he has not been here for several days."

Painful as it might be, it was necessary to arrest Frederick Hamilton. Several officers were despatched upon that unpleasant errand, and his father was sent to acquaint George Hamilton of his melancholy bereavement. The corpse of the murdered factory girl was removed and properly prepared for interment. With feelings that cannot be depicted, they endeavored to obliterate the bloody evidence of the cruel deed. Yet it was only by dint of great persuasion that they could be brought to perform the ungrateful task.

With an agonized heart, the father walked slowly towards the house of his elder son. He could not bring himself to believe that Frederick had committed the murder; for with him he had always been an especial favorite for his manliness; his urbanity, and his entire abhorrence of any conduct that savored of dishonor. The whole affair, to his mind, was wrapped in a mystery the most profound.

The old man arrived at the house of George Hamilton. Luckily the servant did not answer the bell; or, in obedience to his master's orders, he would have denied the old man admittance.

Hamilton had just left his room, and his favorite servant was attending him at breakfast.

"Tell George that I have awful news to communicate, and that I wish to see him," said the old man, seating himself in a chair in the hall, although the servant invited him into the parlor.

Hamilton had been momentarily expecting the intelligence of the murder since he had awoke from his slumbers.

When the servant announced the message of the old man; he endeavored to fortify himself for enacting his part in such a manner as to appear horrified and surprised. He bade his menial admit the messenger.

With a solemn, hesitating step, the old man entered the breakfast room, for he always squared his actions with the state of his feelings. He seated himself, and Hamilton, without raising his eyes from the plate he was using, inquired,

"You say you bring me bad news, father. What is it this time, for you are always a chilling messenger?"

The old man observed his downcast look, and a horrible conviction seized upon his mind.

"The girl is dead!"

"Dead!" exclaimed Hamilton, raising his eyes and staring at the old man with a look of well-feigned surprise.

"She was found in the stream this morning, murdered in a most horrible manner."

"Murdered! God deliver us. Can it be possible!"

"It is even so," said the old man, who had not once taken his eyes from Hamilton's countenance.

The eldest son had schooled himself for his part, and he acted it with skill. He paced his room apparently in great pain; then taking his hat, he told the servant to inform the family of his loss, and walked swiftly down stairs, leaving the old man alone in the room. He was not long alone, however, for the servants had overheard enough of his errand to know that some one was murdered, and a half a dozen females of the establishment were soon around him, listening to the heart-rending details.

With streaming eyes, the old man concluded his doleful tale, and returned to his home as doleful and as sad as if the only friend he had upon earth had left him to sorrow and desolation. He wandered around the solemn house without any object in view, like one possessed of a troubled spirit that could not find repose. Hamilton had already arrived, and was exhibiting every symptom of grief that could be thought of. He shed tears in the greatest abundance, and refused the consolation of several of his acquaintances who had called to comfort him under his misfortunes. Strange it is, that the human heart cannot arrive at such consummate perfection in goodness that it does in evil.

The officers despatched to arrest Frederick Hamilton. When the officers in quest of him came to his house, he was slumbering, unconscious of the fate that was hanging over his head.

The minions of the law were promptly admitted, and with feelings of alarm the wife and daughter, who were seated in the parlor, heard their inquiries for Frederick. In a moment all fears vanished from the wife's heart, and she hastened into an adjoining room to awaken her husband.

She was followed, however, by an officer, who passed rudely by her, and shaking Frederick roughly by the shoulder, he aroused him.

"What is your errand?" he asked, rubbing his eyes and yawning.

"You are arrested for the murder of Mary Bean, sir."

"What!" cried Frederick, "Mary Bean!" and he stared wildly at the policeman.

"Yes, for the murder of the missing factory girl."

Mrs. Hamilton fainted. A servant was called, and she was borne from the room. When she was gone, Frederick essayed to follow her; but he was prevented by an officer.

"Poor Mary murdered," slowly repeated the wretched man, as his brain reeled, and the objects around him grew dim and indistinct. "Poor Mary murdered."

"I repeat it, sir; and you are arrested for the murder."

With a groan that moved even the hardened wretches around him, Frederick Hamilton sank upon the floor.

Whilst the officers were endeavoring to restore animation, Mr. Bigelow entered the room, having been advised by the daughter of his partner's arrest; and he asked, in no very conciliatory manner,

"What means the invasion of these premises? What have you done to that person?" and he pointed to the prostrate form of Frederick.

"We are here upon duty," replied the leader, "and we are not to be deterred from performing it."

"What have you done to that man, I repeat? Duty or no duty, you will not abuse him in my presence."

"You may dispense with your alarm, sir, he has only fainted, and will soon recover."

"What is your duty with him?"

"To arrest him."

"Arrest him! for what?"

"Murder."

"Murder!" echoed Mr. Bigelow, perfectly astonished.

"For the murder of Mary Bean," returned the officer.

Bigelow nearly fainted—not that he for a moment supposed his friend guilty of the awful crime—but from his excess of wonder and fear. Wonder that so excellent a man should be even suspected, and fear that he was the victim of some hellish plot.

Hamilton, during this time, had recovered his consciousness; but he was so weak that he could hardly stand. He turned an imploring look upon the kind face of his partner, and the tears filled his eyes, and slowly trickled down his cheeks.

"I am ready, gentlemen," he said, in a faint voice. "Take me where you like. Of the crime with which you charge me, God knows I am innocent, and he will defend me."

The officers made no reply, but supporting Frederick, they left the cottage. When the prisoner reached the door, he turned to his friend, whose face was covered with his hands to hide his emotion, and said, with a voice choked with emotion,

"I leave my family in your charge, Bigelow; be kind to them, and console them, for my sake."

His friend dared not trust his voice to make a reply, and Hamilton was conveyed to prison. Finding their captive very weak from the sudden and terrible shock he had received, they had called a coach, and, as a consequence, the distance was soon traversed.

Frederick Hamilton was securely confined in a room, of which he was the only occupant, and he was therefore left to solitude and his own reflections. On his progress to prison, he had been informed by the officer, that the reason for his arrest originated in the circumstance of his gloves and handkerchief being found in the murdered girl's bosom. This explained to him at once the reasons for his arrest, and he felt convinced that he was the victim of a conspiracy.

Hope and confidence are the last friends to desert innocence; and Frederick calculated on a speedy release from confinement. Poor man—he could not foresee the intricate and tangled net with which he was surrounded, else he would have been compelled to acknowledge the extreme danger of his situation. He relied entirely upon his innocence, and the ease with which he could make it appear. Every circumstance, however, was decidedly against him. He had been absent all night, and had returned to his home at a late hour in the morning; he had been met by a watchman, and that too in front of the very spot where the body was found, and to his questions, had returned wild and incoherent answers. There was a terrible array of circumstances against him. Did he imagine that he could explain them? He never doubted it for a moment. He remembered the circumstances of his gloves and handkerchief, and the remarks that had induced him to leave them at the Brown Jug. He could show, conclusively, that he had never returned for them, and consequently that they could not have been left through his agency. How little he knew of the master-spirit that was sporting with his destiny, as a child plays with a toy.

Throughout all that day, nothing was talked of but the murder, and the subsequent arrest of the unfortunate Frederick. An hundred speculations were afloat regarding the cause that had prompted him to the rash act—for like all criminals, or rather all who were accused of crime—he was deemed guilty of the heinious offence. All were agreed that it was the most atrocious outrage ever perpetrated in the city, and the monster deserved a thousand deaths.

To the news-venders it was a perfect windfall. Edition after edition was published, containing an account of the horrid transaction, each one claiming to have some additional particulars, and the insatiate public bought and read them with anxiety.

Geographically, indeed, was the murderer's conduct depicted at the time of his arrest; and it was also said that no pen could describe the awful agony of that distinguished philanthropist, George Hamilton, who had lost a brother whom he tenderly loved, but who was said to have met his fraternal advances with vindictiveness and scorn.

How blindly the populace worship and grovel at the shrine of wealth and ostentation.

Amid all the exciting conversation attendant upon the state of affairs, not a voice was raised for Frederick Hamilton, who was incarcerated for the commission of the crime. Not a press, not a private individual proposed that public opinion should be suspended until the trial should take place, and the matter sifted to the bottom by the proper authorities. Not a single good property of his heart was mentioned, but brains and memories were raked and ransacked to find some little incident that might be made to tell against him.

How truly has it been said, that prosperity brings us friends, and adversity tries them.

We have said that there were no voices raised in his behalf, but we were wrong. There were two friends that upheld his innocence—two that did not hesitate to denounce his accusers—these were his partner and broken-hearted father. What could their voices avail to stay the storm that so desperately beat against his reputation. Were they rich? Were they powerful? Did they wear purple and fine linen?

Tarrying a moment to comfort the distracted wife and daughter, and then hastening to his store, to give instructions to his clerk, Mr. Bigelow then set out to visit his friend, in prison. By dint of much persuasion he obtained an interview, but it was only granted on the condition that the jailor should be present during the whole of it. To this Mr. Bigelow made no objection, and he visited the prisoner in his gloomy room. To him Frederick detailed every particular, all of which his friend noted down, and when he left him, promised to seek a counsel, and when he had made all the arrangements for his examination, to visit him again.

He had the most unshaken confidence in his friend's innocence; yet when he weighed the desperate chances against him, he felt his heart grow cold within him. He resolved to do all in his power, notwithstanding the array against him, and he accordingly sought the office of an eminent attorney, in the lower part of the city.

The attorney was a kind-hearted, frank, and benevolent man, and an ornament to his profession. He had heard of the murder, and was deeply moved by the history that Bigelow gave him of his partner, and he did not fail to add, in his details, a list of his many virtues. He concluded by giving the attorney Frederick's detail, and he then solicited his aid in extricating his friend from his perilous situation.

Mr. Oakley, the attorney's name, heard the narrative through to the end, and then shook his head in a doubtful manner. He did not for a moment doubt the truth of Hamilton's statement; but he too was convinced that the unfortunate man was the victim of a plot, and was fearful that the net was so artfully woven as to defy all attempts to break it. He expressed his fears to Bigelow, and that worthy man could not resist the acknowledgment that they were just.

"The great difficulty," said the attorney, "lays in the absence of proof. Without that, the assertions of the prisoner, no matter how true they may be, go for nothing."

"I know it," replied Bigelow, in a desponding tone; "but what course would you recommend?"

"I'll tell you. The prisoner is in a custody, and we cannot urge him to an examination until he is prepared. We must, therefore, have that proceeding deferred until we can make an effort to obtain the testimony that is to substantiate his story."

"I see," said Bigelow, "but will that time be allowed us? Will they not push the matter forward?"

"Who?"

"The magistrate."

"No. I will see to that; you call here to-morrow, and we will visit the prisoner in person."

"I will call!"

"I feel interested in him. His situation is both singular and painful in the extreme. How does he bear his misfortune?"

"Bravely! not a murmur: not a complaint."

Mr. Bigelow left the office, but his mission was not yet executed.

After all the efforts that had been made, nothing of any importance had been secured for Frederick Hamilton.

Mr. Oakley felt that this circumstance would tell fearfully against his client; and he regretted that the measure had been pursued, but it could not be remedied, and regrets were useless; the day of the examination was close at hand, and he prepared to meet it in the best manner possible; yet he knew that his client would be remanded to prison to await the action of the Grand Jury, and the final arrival of a trial.

The day of examination arrived; the excitement with regard to the murder had not abated in the least, for a variety of circumstances had contributed to keep it alive. First among these was the funeral of the deceased, which was attended by thousands, who took that means of expressing their horror of the detested crime, and then came the efforts that had been made by the police to find some corroboration of his story.

At a very early hour in the morning the steps of the court rooms, and that portion of the ground, immediately in front of them, were filled with a dense mass of human beings, waiting with the utmost impatience for the doors of the court room to open and admit them.

Around the entrance of the building, were groups of police officers, armed with heavy batons, which they were frequently obliged to use vigorously to keep off the excited crowd, who attempted several times to rush into the court room; so anxious were they for a sight of the prisoner, and to listen to the details and circumstances of the murder.

The witnesses and attorneys engaged in the matter, affected an entrance into the court room by a private passage; and so, also, had the officers conducting the prisoner. When the magistrate announced himself in readiness to proceed, the police withdrew from the doors, and the rushing, yelling, and screeching that ensued among the crowd, beggars all description. Like a living torrent the mass formed into the halls, offices and apartments of the vast pile, filling it to its utmost capacity with interested and excited persons.

Nearly an hour expired before order could be restored, the police mingled with the crowd, and commanded and entreated alike in vain. There was such an anxiety to see the prisoner, such a desire to gaze at the individual, who was so lost to every sense of principle, gratitude and honor, as to slay the innocent girl, that the curiosity could not be allayed without gratification.

—But the murderer was not there.

George Hamilton had been notified of the examination by the magistrate, and had been requested to attend; but he did not attend; he dared not gaze into the face of his victim; he begged to be excused on the ground of his feelings; his brother was in the custody of the outraged law, and he had no desire to listen to a history of the circumstances, by which this unfortunate state of affairs was brought about. The people applauded his forbearance toward his brother, and commisserated his grievious afflictions.

Poor Frederick could hardly contain himself during the long and tedious examination that followed; to be placed in the dock of a malefactor, to be pitied by some, to be scorned by others, and to be abhorred by all, was indeed the acme of suffering to his proud and sensitive spirit. Appalled and astounded at the terrible array of circumstances that pointed directly at him, as the perpetrator of the crime; and from which he saw no escape, his proud heart gave way, and he covered his face and wept.

"He is contrite at last," said one.

"I'll bet a dollar that he confesses the whole affair," said a most inveterate gambler.

"The evidence of his guilt is irresistible, and he knows it," said a third.

"Murder will out," said another.

And thus the opinions of that vast auditory were all averse to an individual, in all respects as guiltless as themselves.

We shall not detail the circumstances and facts, that were brought forward to establish Frederick's guilt, for the reader is already acquainted with them: suffice it to say, that after the examination was ended, the magistrate promptly ordered his return to prison, there to await his trial for murder. Frederick felt that it was ominous of his future fate, and with a sad heart and a burning eye he accompanied the officer to the dreary prison.

To Oakley, the attorney, and Bigelow, the steadfast friend of the prisoner, and to the crowd of spectators in the court room, this was anticipated as a matter of course: but to the heart-broken wife, and the loving daughter, the blow came with a crushing force.

When the result of the examination was made known at the house, Frederick's wife fell fainting on the floor, and when she was placed upon a bed, and animation restored, it was found that her reason was destroyed and she was a maniac.

Medical aid was speedily obtained, but what can art do for a diseased soul; in spite of skill, and the unwearied application of every known remedy, the aberration continued, and she raved furiously, or wailed piteously of her absent husband.

As the nature of the young are more pliant and elastic than those of years and maturity, they better withstand the blasts of adversity, and misfortunes that overtake them; they bend to its violence, and when it has passed over, assume their natural positions.

The truth was fully exemplified in the case of Sarah Hamilton and her mother, whilst the latter resisted the storm with all the pride and affection to be found in the heart of a wife and a mother; and was in consequence, riven like a tempest-torn oak: the former bent both head and heart to the floor, and although her agony was keen and frightful, and her tears as bitter as blood, yet she arose after the suffering, and if she was not as happy and joyous as formerly, she was calm and composed.

Bigelow frequently visited his friend in his cell, but he dared not inform him of the condition of his wife whom he so tenderly loved; he rightly conceived that the calamity would prove too much for him, and that he already had enough of adversity to contend with; when, therefore, the prisoner asked concerning his wife and daughter: he was forced to disguise the truth and answer,—

"They are as well in spirit as can be expected, in view of the situation they are in."

To the wants of the family Bigelow most scrupulously attended. He often wandered through the streets, and throughout the degraded portions of the city, stopping at the rum dens, and the public rooms, listening to the conversation, and securing the facts of the residents in hopes to obtain some information; but a more acute and experienced searcher than himself, would have failed under the same circumstances; and it was left to time and fortune, to unravel the fearful mystery.

CHAPTER II.

There was not, perhaps, a more shrewd and observing judge of human nature in Saco, than Bowen. He knew a man in all his leanings, after a slight acquaintance.

George Hamilton had misjudged this loving friend of his most egregiously—whilst he had imagined that the burglar was a mere tool in his hands, to be applied to any purpose he chose, that worthy individual had read his very soul as clearly as if it had been a printed page, and had acted accordingly. The moment he had heard of the murder, he knew the author of it; he knew the motives that prompted it, and he knew also that it had been a long time in agitation. Perfectly acquainted with crime, himself a daring criminal, he knew at once the artifices that had been used to fasten the appearance of guilt upon Frederick Hamilton.

Bowen also knew that Hamilton had an accomplice in the matter, and he rightly judged that the Doctor was the man. He determined, however, to satisfy himself fully upon that point, and for that purpose he resolved to visit the Big Tanker, which he knew to be the usual resort, and, in fact, the home of his worthy friend, and see if his suspicions were correct. A knowledge of this transaction—that is, a certain knowledge of the author of the murder—would give him as unlimited a control over Hamilton as if he had owned his soul. He resolved, therefore, to obtain this knowledge, and use it for his own purpose.

On the evening of the day on which the murder was discovered, Bowen replenished his inward man with several potations of his favorite liquid, and arming himself with a stout cane, wended his way to S— Street. He entered the tavern of the worthy Mrs. Clark, but was greatly surprised to find it occupied by no one but the landlady, who stood behind her bar, supporting her face with her hands, and looking very disconsolate and melancholy, as if her last customer had departed to the land of spirits, without calling at her inn and paying up his score. Knowing that his presence would not be regarded with very charitable feelings unless he was a bona-fide patron of the bar, he stepped up to the counter, and as the face of Mrs. Clark relaxed into a smile, at the prospect of a business transaction, he called for a glass of the best brandy that her establishment afforded.

This was furnished without delay; and Bowen, suspending his breath, and repressing a spasmodic action of the stomach, threatened a violent upheaval of its contents, gulped down the villainous compound, and threw himself into a seat in an obscure corner of the room.

Half an hour passed in perfect silence, and during that time no one entered the apartment. The burglar entertained fears that he should not discover the individual for whose sake he had not only walked from C— Street, but had voluntarily swallowed a potion that would have induced combustion in any stomach, not previously used to the reception of such inflammatory guests. He was not doomed to disappointment, however. The little door leading to the parlor and the sleeping-rooms above were presently opened, and Dr. Savin, pale as a ghost, and apparently shaken by a violent ague, hastened to the bar, and called for rum.

The suspicions of Bowen were confirmed, there was such a change in the person before him, from the hardy, daring and reckless villain, to the trembling and affrightened novice that quakes and starts at sights and sounds emanating from his imagination, that it implied guilt of a heavier and more harrassing description than any ever felt before.

The Doctor's potation was heavy; he turned to seat himself, after he had paid for his beverage, and for the first time, discovered the person of Bowen, enveloped in the gloom of a smoky and indistinct corner of the apartment.

Not recognizing the features of his friend, the guilty wretch started, and his wild and haggard features became if possible a shade paler; he started to leave the room, and then, as if ashamed of his fears, he returned and seated himself.

Bowen did not speak, but enjoyed the fears of his brother villain exceedingly. The Doctor endeavored in vain to obtain a full view of his features, and at last, being fully determined to ascertain who he was, he cleared his throat and spoke:

"A very pleasant evening, sir?"

"Yes;" replied Bowen, in an assumed tone.

"Anything new in the city?"

"You've heard of the murder, I s'pose?" answered Bowen.

"Yes;" replied the Doctor, in a faint tone, "and I believe they have secured the murderer?"

"No;" replied Bowen.

"No!" repeated the Doctor, with a sudden start, and with great interest depicted on his features; "the papers say as much."

"Is it a strange matter to read a lie in the newspaper?" queried Bowen.

"No;" returned the culprit, whose countenance fell wonderfully; "but I could not suppose they would dare to publish the arrest of a man for such a crime, unless it were true."

"Oh! there has been an arrest, I admit."

The Doctor brightened up.

"That's what I said. He was arrested for the murder, was he not?"

"Yes, I presume so; but he is not guilty."

The Doctor started, and looked more intently at the burglar. He could not identify him.

"What makes you think he is innocent?" he asked.

"Several circumstances."

"What are they?"

"I'll tell you the principal one, if you like."

"Do so."

"Because he was not there," replied Bowen, in a hoarse whisper.

The Doctor arose hastily, as if a galvanic battery had been applied to him, walked rapidly towards the door, then hastily returned to the bar, and asked for more rum. Bowen witnessed the unequivocal symptoms of guilt with delight the most refined.

When he had drained his glass, the Doctor again seated himself, but this time so near the person of Bowen as to recognize his features. He grasped his hand most affectionately, as if rejoiced to see his friend, and exclaimed,

"D—nation! man, why do you seek to disguise yourself from me. Are you a police agent?"

"I have not disguised myself, my good man, you have had reason to be thankful before now that I was a police agent."

"Say no more about it," said the Doctor, attempting a laugh. "To tell the truth, you frightened me."

"You flatter me; I was not aware that there was anything absolutely frightful in my appearance."

"No, no, not that! I did not know but you were a police officer—that's what I meant."

"Suppose I had been, why are you afraid of a policeman?"

"Well, you know, I suppose," and the Doctor dropped his head upon his breast, to avoid his comrade's piercing gaze, "that I don't care to be recognized by the gentlemen with canes."

"You, I hope, are not guilty of this murder that you are so easily alarmed?"

"No;" exclaimed the Doctor, looking inquiringly into his comrade's face. "No, no; I am not the man."

"Nor concerned in it, I suppose?"

Another glance of inquiry, and the Doctor said, "Why ask these questions, Bowen?"

"Your face evinces guilt."

"Pshaw! I tell you I am unwell, and have been so for many days. Mrs. Clark will tell you so."

"Will you take my advice?"

"What is it?"

"You had better place yourself under the care of Dr. McRey a short time at least. He is eminently successful in cases requiring rest and quiet."

"I understand, do you really think so?"

"To be sure I do; there will be a great noise in the town before long. I am afraid it will disturb you."

"Have you seen Hamilton lately?"

"I have not."

"If I could see him a short time, I believe I would take up with your advice."

"I will see him for you if you like."

"You cannot tell how much you would oblige me."

"Well, I'll see him in the course of tomorrow. In the meantime, you had better not expose yourself to the public gaze."

The burglar had accomplished the purposes of his errand, and he retired from the Big Tanker. He resorted to a bottle of Madeira immediately on arriving at home; and as he sipped it at his leisure, he mused as follows:

"Just as I expected. The Doctor and Hamilton are the men. The Doctor has not the bottom to bear an investigation, and ought not to be left at large. The Fountain is his proper place until he can be sent out of the country without exciting suspicion. It will not be to my interest to let Hamilton be destroyed, until after I have received my share of the plunder of the Farmer's Bank; therefore I'll assist him a little."

Then the daring villain guzzled wine until his brain was sufficiently muddled to induce drowsiness, when he retired to his bed to sleep soundly until morning.

After he had breakfasted, when the morning came, he held a debate with himself which he should do; write to Hamilton to assist him, or proceed at once to his house and confer with him.

"The fact is," said he, "I had better go and see him. He promised to be here some days ago to see about the plunder of the cashier of the Farmer's Bank; but he has not been here. The lord knows that if anything would induce him to keep a promise, it would be the prospect of receiving money. That has failed, and I will call upon him."

He accordingly walked to his friend's home. Hamilton was at home, and was surprised, and, in fact, not pleased with his friend's visit. He did not wish to be seen by any of his acquaintances until the thousand rumors and anecdotes with regard to Mary Bean's death were forgotten; for their recurrence was painful, and often caused him to start and appear disconcerted when he most wished to look calm and collected. He, therefore, received Bowen coldly, which the latter was not slow to perceive.

"I should not have disturbed your profound grief," he said, piqued at the manner of his friend, "if important matters had not required it at this juncture."

"I am in but a poor state for the transaction of business matters," replied Hamilton.

"Of course you are," said Bowen, coldly, "Yet I suppose you are capable of an effort, if safety requires it?"

"What do you mean?" asked his friend.

"I suppose you are accustomed to the calamities of the world, and are philosopher enough to retain your faculties under the heaviest of them. Much as your mind must have endured, you are aware that a great calamity can befall you."

"Be pleased to speak plainly; I am not good at solving riddles," replied Hamilton, displeased with the perfect coolness with which his friend spoke of the murder of Mary Bean.

"Just so, indeed. Precisely so," said Bowen, more than ever determined to torment his companion.

"Will you enlighten me upon the subject of your errand?"

"Have you seen the doctor lately?"

Hamilton turned pale. "No."

"I have."

"Well, what of that?"

"Why, you had better see him, too."

"What have I to do with him?" cried Hamilton, evidently alarmed.

"You know best."

"Speak out, for God's sake!"

"I say you had better see him at once."

Hamilton was thunderstruck. Where could Bowen have learned the fatal secret? Had the doctor disclosed?

"You talk strangely, sir; I do not know that my safety depends in any manner upon Savin. To tell you the truth, I am not aware that I am in any very great danger any way."

"You are your own judge, not me. All I shall say, I have said. If the doctor was a particular friend of mine, and I was in your place, I should make it my business to place him under the care of Dr. McRey until his nervous excitement passed away, and the public mind was settled; then I should let him rusticate among the woods and prairies that he has talked so frequently about of late. I should do so; you are your own judge. Permit me to bid you a very good morning, sir."

Bowen took up his hat and made a very profound bow, and turned to the door.

"Stop a moment! stop a moment!" cried Hamilton.

"Excuse me, you are in no situation to transact business, or see your friends. I bid you good morning."

Hamilton was in the agony of doubts and fears. What was the matter with his friend, that he should act so strangely? Did he know of the perpetration of the murder? What was the meaning of this singular warning?

Meantime, Bowen had succeeded in his purpose. He had given Hamilton a warning, and was confident he would attend to it. He had also excited his suspicions with his knowledge of the murder, and engendered in his mind a dread that would enable him to move him like an automaton. He fairly laughed at the power thus singularly placed in his hands by an unforseen turn of fortune.

Of a certainty we sometimes laugh, and are generally the most reckless when nearest to danger.

Hamilton paced his room in an unenviable state of mind. At last he took up his hat and resolved to see the Doctor himself let the consequences be what they might. When he gained the street, he looked around for Bowen, but that worthy had entered one of the numerous shops beside his path, and was nowhere to be seen. Hamilton was mortified and chagrined; but he pursued his way along the street.

His walk to the Big Tanker was provoking in the extreme. Every acquaintance he met—and their numbers were not few—detained him with an hundred inquiries about the murder, the arrest, and the probable cause of the crime. The hardened villain was compelled to answer these inquiries, and listen to the condolence that was proffered him in consequence of his own damning crime.

At last, wearied and sick at heart, and dreading to meet an acquaintance, he arrived opposite the Big Tanker. As usual he carefully looked up and down the street to see that he was not observed, and then with the rapidity of a criminal fleeing from justice, he darted into the miserable den, and was glad to find that the landlady was entirely alone in the bar-room.

"Good morning, ma'am."

"Good morning, sir; and very pleasant it is, too."

"Very," said Hamilton. "Where is your friend, the Doctor? Is he absent?"

"Ah!" sighed the woman, "the poor Doctor is in a very bad way. To tell you the whole of the blessed truth, I believe he's possessed with the devil."

"Indeed. Is he sick?"

"Not so much in body, bless the poor man, as in his mind, sir."

Hamilton was alarmed.

"Where is he?"

"Oh, he's in his bed, poor man. I have beseeched him to have a physician called, but he will not consent to it. Only to think, sir; and he used to be so gay and so lively."

"I should like to see him for a few moments. Perhaps I could find out his malady."

"God bless you, sir, if only you could, I should be delighted; for I must say, that the Doctor was a favorite of mine; quite a favorite, indeed sir."

The armorous landlady attempted to look very sad and pensive—and her step was slow as she came out from the bar and opened the little door that led to the upper rooms.

"I will conduct you to his apartment, my dear sir," she said, turning towards Hamilton.

The murderer followed her—and was soon in the presence of the miserable Dr. Savin.

After Mrs. Clark had smoothed the pillows and spread the dingy counter-panes, she made a low curtsey, and left the chamber to the two murderers.

Hamilton was forcibly struck with the altered appearance of his accomplice. His cheeks were pale and sunken—his brow—tight and shining, and his lips parched and white. In the eye, however, there was the greatest change: it was greatly enlarged and protruded from his head as if thrust out by some artificial agency; it was bloodshot, and looked wild and, at times, fierce.

When the landlady departed, he thrust his trembling hand towards Hamilton, and a ghastly smile played upon his features.

"I am glad you have come; Bowen said he should send you here to see me."

At the mention of Bowen's name, Hamilton started: "Curse the villain," muttered Hamilton, between his clenched teeth: "is he on my track, he had better beware!"

"I will know his errand before long! but now, tell me why you sent for me:—first however, tell me what ails you."

"I am sick," replied the Dr., "very sick, and I want to leave this place!"

"Where do you wish to go?"

"Anywhere but this place, I can't abide in."

"I am sure I think it very comfortable."

"Why don't you come here and live then! I'll give up my room to you, without a word of complaint," said the Doctor reproachfully; "see then if it is comfortable."

"But what is the matter?"

"Ah! I tell you I was never made for murder; It was an accursed hour when I engaged in it; I can rob or steal without any particular qualms of conscience, but when it comes to murder, I am not the man."

This grated harshly upon the ears of Hamilton, he keenly felt the reproach it conveyed.

"Where do you wish to go?"

"To the Fountain House, let me stay there until this matter is past, and I am recovered, if it please God to restore me; after that I shall seek some other region."

"Well, prepare yourself; to-night I will call for you, and you shall be taken to the Fountain House. In the meantime take this purse, which you may need before I am able to pay you your share of the booty we have gained."

The Doctor took the purse, and Hamilton left the Big Tanker. The Doctor arose from his bed, and, with trembling steps, made his way to the bar-room.

CHAPTER III.

The Doctor was greatly rejoiced to arrive at the Fountain House. He was also rejoiced to find that celebrated receptacle of the unfortunate so full of inmates; for he dreaded solitude as he dreaded death. Besides the consolations afforded by company; he had nothing to fear from his companions, for they were all like himself, stained with crime, and dodging from the vengeance of the law.

The worthy keeper of this miserable hole, had been ordered to furnish the Doctor with everything he desired, except it might be liberty; who consequently could indulge in eating and drinking to his complete repletion; for the worthy landlord, in whose custody he was, was not without the prominent characteristics of his profession—avarice—and unscrupulousness; for a few days the villain enjoyed himself. The conversation of his comrades, and the fumes of bad liquor contributed to drown his remorse; but by-and-bye these palled upon his taste, and despite his exertions, he would become melancholy, and even sad. At night especially, after he had retired to his bed, strange phantoms would congregate round his pillow, and terrify him with their haggard and awful appearance, or by the uncouth and horrible sounds that were emitted from their fleshless jaws; he grew pale and wan; his knees trembled, and his eyes assumed a strained and unnatural appearance. The room in which the Doctor lodged, was immediately opposite, and adjoining the one occupied by Mr. Leslie, an artist, only a very slight partition separated them, and the least possible noise made in the one, could be distinctly heard in the other. The artist was consequently, frequently aroused in the night by the groans and sighs of his neighbor; often, too, through the day; Leslie had noticed the singular appearance of the Doctor, he soon came to the conclusion that something weighed heavily upon his conscience, and that it was in all probability the recollection of some deed of blood, in which he had participated. One night, soon after he had embraced these conclusions, the Doctor was more restless than ever; indeed, both his physical and mental strength had been failing for some time; on the particular occasion to which we allude, his groans were louder and more frequent than ever, and at last, unable any longer to endure his agony alone, he sprang from his wretched bed, and rushed into Leslie's room with the desperation of a maniac.

"For the love of God," he exclaimed, in a voice hoarse with terror, "get up and strike a light, if you have any mercy on me, I can endure these cursed spectors no longer."

"What is the matter," asked Leslie in a soothing tone, "are you ill?"

"Oh, yes, I am sick; sick in both body and mind. Do get up and strike a light, then I am sure these d—d visions will depart."

Leslie arose and lighted a filthy lamp, standing upon a rickety table near his bedside. The Doctor had thrown himself into the only chair in the room, and with a ghastly paleness spread over his features, was trembling in every limb. Leslie pittied him; "What is the matter with you?" he asked, "I have observed, for some time past, that you were very ill: can I do anything for you?" The Doctor gazed at him with the wonder of a child; Leslie's words were the first kind words that had fallen upon his ears for years. There is a mysterious influence connected with human sympathy; in a moment the Doctor looked upon the artist as his best friend; something seemed to whisper to him also, that the remorse

that preyed upon him so painfully, would be assuaged if he disclosed
the frightful secret with which his bosom was laden; once or twice he
resolved to tell all, but when he endeavored to speak, his courage failed
him, he thought of a frightful incarceration in a dungeon—of a death
on the gallows—of the power of Hamilton; and he dared not disclose.
Leslie talked encouragingly to the wretched man.

He had been an inmate of the Fountain long enough to know the kind
of characters it contained, and he rightly divined the disease that caused
the Doctor's misery; he rediculed all belief in ghosts and hob-goblins,
showed how they had their origin in a troubled mind, and then pointed
out a few simple rules by which their appearance could be avoided; the
Doctor listened with a wrapt interest, and finally ventured once more to
return to his bed where he remained quiet until the morning. We have
said, there is a mysterious influence connected with human sympathy,
there is also a mysterious influence—a resistless overpowering influence
connected with the workings of conscience; the daylight removed many
of the imaginary fears that had so tormented the poor Doctor; but, alas for
him, his conscience was thoroughly aroused, and although he made every
exertion to force a species of insane and unnatural gaiety, he could not
still its voice which whispered—oh, how fully distinct—guilt! guilt! guilt!
Again he resorted to the bar, but the liquor of the worthy host seemed to
have lost its power; his deepest thoughts failed to produce a symptom of
intoxication, and, with the feeling of a condemned criminal, he saw the
shades of another night approaching. He lingered in the bar room until
the last of his companions had retired, and then with a trembling step,
he went to his bed; his distress was even greater than on the previous
night, he groaned and tossed upon his wretched pallet until it seemed to
be a bed of embers, and yet, every moment seemed to increase his agony.
Leslie was usually the first one in the house to retire.

There was nothing in the company of the landlord's customers to at-
tract him—on the contrary, there was much to disgust and sicken him.
This night he had retired to his sleeping apartment earlier than usual; but
he found it impossible to sleep. Throughout the day he had watched the
Doctor closely. He saw plain enough the misery he was enduring—saw
the steps he took to conceal it; firmer than ever, was he convinced that
a crime of great magnitude could alone disturb so effectually a man who
had long been familiar with transgression and sin. He was thinking upon
this matter when the Doctor came to his room. He heard the groans of
the wretched man—heard him tumbling and tossing on his bed—and

felt his sympathies strongly drawn out in his behalf. He listened to the melancholy noises until near midnight—when he heard the Doctor bound from his bed and alight upon the floor, and in a moment after, he entered his own room, pale, ghastly, and trembling in every joint.

"Oh! in God's name, my dear friend," he said, "I can remain in that room alone no longer. I could not live till daylight."

Leslie knew not what to say. The cadaverous cheek, the sunken eye, and the colorless lip of the Doctor showed the depths of his sufferings.

"Are you ill again?" he asked.

"Ill!" repeated the Doctor in a hoarse whisper, "my God! I am ill—ill enough—but not in body—it's my mind—my conscience, that distresses me. I should not mind being sick in my body at all; for I can endure as much as most men; it's the horrible and awful trouble on my mind that's killing me out and out. Oh, you know not what I suffer."

"I know you suffer," said Leslie, in a soothing tone; "it cannot be otherwise. If I knew what could be done for your relief, I would cheerfully assist you; but a diseased mind, it is said, is beyond the reach of medicine."

"I know it! I know it!" exclaimed the Doctor, vehemently. "If medicine could cure me, I would spare no expense. Even Hamilton would be prompt to assist me, I am sure."

"Who?" asked Leslie, in amazement.

"Hamilton," said the Doctor.

"What Hamilton?"

"George Hamilton."

"Great God!" thought the artist, "can this be another of the villain's victims?"

"You seemed surprised," said the Doctor. "Do you know the man I refer to?"

"I am somewhat acquainted with him," Leslie replied, evasively; "but I lay no claim to a particular intimacy; it appears that he is your friend."

"He ought to be so," replied the Doctor; "God knows he ought to be."

An awkward pause ensued. Leslie gazed at his trembling companion, wondering what crime he had been induced to perpetrate by the consummate villain he had named as his friend. The Doctor, too, was silent, and seemed fearful that he had committed an unpardonable sin in mentioning the name of his employer aloud. Leslie finally opened the conversation again, as he felt a strong curiosity to ascertain the nature of his comrade's guilt.

"Have you known Hamilton long?"

"For some time," replied the Doctor.

"Does he know of your situation here now? I mean, does he know that you are in this place?"

"To be sure: he came here with me."

"But he cannot be very attentive to you, for he has not called upon you, as I am aware of."

"No, he has not been here, sure enough," and a groan escaped from the bosom of the accomplice.

"In times of distress and trouble, such as you appear to suffer from now, the sympathy of your friend is truly valuable. To a diseased mind, it is invaluable."

"Just so," cried the Doctor, with a kind of nervous start. "It is very true; but I suppose he is busy now, since the death of Mary Bean."

"Then the girl is dead," queried Leslie, affecting surprise, although he knew she had been murdered.

"Yes," said the Doctor, "she is dead."

"Did she die suddenly?" asked Leslie, fixing his keen eyes full upon the face of his companion.

The Doctor felt the power of that searching glance, and his very soul quailed beneath it. If possible, his pale face grew a shade paler; and his voice was husky and tremulous, when he stammered—

"Yes, she was murdered."

"Murdered!" repeated Leslie, in a deep, solemn tone. "Is it possible!"

The Doctor turned his face from the gaze of the artist. Again did an unknown and unnatural impulse prompt him to embrace the present opportunity, and confess all as a matter of relief to his pained and aching breast.

"Is any one suspected of the crime?" continued Leslie, striving, but in vain, to catch his companion's eye once more.

"Yes," replied the Doctor, without turning his head; "George Hamilton's brother Frederick is arrested for the murder, and will be executed; but he is not guilty."

"You surprise me," said Leslie. "But perhaps the wretched man is guilty."

"Oh, God! oh, God!" groaned the accomplice, "I tell you again that he is not guilty. I know that he is not guilty of the awful crime.'

"But have you revealed as much where it can avail the prisoner on his defense?" asked Leslie.

"I have not."

"But, man, do you intend to withhold such testimony, and permit an innocent man to die, and to die dishonored? Know you not that it makes a murderer of you—aye, worse than murderer?"

The Doctor buried his face in his hands, and his frame trembled violently from the intensity of his emotion. He rocked his body to and fro, as if to lull the throbs of agony that racked his guilty bosom.

"What can I do?" he cried at length. "What can I do? To disclose what I know, is certain destruction to myself: it is either my life or his."

A horrid suspicion flashed upon Leslie's mind. He was fully aroused, and said—

"I cannot see how it can affect your safety at all. If you are not the murderer yourself, the law will protect you in your disclosures—and good and virtuous men, everywhere, will give you their support. You have nothing to fear, I say, unless you perpetrated the deed yourself."

"I did not do it!—I would not do it!" gasped the Doctor, sliding along close to the artist. "I refused to do it."

Leslie comprehended the case.

"Then, by all means," he said, earnestly, "confess what you know. No harm can come to you, and your mind will at once be relieved of all these horrible pangs of remorse; I wonder not at your sufferings, if you have permitted this unhappy man to remain even for a day in a gloomy dungeon for a crime that he never committed. You must not hope for peace or for comfort, until you have done justice to the case.—No, no! you are more than twice a murderer, if you do not at once proclaim the truth."

The Doctor was singularly affected during this appeal from Leslie. The hot tears rolled down his sallow cheeks, and he sobbed like a grieved infant. He seized one of the artist's hands, and, as he held it between his two burning palms, he gazed into his face with such an expression of anguish, that Leslie himself could scarce refrain from weeping.

"Oh!" cried the Doctor, "this is a fearful struggle. I dare not disclose."

"Why not?" asked Leslie.

"George Hamilton would hunt me from the face of the earth in case I did."

"My God! is not the suspected man his own brother?"

"He is."

"And does the unnatural hell-hound wish him to die a felon's death?"

"One or the other must!" the Doctor almost shrieked.

"This Hamilton is the murderer!" said Leslie; "you have disclosed enough."

"Do not betray me—do not betray me!" the Doctor whined most piteously; "at least, do not mention this until I am safe from Hamilton's vengeance."

"On one condition I will not."

"Name it at once."

"If you will reveal all, my lips will be sealed until you are removed to a place of safety—and until a provision is made by the proper officers for your legal safety—you shall become an evidence for the state; and in that capacity be sheltered from persecution."

"But can you do all this?" asked the Doctor, eagerly. "Can you do what you promise?"

"If I do not, your secret shall be safe with me; I promise not to divulge it."

A smile, ghastly to be sure, lit up the Doctor's altered features, and he squeezed the artist's hands affectionately.

"I will confess," he said, "I will rid my mind of this horrible load—I will do justice to the innocent, and let the guilty suffer. God will give me credit for the motives that prompt me. I am a great villain, and a hardened one; but the crime of blood is more than I can endure."

And the Doctor related every incident connected with the murder, without disguise or palliation.

Leslie was astounded. He knew George Hamilton to be a villain—an arch, designing villain; but he was not prepared to hear of such utter and complete depravity. He knew him to be leagued with counterfeiters and villains of that stamp—but he had never thought him enough the fiend to murder the deluded girl, and then coolly seek to have his brother executed for the crime.

"Surely, surely," he said, when the Doctor concluded his narrative, "such cold-blooded villainy was never heard of before. The punishment of such a man is indeed to be prayed for. Believe me, my friend, although you are not without your share of guilt in this transaction, you will merit, and receive the thanks of every orderly member of society for this exposure of an awful and horrid monster."

"But how can my confession be made available?" asked the Doctor. "We are as much in prison here as if we had been properly committed by a magistrate."

"We will see about that," said Leslie, in a determined tone. "I will know soon if this landlord will dare attempt to detain me against my will. You must on no account attempt to escape. If I succeed, I will do all I promised you for your protection, and then I will return to this place with a sufficient force to take you out."

"And you will not leave me here long? I am sure I shall die if you do."

"No, you shall not be left here long. I will proceed at once with my business, if I can but effect my escape; I will endeavor to repair society for the wrongs I have inflicted upon it, by saving the innocent and bringing the guilty to punishment, with your assistance."

The Doctor smiled again; indeed his disclosures brought him relief; besides this, the confident assertions of Leslie had impressed an amount of hope into his mind that he had long been a stranger to. He felt that his confession made before the world, and rendered subservient to Frederick Hamilton, would be in a great part an atonement for his participation in the murder of the helpless girl.

For arranging the plans for Leslie's departure, and in conversing about the murder, the Doctor and his comrade spent the hours of the night. Just at the dawning of the day, they retired to their respective beds to obtain a few hours of needful and refreshing repose.

The Doctor obtained some refreshing sleep, and when he awoke he felt better, both in body and mind, than he had since his residence in the burglar's den. He descended to the bar-room, and after performing his ablutions, looked around the familiar circle of faces for his friend Leslie; the artist was not to be seen. Leslie's mind was so full of the frightful secret the Doctor had imparted to him, and so much agitated concerning his intended escape, that he found it impossible to sleep soundly. He had unpleasant dreams—he grew feverish, and finally he arose and entered the bar-room. Here he found no one but the landlord—and that worthy, from the effects of his morning's potation, or from some other cause, was most unusually good natured and amiable. He made a bow to Leslie, and politely asked him to drink.

The artist was about to refuse this kindly proffered delicacy, but a sudden impulse prompted him to comply, in the hopes that he might thereby take advantage of the landlord's unusual good feeling.

"With all my heart," he replied, with as bright a smile as he could conjure up for the occasion. "With all my heart, sir, if you are to indulge with me."

"That's of course," returned the landlord. "And I shall also drink to our better acquaintance."

Mentally damning the sentiment that the publican proposed, and wishing from the bottom of his heart that their connection might soon cease forever, Leslie drained his glass, concealing his grimaces as well as he could, and seeming to take his companion's toast in high compliment; he then walked from the bar, and passing through one of the high narrow windows that admitted a dull uncertain light into the room, he appeared to be lost for a moment in reflection. Suddenly he turned around so as to face the landlord, and said: "Is there no yard connected with the house, in which I could take a turn or two for some fresh air? Upon my word this confinement is irksome, and I feel that a half-hours exercise would benefit me vastly."

"A yard," said the host, "you may well say that; a finer one than I can lead you to is not to be found in this region, it is a perfect park, come this way and I will show you."

Leslie joyfully followed the landlord, after wending through a variety of narrow passages, and crossing some half a dozen dark and filthy rooms, they at length emerged into the open air, and in the rear of the mansion.

"Look at this now!" cried the landlord, as if he was about to exhibit the pleasure-ground of Buckingham Palace, "could the heart of a man ask a finer spot for a morning's exercise; it's very fine, and better than all, it's entirely sheltered from observation."

The eye of the artist ran over a muddy narrow yard, surrounded by a low and broken rail-fence, and discovered several litter of pigs and not a few heaps of reeking and disgusting offal scattered about in different directions. He concealed the loathing that the place excited, and said, "Very nice: surely, as you say, it's finely sheltered from observation, and with your permission I will walk through until the breakfast bell rings."

"As long as you please my good fellow, and when you please," replied the landlord, "only bear in mind, that it is against the rules of the house to leave the enclosure."

"I shall remember," said Leslie, and he commenced his promenade forthwith, the landlord re-entered the house, and made his way to the bar, muttering as he went along:—

"That chap turns out to be a d—d fine fellow after all, he rather looked high when he first came here, but now he's really sociable. G—d he'll make a regular trump, if Hamilton permits me to give him more tuition!"

Leslie was not long in ascertaining the departure of the landlord; he gazed upon the vacant fields beyond the narrow boundary of his prescribed limits, and said, "another such opportunity may never occur, I'll improve this chance, and if I only succeed in gaining the highway, I shall be safe. The landlord would hardly dare to use force in order to gain possession of me again." This resolution once taken, he leaped the low fence, and with rapid strides he made across the town, and soon left his hated prison far behind him; at last the rattling of cabs, omnibusses, carts, and the hum of industry reached his ears, he thought it the most harmonious that had greeted him for months, and he almost redoubled his speed. After entering the city a short distance, familiar objects greeted his vision, and seemed like long lost friends just returned. When he reached the vicinity of S— Street he halted, and leaning against a post he considered what course he should pursue to effect the objects he had in view.

Chapter IV.

Wenton, the burglar, was still in prison. For a long time after his arrest he was a lunatic. The fearful shock he had received in the perpetration of the murder of Mr. Parsons, treacherous and unworthy as he proved to be, was too much for his deep, nervous temperament, and his brain wandered. There was something inexpressibly touching in his sayings; they were not wild and boisterous, but were the melancholy moanings of an agonized spirit. His very soul seemed racked and tortured with intense and ceaseless pain, and even the rough and unfeeling turnkeys and others employed about the prison, sympathized with him, and commisserated his misfortunes in their rough way; violent passions most irresistibly exhaust themselves, and eventually, Wenton became calmer. He was dull, spiritless, not communicative, and seemingly dreaded society, yet his eye had lost the wild glare—his speech was coherent, and his prison physician pronounced him convalescent; consequently, the magistrate resolved that he must go through the trial. Wenton was duly notified of these arrangements, but was entirely unmoved thereby; he expressed no anxiety as to its termination, nor suggested any evidence that might avail him in his dilemma. When asked for his friends, he invariably replied that he had none in the world.

But the reader has already seen that if Wenton had no friends, there were some who were interested in his welfare. True, their interest was entirely selfish, but nevertheless, the selfish friendship is after all, the most to be depended upon of any; it was not safe for either Hamilton or Bowen to permit Wenton to be detected in his crimes, and therefore, powerful motives induced them to exert themselves in his behalf. The evening previous to the examination, Bowen visited Hamilton at his residence, he was not refused admittance, but when he entered the apartment in which Hamilton was sitting, the murderer became pale, and avoided looking him in the face; his manner also was restrained and cold, yet he would fain have appeared warm and friendly to his associate; Bowen was not disconcerted in the least, confident of the power he held over Hamilton, a keen and ready reader of the human heart withal, he saw at a glance the feelings of his companions toward him, he knew that Hamilton dreaded him for the secret he possessed, and clearly foresaw that in a little time he would heartily hate him.

"I have called to see you," said Bowen, "about that Wenton affair, to-morrow is the day for the examination, of course you will be present!"

"I have procured able counsel for him," replied Hamilton, "and can do as much for him away from the court-room, as I can there. I have no desire to appear in public just at present, especially as the champion of men of the character that Wenton will probably bear there."

The thief opened his eyes, stared wildly about him, and then threw himself into a chair. He finally drew a long breath and seemed suddenly to have recovered his bewildered faculties.

"Ah! yes, I see, you now profess pride," said he, "of course now you would not like to associate with a common criminal like the poor burglar—you do a bigger business!"

This stinging retort reached the very soul of Hamilton; he started fiercely from his chair, and exclaimed, "D—nation, what do you mean sir, by using such language to me—what do you mean, I repeat!"

"'Pon my soul: the man is crazy," replied Bowen, as if addressing a third person; a moments reflection had cooled Hamilton amazingly. Well he knew that it would not do to trifle with his comrade, for he possessed the power of life and death, and dishonor, with regard to him; with an expression of real sorrow, he said "At times, Bowen, I think your conclusions are correct, I am often really fearful that I am insane, I hope I may so far presume upon your friendship as to ask your forgiveness in this matter—lately you use singular language to me, and I freely confess that it is irritating me."

"You are in a deplorable condition," replied Bowen, coolly, without looking at his friend. "A very singular condition you are in. When I was here before you promised me that you would be present at the examination of Wenton."

"So I did," replied Hamilton greatly softened—"and so I will, it was the suggestion of my attorney that I should keep away—I will go, however."

"If your attorney knew all, I am sure he would be satisfied that you are as much interested in the matter as I am. A man cannot watch his own safety through the instrumentality of others, not at all times, at any rate."

"True enough, and I think I had better be there in person, indeed you may depend upon me."

"Well I shall depend upon you, I apprehend no danger; to be sure, but then we must look well to Wenton, for he is not exactly in his proper mind."

Bowen departed, and for once they separated without drinking wine together. Hamilton did not regret his companion's departure, and Bowen himself felt that a longer interview might lead to something unpleasant.

Early on the morning of the examination, Bowen appeared at the office of the justice; he had not been long in attendance before Hamilton entered, followed by his attorney, who carried several formidable looking volumes under his arm, and acted as if the destinies of the nation were resting upon his shoulders. Bowen barely recognized them, and then engaged the acting magistrate in conversation, as Bowen had reckoned, when the court, as it was termed through courtesy, was convened for the transaction of business, he was politely requested to take a seat upon the bench, he at once complied with the invitation, and with an air of well conceived sanctity, he assumed the functions of the magistrate.

Several cases of petty offences were first called up and disposed of before Wenton was called for; when, however, the case of the burglar was reached, the attorney arose from the chair in which he had been sitting, apparently reading a newspaper, and with a cringing and deferential bow, announced to the court that he appeared as the council for the prisoner.

"At his request?" asked the magistrate. The crafty attorney was somewhat disconcerted by this unexpected interrogatory, but he answered—

"By his friends' solicitation, sir; they have heard that the prisoner is not in a capacity to select for himself, and have requested me to assist him."

"Very well, perhaps you would wish for an interview with your client before the trial commences?"

"I should sir!"

"Officer, lead this gentleman to the prison, of Wenton the burglar, the court will await his return."

Hamilton and Bowen exchanged significant looks, as the attorney left the court room, the murderer at once comprehended his friend, and he followed the attorney.

"Let me speak to you one moment," said he, as he emerged into the open air. "Perhaps I may be absent when you return, and shall not enjoy another opportunity."

Hamilton seized the attorney by the arm, and retiring beyond the hearing of the officers, he said "Strangely enough, I have neglected to inform you how Bowen and myself became interested in this case, it is necessary that you understand the matter fully, you know, to be sure,—This Wenton has been a great deal in my employment, and has also been assisted by Bowen; since the loss of his reason, I have not seen him, but both Bowen and myself are fearful that in his ravings he may use our names, this would be annoying, and afford a fine pleasure to many envious persons, now I want you to be careful of my name and Bowen's."

"No fears about that," said the attorney, with a professional smile. "I understand that." Hamilton returned to the court-room, and the attorney proceeded to the cell of his client. Wenton was reclining upon his coarse straw pallet, when the policeman and the attorney entered. He paid no heed to their arrival, and the officer said—

"Come, Wenton, your examination commences to-day, and here is a gentleman that your friends have employed to defend you. Rouse up, he wishes to see you."

"My friends," said the burglar, rising from his couch and staring at the officer.

"Yes, your friends."

"Strange enough. God knows I have none in the world. No, not one."

"Well, then, be thankful for this one that you have just found, and tell him your story quickly." The officer left the prisoner, securing the door of his cell, and leaving the attorney alone with the burglar.

The crafty attorney soon saw that Hamilton and Bowen had nothing to fear from his client, and the interview was of short duration. Although earnestly pressed on the support, Wenton refused to utter a word about the murder and robbery; or to give any account of the manner in which he entered the house of Parsons.

The attorney was delighted. An excellent client, thought he. This matter will prove but a light affair.

When the officer returned, Wenton was conducted to the magistrate's office, and the attorney followed. He smiled encouragingly upon Hamilton as he entered the court-room, and the worthy man felt a load removed from his bosom in consequence. Wenton was arraigned forthwith, and the witnesses for the prosecution called.

Nothing could be proved against Wenton, not the slightest circumstance that could connect him with the robbery. He was deemed by every one who had seen or conversed with him since his arrest as a maniac, incapable of planning or executing a robbery of any kind, either great or small.

He was consequently discharged. When told that he was at liberty to go where he pleased, and that the law had no more demands upon him, he stared wildly at the magistrate for a time, but finally seemed to comprehend the purport of the language, and he left the room. He soon disappeared in one of the obscure alleys of that quarter of the city in which he had been confined. Hamilton seemed perfectly satisfied, and the companions adjourned to a neighboring hotel to take wine. After indulging in a bottle they separated, each one returning to his home. Bowen's sagacity had for once met with its equal. During all the examination of Wenton, and during their subsequent interview—nay, whilst they were drinking their wine, they had been carefully and closely watched by keen eyes.

CHAPTER V.

Who can tell the anguish endured by the innocent and down-trodden in prison cells. The many sleepless nights, the long monotonous days, the dull oppressive air, the fluctuations of hope and fear—who shall paint the picture? Heavily and wearily wore away the time to Frederick Hamilton after his examination—alone in his narrow cell, with only a dull and a spiritless light that stole through the heavy iron bar surrounding his little window, to solace him in the day time, and plunged in a pitchy and oppressive darkness in the night; he sat and brooded over the misfortunes that had dogged his footsteps through life. At first hope had buoyed him up—he knew that he was innocent of the crime wherewith he was charged, and he did not doubt his ability to make that innocence appear after his examination. After his failure to obtain the proof upon which he relied for his acquittal, hope left him, and he gave himself up to a moody despair. He saw plainly that he was the victim of some diabolical plot, and he felt that it was useless to struggle any longer against his destiny. He regarded his doom as sealed, and looked upon death as an event that would rid him of misery and anguish, and consequently as a consummation devoutly to be wished. Sometimes he thought of his wife; she who had so long been the pride and the light of his existence, and then his heart gave evidence of sensibility, gave the token that there yet was feeling in its depths. What a blow his incarceration must be to her—how her fond and sensitive heart must bleed over his misfortunes. Alas! the wretched prisoner knew not of the calamity that had befallen her, and it was well that he did not. The time for the trial was fast coming on. Bigelow, the indefatigable friend of the prisoner, and Oakley, his talented and determined attorney, visited the prisoner frequently; but they could hold out no hope to him. Every effort to discover the Dr. on the evening of the murder had proved unavailing; and although Bigelow whispered hope, and the lawyer spoke encouragingly of the case, neither of them could deny the motive that induced them to do so. They could not bring themselves to warn the prisoner to prepare for an ignominious death. Yet, as we said before, they could hold out no hope to Frederick, for he at once perceived that their language was but the pardonable deceptions of kind hearts, dreading to give him pain.

The court was at length convened, and, at the opening, Frederick Hamilton was arraigned for the murder of Mary Bean. All the excitement that had so agitated the city at the time of the murder was again aroused. Again the press teemed with accounts of the horrid transaction, and men in every public place denounced the murderer. Again was George Hamilton, Frederick's brother, drawn before the public—again was his many virtues commented upon—and again was the warmest sympathy of the public bestowed upon him.

How often, truly, do the wicked flourish like a green bay tree, while the innocent meet with execration and abhorrence.

As soon as it was known that the trial of Frederick Hamilton would be the first one of the session, the court and the adjacent grounds presented a continuous scene of riot and confusion. The crowd was tremendous; and the police force, with all the aid of their long staves and their authority, was found to be inadequate to the task of preserving order, and keeping the halls and the lobbies of the court clear from intruders.

Among all the mass of human beings, not one raised a voice in behalf of Frederick Hamilton. Not one uttered a word in commendation of his previous character, or possessed sufficient moral courage to point to one good or generous action.

And why was this so? Why is it so in such cases? Men in these days style themselves Christians. They wear long faces, they build great churches with tall steeples, they pay eloquent men great salaries to disseminate the tidings of God's love to man, they are punctual in their attendance upon churches, and yet the soul and life of their devotion and adoration is gold.

No one doubted the conviction of the prisoner, that was already past a doubt, yet every one felt anxious to hear his defense, to ascertain upon what points he relied for acquittal. Mr. Oakley, Frederick's counsel, stood high at the bar. He was very eloquent, searching, and profound. Every one knew that he would make a most desperate attempt to clear his client; yet all thought that, in this instance, he had overtasked his conceded powers.

Not until the prisoner had been brought into court, and seated in the dock, were the crowd admitted. The policy of this arrangement was soon apparent; for in a very short time every avenue and corner were filled with a dense and interested multitude, as compact as might and force could make them; they stood before the prisoner, like so many savages thirsting for his blood.

Before the commencement of the trial murmurs of dislike for the prisoner, and criticisms upon his hardened and careless appearance, were quite common among the audience; but the moment the proceedings of the law commenced, all was as hushed as could be expected from so vast a congregation.

As we have stated elsewhere, Frederick Hamilton was pale and emaciated from his long confinement, but to the eye of an unprejudiced individual, had one been there, his bearing was bold, even noble and commanding. He listened to the reading of the indictment, wherein he was charged with the commission of a revolting crime, in every possible form that legal ingenuity could suggest. With an unblanched cheek and unquailing eye when commanded to plead to its wretched contents, he answered, in a deep manly voice, "Not Guilty."

These evidences of his innocence, of the triumphs of a wounded heart, were thrown away upon the assembly; indeed, in the minds of those present, it was an aggravation of his offence, for they argued it exhibited a brazen impudence in guilt absolutely shocking to behold. The Jury who were to judge of the prisoner's guilt or innocence, was soon empannelled, although it was supposed, generally, that Oakley would be extremely careful in their selection, and use the prisoner's privilege of challenge to the utmost, but he never raised an objection, and permitted them to be sworn as they were called. This conduct excited surprise.

The District Attorney opened the prosecution with a glowing and eloquent disquisition upon the enormity of the offense, and the cold-blooded and premeditated audacity with which it had been committed. He seemed to labor most energetically to get up a powerful feeling against the prisoner before any evidence to prove his guilt had been brought forward; he sat down after what the press termed a powerful effort, a long pause ensued after the opening of the public prosecutor, but whether it was to give time for his eloquence to work its effect, or whether it was unavoidable did not appear. At length he proceeded with great pomposity to call up the evidence, it was entirely circumstantial, but so acutely and ingeniously had George Hamilton, and his confederates, wove their web, that for Frederick the details were absolutely damning. It seemed to fix the infamy and guilt of the deed upon him without the shadow of doubt. At the close of the first day, the manner in which Oakley conducted the defense was the subject of universal wonder and remark. Throughout the day he had not made one remark, had not asked a single question of the witnesses, had not taken a note of the evidence that had been placed before the jury. What could it mean? It was very singular, nay, it was mysterious. The love of mystery, of the dark and inexplicable, is a powerful passion in vulgar minds. The public prosecutor made ample amends for Oakley's silence; he was prolixity personified; he seemed to be deeply vexed at the taciturnity of his opponent, and started question after question, argument after argument, merely for the love of the thing; he invariably had both sides of the question, affirmative and negative, and to do him justice, we must say that he did each side equal credit.

Three entire days were so consumed in this manner, and then the public attorney pronounced the evidence closed for the people. All eyes were instantly turned upon Oakley—now the eventful crisis had come—now the mystery of his defense would be explained—now the public would witness the ingenuity and eloquence of genius in a desperate case. The interest of the vast crowd in attendance was actually wound up to horrible tragedy point.

Mr. Oakley arose slowly and calmly; he gazed at the jury for a moment and said, "The defense has no evidence to offer." A message from the eternal world would not have created a greater surprise than did this simple announcement: instead of an explanation of the mystery that had been looked for so earnestly, here was a new edition of it. Why had citizens and policemen been summoned on behalf of the prisoner if their evidence was not desired?

Was the evidence of the wretched man's guilt too damning, too overwhelming, to admit an attempt at palliation?

Whatever the occasion of the proceeding, Oakley did not explain, but resumed his seat as cool and collected as if nothing of importance had occurred.

The District Attorney shared in the general surprise, indeed it was some time before he recollected himself, so completely was he taken aback. At last he requested that if there was no evidence to offer, the defense would proceed to sum up the matter.

Oakley again arose, and informed the court and jury that "the prisoner's counsel had no remarks to offer." This disclosure completely nettled the public prosecutor; this arrangement would detract one half from the unfading laurels he had designed to win, and it was absolutely annoying to have a victory over such an opponent as Oakley thus shorn of its glory. There was no hope, however, and he was compelled to commence his own argument, for argue he would, like Goldsmith's Schoolmaster, "e'en though vanquished."

Who has not witnessed, in some of our numerous courts of justice, the vehement and nonsensical outpourings of lawyers, whose sole claim to the privilege of existence is based upon that declaration of justice, that makes it criminal to take the life even of the meanest of God's creation unnecessarily—men of brass and froth, whose field of action is confined to the miseries and wants of suffering humanity, the human carrion bird.

After four hours of muddy rant, four hours of excruciating mental agony, the case was submitted to the jury, and the vast throng separated to await the announcement of the verdict.

The public were not kept long in suspense, for the jury soon agreed upon a verdict, and returned into court.

On the announcement being made public, the crowd again rushed in, and once more a multitude was congregated.

Frederick Hamilton was pronounced guilty. There was a perfect silence for several moments after this awful announcement, and then all eyes were turned upon the prisoner to see how it affected him. Not a feature moved. There was the same pale, placid, pleasant countenance that had been turned upon the jury through all the tedious trial. Neither was Oakley in the least disconcerted or surprised.

The audience was strongly disappointed, as they passed out of the hall, they muttered—

"What is the meaning of all this?"

The morning after his conviction, Frederick Hamilton was sentenced to be hanged until he was dead.

Chapter VI.

Leslie stood leaning against the post in S— Street a long time, at a loss how to proceed; he was convinced that he had not weighed all the difficulties of his mission, while he was in the Fountain. After hearing the confessions of the Doctor, he had been prompted by an impulse common to every feeling mind, to rush to the rescue of Frederick Hamilton, who was unjustly suffering for the crime of another. He had escaped the surveillance of George Hamilton's agent, but what was he to do! He was a stranger in the city, poor and unknown, and himself a partner in crime with the man he was about to denounce.

To whom should he apply for aid under these circumstance? To whom could he apply? Who would believe his story?

People would at once say that he invented the story on purpose to secure the reward of Frederick's friend.

All these thoughts, and a thousand others equally discouraging, suggested themselves to the mind of the artist, and he was fairly bewildered. He quitted his recumbent position against the post, and walked down the street without paying any heed to the glare, pomp and bustle that surrounded him. He was not aroused to a perfect consciousness of his situation, until the calls of hunger assailed his sensibilities. He had a small amount of money in his pockets, and he looked around for an eating house; his eye at length caught a sign suspended across the walk, and he entered one of these provision saloons, so common in the city, he ordered a plain, but substantial meal, and retired to a box to eat it in quiet; when his appetite was satisfied he paid his bill, and again set out upon his wanderings. Night at last overtook him, and he was as far from the accomplishment of his errand as he was in the morning, he sought out a lodging-house and retired to rest, hoping that the dawn of another morning would find his mind quiet and capable of forming some effective determination. Leslie experienced one great difficulty, he did not know a single friend of the unfortunate prisoner, and when he asked for information upon this point, the usual answer was, "D—n him, he has no friends,—a man that would murder an unsuspecting girl deserves no friends."

How the artist's heart sympathized with Frederick Hamilton, he knew that he was innocent of the crime laid to his charge, for another had perpetrated it; he thought of the sufferings of the wretched man in his gloomy prison, and then he remembered the agony he had himself endured. After all the talk about philanthropy and disinterested friendship, there is nothing like experimental suffering to open the human breast, and cause it to sympathize with distress. Determined not to be foiled by the repulses he had met with; Leslie persevered in his enquiries. He wandered from street to street, asking every man he met who were the friends of Frederick Hamilton. Another night found him wandering still, without having acquired the information for which he was so earnestly seeking. Almost discouraged, he again sought lodgings.

Curse the heartlessness, the selfishness, the heathen barbarity that prevails in these cities; such exhibitions as I have witnessed this day are enough to make one hate his kind; high and low, Jew and Gentile, it is all the same.

Man is social in his nature, and pines and droops when deprived of the society of his kind; yet in cities, all the rough, unfeeling, and selfish points in human character are drawn out in bold relief. For a long time after his head was upon the pillow, he did not sleep, he was racking his ingenuity to discover the friends of Frederick Hamilton, if indeed he had any friends, sometimes he thought that the man was doomed, for every one seemed to bear him the most inveterate and determined malice.

In the morning, as soon as he had breakfasted, he again started in quest of Frederick's friends, for several hours he walked the streets, and, although he met many people, he could not bring himself to ask a question, he feared a repetition of the former answer, and it shocked his feelings. At last he entered I— Street, here a living throng presented itself, but every man, woman, and child, walked as if the salvation of souls innumerable depended upon their diligence, and upon the brow, or in the eye, or on the lip of each one, the sentence seemed to be impressed, "keep off."

There was not a kindly look, not a civil expression to be seen any where; the poor artist was perfectly disheartened, and turning into S— Street, he left the frigid crowd walking along in a fever of anxiety and excitement, he espied an old man, whose silver locks, and slow and regular step seemed to hold out some encouragement. Leslie remembered that old age is usually garrulous, and the appearance of the old man denoted him to be of comfortable circumstances, and possessed of intelligence. Leslie eagerly approached and accosted him, "Do you reside in the city sir?"

The old man stopped, leaned upon his staff, gazed into the artist's face, and answered, "I do."

This was the first civil reply that Leslie had received since the commencement of his inquiries, he was encouraged.

"Perhaps you can tell me something of Mr. Frederick Hamilton?"

"Frederick Hamilton!" replied the old man, musing; "what business is he engaged in?"

"He is in prison, now," said Leslie, with a faltering accent, fearful that the old man would insult him as others had done; "you may remember, that he was arrested for the murder of Mary Bean, who resided in Manchester."

"Oh! yes, yes," replied the old man. "I remember now, and a very distressing case it was, too. He is in prison, sure enough, and his trial will soon come on."

"Do you know aught of him?"

"No, I never knew him."

"Do you know his friends?"

"Oh! Yes, I know several of them."

"Will you direct me to them," said Leslie, smiling for joy at the double discovery he had made—the friends of Frederick Hamilton, and one civil pedestrian in the city.

"Certainly," replied the old man. "In the first place, his brother George lives in W— Street, in the upper end of the city."

Leslie's hopes fell. George Hamilton was not friendly to Frederick; he was his most unrelenting enemy.

"No, no," exclaimed he eagerly. "Not him, I mean those friends that interest themselves in his behalf."

"Why, surely," said the old man in surprise. "Who would be his friend, if his brother would not?"

"I assure you that his brother is not," replied Leslie. "But perhaps you could tell me the name of the attorney for the prisoner; he is the man I desire to see."

"I do not know him."

"Nor any other of his friends?"

"No—ah—yes; there is his partner."

"Whose partner?"

"Frederick's."

"Will you tell me his name?"

"His name is Bigelow."

"Does he, too, believe Frederick guilty of the crime of the murder?"

"No. He is his fast friend. Now that I remember, he has offered a large reward for the discovery of certain evidence that is favorable to his partner."

"Where can I find him?"

"I do not remember his place of business; a reference to the directory would inform you."

"In the city of course."

"Yes."

Leslie thanked the old man for his politeness and information, and at once started for a directory. Fortune still favored him, for he soon found one, and through its instrumentality, ascertained the location of Bigelow's store.

He started out in pursuit of it; on his way he halted at a refectory to procure refreshment, and while eating his solitary meal, he overheard a discourse between two men relative to Frederick's case. He became deeply interested, in their arguments, pro and con, and the afternoon was far advanced ere he started on his journey. His route again lay through S— Street; but this time he heeded not the cold and thronging denizens that met him. He had at last succeeded in ascertaining the whereabouts of one man that was reputed to be the fast friend of a wronged and persecuted man; to save whom he again visited the city, the scene of his most bitter and poignant griefs.

Surely, he thought, the reward I shall receive for this act, will blot from my mind the remembrance of those sins for which I have so bitterly atoned. It is a reward, too, that gold and power can never purchase. At the upper part of S— Street, he observed the crowd scattering in every direction, and uttering shouts of terror. He stopped to ascertain the cause of the tumult, and saw two frantic horses with the remnants of a carriage dangling at their heels, making directly toward him with the most desperate speed. They were upon the walk, and had already overrun and trampled upon several.

To avoid these animals, the artist rushed into the street. Just at the moment that he did so, the horses changed their course, and ran directly upon him. He was knocked down, frightfully bruised, and left insensible upon the rough pavement.

The horses passed on down the street, and a crowd assembled around the fallen man. None knew him, and none offered to assist him; but a policeman, happening to pass at the time of the accident, ordered him to be conveyed to the hospital.

Leslie was lodged in the ward of a hospital; for a long time he was insensible; but as the signs of life were visible, the surgeons who attended him spared no effort in his behalf, and he finally revived.

He revived, but oh, what a waking.

The pain he endured was most excruciating. Death itself would have been a relief to him, and he prayed for it loudly and earnestly. In his fierce agony he forgot Frederick Hamilton—forgot the generous influences that had drawn him from the Fountain, and placed him in the way of danger.

The injuries that Leslie had received from the frantic steeds in S— Street, had occasioned him a long train of suffering and pain. By dint of good treatment, and the powers of a vigorous constitution, he eventually recovered; and the day after the condemnation of Frederick Hamilton, he left the hospital.

He knew nothing of the trial or of the conviction of the man he had come to save. As soon as he could, and as fast as enfeebled limbs could carry him, he sought the address of Bigelow, in order to disclose to him the precious evidence he was in possession of. The artist reached the merchant's office, and found the man he was in quest of alone. This was what he desired, and at once opened the object of his errand.

"I understand you are the friend of Frederick Hamilton, in prison for the murder of Mary Bean."

"I am."

"I have important news for you."

"Of course you know the prisoner is condemned."

"Great God! Then I am too late."

"Perhaps not," said Bigelow, interested in the artist's manner.

"I am in the possession of evidence that will prove him innocent of the charge."

"How?"

"He is not guilty."

"But he has been condemned."

"Is it then too late to save him?"

"Perhaps not," said Bigelow. "Go with me to the office of his attorney, and make your revelations there."

And together they proceeded to Oakley's office, where Leslie related the confessions of the Doctor.

Oakley was astonished, and Bigelow, unable to restrain his emotions, threw himself into a chair and burst into tears.

"The first step to be taken," said Oakley, maintaining his self-command, "is to proceed to the place where the Doctor is secreted, and obtain the custody of his person. For this purpose I will seek the assistance of the chief of police, whilst you remain here."

And the overjoyed attorney at once proceeded in quest of the officer.

The policeman, from his confidence in the attorney, resolved to proceed on the errand at once. He therefore selected a strong force to accompany him, procured carriages for their conveyance, and appointed a place from which to set out. Oakley, the artist, and Bigelow, also procured a vehicle, for the purpose of accompanying the officers. Both parties met at the appointed rendezvous, and started together for the Fountain House. Whilst they are on the road, let us enter this home of the hunted and look about us. After the Doctor had revealed the terrible secret to the artist, his mind was easier. The hope that he should soon be relieved from the society of criminals, which he now dreaded as much as he had once desired it, and be removed from the terrible suspense and uncertainty that were hanging over his head, and tormenting every moment of his life, seemed to afford him some consolation; and after the departure of Leslie he was more cheerful. But when day after day passed away, and he had received no tidings from him, he fancied himself deserted to his fate, and again became despondent.

On the evening in question he was as usual seated in the bar-room of the establishment; the companions of his imprisonment were seated around him, some drinking, some playing cards, and others singing ribald songs, or rehearsing stale and obscene jests and anecdotes.

The Landlord was standing behind his bar, supplying the wants of his customers, and occasionally uniting with them in a chorus, or in the draining of a bumper.

Presently there was a rap at the door. In an instant the sounds of revelry ceased, and the startled inmates of the den looked at each other and listened. The sound was repeated louder than before, and of longer duration. The landlord left the bar and proceeded to the door, whilst his lodgers, with the exception of the Doctor, took their departure to their respective rooms.

"What is wanted?" asked the landlord.

"Let me in at once," exclaimed the familiar voice of the artist. The Doctor started with a joyous surprise, and the landlord exclaimed. "By the Gods, it is our quiet friend returned again. After all he cannot leave the shelter of the old crib."

"Will you admit me?" asked Leslie.

"To be sure I will, you are one of us. Be patient for a moment and you shall be gratified;" the landlord hastily unbolted the door and threw it open. "Come in," he cried.

Leslie entered, but at his heels followed a strong body of policemen. The landlord endeavored to close the door, but a well directed blow, from a short club in the hands of one of the officers, laid him senseless upon the floor.

"Thank God, you have come at last," cried the Doctor, seizing the artist by the hand. "This is the man," said Leslie, turning to the chief of police. "Then let us move at once," he replied; "At some future time I may examine this place more closely." And, accompanied by the delighted Doctor, the police party left the miserable Inn, and seating themselves in their carriages, were rapidly whirled towards the city. On arriving at the court of justice, the Doctor and Leslie were provided for, by the order of Oakley, and further proceedings deferred until another day. Early the next morning the Doctor was examined by Oakley, in the presence of the chief of police, Bigelow, and the artist. He gave, under a promise of protection, a full and accurate history of the murder, from the time it had been first agitated, up to the moment of its perpetration; and when he announced that George Hamilton with his own hands inflicted the fatal wound, a general exclamation of horror and execration escaped from his auditory. The Doctor related all the particulars, and the objects for which the fraud was committed. The day after the examination of the Doctor, Oakley and Bigelow were conversing together over the success. "You will proceed at once to the Governor and obtain the pardon, if it be possible; you will then return at once to me. The condemnation of Frederick will lead the perpetrators of the plot to suppose that all danger is past, and they will commence upon the plunder they have acquired. The witnesses will return, and as no one will dream of a pardon, they will become careless, and we, by a strict watch, will be enabled to entrap them."

"I will proceed at once, this very day."

"Of course this matter will be kept a secret."

"Of course."

"Our success in detecting the murderers depends upon our secresy. We must endeavor to wipe the stain from Frederick's character, it can only be done by showing him innocent."

"True enough," replied Bigelow, "with the odium of this crime attached to him, life itself would be of no value."

The conference closed, and Bigelow departed to see the Governor. This interview with him was necessarily brief. Oakley returned to his office to mature the plans he had roughly devised for the detection of the murderer and his accomplices.

The condemnation of Frederick Hamilton seemed to quiet the public mind. The great fever was passed, and men once more resumed their occupations and ceased to converse either about the doomed man or his late trial.

If the public were satisfied with the termination of the matter, George Hamilton was delighted. Startling as this announcement may appear, he was delighted. All his schemes had succeeded. His brother was destroyed.

When Oakley returned to his office, there, seated in the window, with a complacent smile on his features, he discovered Bigelow.

"Returned so soon!" cried Oakley, "then of course you were successful."

"I was."

"And have secured a pardon."

"I have secured the precious document in my pocket. And the Governor, unlike the majority of great men, had not forgotten his obligations to you."

"No."

"Singular enough, we have now the evidence that completely exculpates Frederick, and points to the author of the deed."

"God be praised!"

"He has need of it," replied Bigelow; "luckily he has been prevented from committing a double murder."

"And is this testimony safe?"

"As safe as stone walls can make it."

"Surely."

"Then it is indeed a remarkable intervention."

*   *   *

Let us return to George Hamilton. The evening after the sentence of his brother, he was alone in his room. A heavy and familiar tread upon the stairway, however, caused him to start, but before he could utter a word, the door opened and Bowen entered the apartment.

"I hope I do not intrude upon you," said the burglar, "but I have important information to disclose."

"More croaking," thought Hamilton. "Curse this man, I hate him most heartily."

"Leslie has escaped from the landlord's," pursued Bowen. "Wenton is in the city, and swears that he will not leave, but will confess the murder and robbery of Mr. Parsons."

Here was the opposite side of the picture at which the murderer had been complacently gazing.

"Curse my unlucky stars," he cried. "How do you know that you have been correctly informed?"

"The best evidence I ever knew gave me the information, and I could not doubt if I would."

"What evidence?"

"My own eyes," said the accomplice, draining a glass of wine. "From some source or other, Wenton is full of money, and from present appearances, he seems determined to enjoy it."

"Damn this wretch," cried Hamilton, completely off his guard. "I gave it to him myself."

"No matter where he obtained it. I had understood that you were anxious about his absence, and I thought the information would be acceptable. Leslie is also somewhere about the town, for he has just quitted the hospital, where an unlucky accident had confined him."

"And what is to be done in the matter," asked Hamilton, as usual, turning to his associate for advice.

"We must do all that we can. If you will accompany me, we will visit them. With your influence to assist me, I might prevail upon them to act in a reasonable manner. For myself, I have no fears of Leslie; he is not a common wretch."

Mr. Hamilton dreaded to accede to the proposition of his friend, but he could not with propriety refuse. In fact, he was too deeply interested to do so; and, after fortifying himself with several glasses of wine in which his Madeira-loving friend joined him, they sallied out in company in quest of the felons. But a long and toilsome search brought them no reward. They could not discover Wenton.

For once even Bowen was alarmed. He knew the utter worthlessness of a villain's promises; and he knew the danger with which Wenton's presence in the city surrounded him.

Hamilton was thoroughly aroused; after all he had not secured his peace of mind; and he felt for the first time, that the vile and unprincipled wretches that he had brought around him by his villainies, were destined to be perpetual thorns in his side. He bitterly cursed the blind fatality that had induced him to engage with them.

* * *

To return to Oakley, Frederick's attorney. There was but one missing link in this chain of testimony, and that was Wenton. Incited by the discoveries they had already made, the policemen determined upon one more search for Wenton. They sallied out, full of stubborn determination; but as the trail had passed, and that worthy personage had supposed that all danger to himself and his employer had passed with it, he did not put their patience or ingenuity to the test. He was discovered in a gambling den in A— Street, and at once brought to the court.

The same promise of protection that had been given to the Doctor were held out to this worthy; but for a long time he refused to disclose a word; but when he saw that the Doctor was secured, and was assured by that individual in person, that all had been disclosed, he quickly fell in with the overture, and acknowledged his participation in the murder and robbery of Mr. Parsons, even to his last interview with Hamilton, and his reception of one thousand dollars.

"We have them now," exclaimed Oakley, joyously; "and the innocent will be saved. These witnesses must be confined, however, and the matter kept a secret, for we are not yet prepared to divulge."

The policemen acknowledged the justness of these conclusions, and the two witnesses were separately but comfortably confined, and furnished with every necessary that could conduce to their physical well-being.

CHAPTER VII.

The news of Frederick Hamilton's pardon by the governor, burst upon the city like the explosion of a powder mine. At first men could not credit the story. It could not be possible that the Chief Magistrate had dared to thwart the administration of justice, when the guilt was so positively, so incontestibly clear.

They were forced to believe it, however, for the overjoyed Frederick was released from prison, and the newspapers officially published his liberation to the world. He was really free from the meshes and terrors of the law, and in the full enjoyment of his liberty.

If they were astonished at the news of Frederick's pardon, they were actually horrified when they heard that George Hamilton was under arrest, charged with the commission of the offence for which his brother had been condemned.

In the utmost consternation they asked, what can the world mean by such improbable proceedings.

Frederick Hamilton had no friends amongst the public mass; but all were the warm friends of George. Although he was obliged to submit to the mandate of the law, and appear before the magistrates for his examination, yet, the sympathies of the public were with him, and he maintained a bold front. He did not know the evidence upon which he had been implicated, for he had neither heard of Wenton's arrest, nor the forcible rescue of the Doctor.

He was accompanied to the court-room by Mr. Brigham, his counsellor, and a long line of indignant and sympathizing friends. His denouncers were also there, and were fully prepared to substantiate the charges against him.

He was arraigned in the room that had witnessed Frederick's agony.

The crowd was again immense, and the public wondered at the news of the charges brought against him.

It would be idle to attempt a picture of Hamilton's feelings, at the time of his arrest. He had been so long successful in his villainies, had so long escaped even suspicion, that at the first he was indignant, and severely reproved the officers in the discharge of the duty for their impudence. He majestically waived them away with his hands; but when he ascertained that his imperious order was disregarded, he began to reflect upon the situation in which he found himself.

What could have directed suspicion towards him at this late hour? What evidence to warrant his arrest had been laid before the Magistrate? Surely, it could be but some trifling circumstance, seized upon by the friends of Frederick, as a desperate and final effort to save him from the gallows.

At the time of his arrest, he knew nothing of Frederick's pardon.

The examination commenced; Leslie fell back amidst the crowd, and George Hamilton felt that his doom was come.

It was a long time after the excitement, before the business could proceed; the audience were highly excited, and could not be prevented from commenting upon what had just occurred. Order was finally restored, and then Mr. Brigham said: "We are now anxious to confront the testimony which the authors of this accusation against Mr. Hamilton may rely upon, and we would wish your honor to proceed in the matter at once."

"We are ready," said Oakley. And the court called Doctor Savin.

Hamilton started from his seat as this name fell upon his ear, and with a straining eye, gazed about the house in search of the Doctor—he could discover nothing of him however, and fell back into his seat with his face the hue of death.

The Doctor was in an adjoining room, but was speedily brought before the court, by an officer in attendance; he was very pale and haggard, but he was firm and collected, and looked upon the vast crowd assembled without any visible emotion.

An apparition from the world of spirits, could not have affected Hamilton more powerfully than did the appearance of Doctor Savin. With the rapidity of thought the scenes of that terrible night, in which he imbrued his hands in the blood of Mr. Parsons, and also of poor Mary Bean, passed before him, and the knife of an assassin could not have caused a keener pang than did the odious review. Hardened as he was in crime, he discovered that his conscience could yet be reached; he dared not look his accomplice in the face.

The oath was administered to Doctor Savin, with an awful distinctness, every word of which sunk into the heart of Hamilton, as if impressed with a red hot iron. He related a history of the murder. As he confessed his own participation in the crime, the tears rolled down his cheeks, and his voice was choaked with sobs.

The Doctor made no pretentions to morals, laid no claim to weight of character, but there was an earnestness, an air of truthfulness about his narrative, that carried a conviction of its truth to the bosoms of his listeners; confused, terrified, and ashamed, George Hamilton covered his face with his handkerchief.

After the testimony of the Doctor, Wenton was introduced; he detailed minutely the part he had played in Mr. Parsons deep plot, and the reward that had been paid him as hush-money; his evidence closed the examination, and the murderer was committed to prison to await the further movement of the law.

The Doctor and Wenton were also secured. So overwhelming was this testimony, so directly and undeniably did it fix the guilt upon the culprit, that his powerful troupe of attorneys could not find even a loop to hang a doubt upon. They could not produce or urge a single extenuating circumstance in their client's favor, but were forced to surrender him to the strong hands of the law.

Who has not witnessed sudden and complete revolutions in public opinion? Who has not seen the speed with which men will rush from one extreme of sentiment to another?

Frederick Hamilton was perfectly exonerated in the minds of the populace, and was at once regarded as an abused and injured individual. So far did they carry their opinions of the injustice, that had been done him, that they repaired in a mass to his house, and honored him with a full and manly expression of the change in their feelings toward him.

Who can describe justly, the feelings of George Hamilton, now that he was compelled to exchange his place for the naked walls and damp floor of a prison cell. How frightful, how chilling was the contrast. Unlike Frederick in the same situation, he had not the consciousness of innocence to sustain him. When the shades of night closed in upon him, and he could no longer discern the day-light through the iron bars that guarded the solitary window of his cell, his remorse was most excruciating. He threw himself upon his wretched pallet and endeavored to silence the reproaches of his soul in slumber, but he could not; sleep would not visit him, he tossed in indescribable agony, and the sweat stood upon his brow in large beads.

The very torments of hell seemed to have seized upon him prematurely. He could hardly refrain from calling out. There is not in the whole catalogue of miserable beings, a more helpless and despondent individual than a hardened and desperate villain, entrapped in his rascality, and securely confined by the powers of the law.

Bowen's career was speedily closed. He was arrested, and cast into jail, but soon after his incarceration he took sick, and the utmost exertions of the physicians that were called to assist him did not avail him.

He never spoke, but breathed his last soon after the adjournment of the court that committed his friend and dupe to prison.

Through the exertions of his friends George Hamilton determined to make most desperate efforts to escape the punishment that he so richly deserved, and they accordingly raised the cry of persecution and conspiracy. They endeavored to convince the people that Hamilton was the victim of powerful and vindictive enemies, and that the evidence, who were his denouncers, were abandoned and dissolute men, and not entitled to credence from men of influence. But the public, good easy souls that they are, are not easily deceived in such matters. The evidence of Wenton and the Doctor was too strongly corroborated by circumstances to be doubted, and was consequently well received.

CONCLUSION.

The trial of George Hamilton was called up at the next term of court, although every effort was made by his counsel to defer it; these motives did not prevail.

During the period that elapsed between the examination and the day set apart for the trial, the Magistrate had been indefatigable in searching out every particle of evidence that could, in any way, be said to bear upon the case.

All was detected, and various other circumstances were brought to light, which left not a shadow of doubt as to Hamilton's guilt, if there had been any.

It is almost needless to say that the wretched man was condemned.

His counsel labored assiduously in his behalf, but the proof was too damning, and the guilt too flagrant. With all their eloquence and legal tact they could not save him. Although the remorse of the murderer had been keen, although his soul had been most terribly shaken, yet through all his imprisonment, through all the stages of his trial, hope had not deserted him; but when conviction speedily followed the close of the evidence, he did indeed despair.

The weight of his guilt, the terrible remembrance of his past life, the misery of his present condition, absolutely crushed his very soul to atoms.

For many days he was a maniac. He raved of Mary Bean, of Frederick, of the torments of hell he had already endured; only by constant watching was he prevented from taking his own life. "Verily, the way of a transgressor is hard."

Eventually the brain fever, under which he had been laboring, subsided, and he became calm. He gradually recovered his strength, and could pace the narrow boundaries of his prison cell. His keeper no longer watched him, and he was frequently left to the solitude of his abode. One morning the Rev. Mr. Miller, his spiritual adviser, visited his cell, for the purpose of persuading him to confess the crimes with which he was charged, and prepare his soul for death; he saw that he was extended upon the bed, apparently sleeping quietly, he saw his provisions upon the little table with which his cell was furnished, and with as little noise as possible, for he did not wish to disturb him, he quietly retired.

At noon he returned again, but observed that Hamilton was yet lying in the same position, and that the provisions were untouched, his suspicions were aroused and he approached the bedside of the doomed one.

He started with horror as he observed a pool of blood upon the floor. Recovering from the shock, he proceeded to examine the bed more closely, and he discovered that Hamilton was dead. And upon his pillow was found this memoir of the horrid deeds of his past life. He had closed his wretched career by the commission of a crime as daring and heinous as the murder of Mary Bean. He committed suicide in the jail at Saco, Maine, on the 7th day of May, 1852.

Frederick, the injured brother, attended to the burial of the suicide. He was decently interred, notwithstanding he was a murderer.

Doctor Savin was convicted of murder in the second degree, and sent to the state prison for life.

Wenton died in the state prison soon after his incarceration.

THE END.

NOTES

ABBREVIATIONS

AA   *Augusta (Maine) Age*
BB   *Boston (Mass.) Daily Bee*
BI   *Boston (Mass.) Investigator*
BT   *Boston (Mass.) Daily Evening Traveller*
DJ   *Lowell (Mass.) Daily Journal and Courier*
DL   Special Collections and Archives, Dyer Library, Saco, Maine
EA   *Portland (Maine) Eastern Argus*
FC   *Amherst (N.H.) Farmer's Cabinet*
KG   *Kennebunk (Maine) Gazette and Maine Palladium*
LL   *Palmer's Illustrated Life in Lowell (Mass.)*
MA   *Biddeford (Maine) Mercantile Advertiser*
MD   *(Saco) Maine Democrat*
MHA   Manchester (N.H.) Historic Association
MHS   Maine Historical Society, Portland
MSA   Maine State Archives, Augusta
NHA   *Manchester (N.H.) American*
NHD   *Manchester (N.H.) Democrat*
NHHC   New Hampshire Historical Society, Concord
NHP   *Concord (N.H.) Patriot and Gazette*
PA   *Portland (Maine) Advertiser*
PB   *Portland (Maine) Pleasure Boat*
PT   *Portland (Maine) Transcript*
SM   Saco (Maine) Museum
SU   *Saco (Maine) Union*
YCH   *York County Herald*

1. "Excitement in Saco—Dead Body Found," *AA*, Apr. 25, 1850.

2. Janet Farrell Brodie, *Contraception and Abortion in Nineteenth-Century America* (Ithaca, N.Y.: Cornell Univ. Press, 1994), 88.

3. On the cultural work of fiction see Jane Tompkins, *Sensational Designs: The Cultural Work of American Fiction, 1790–1860* (New York: Oxford Univ. Press, 1985).

4. "The Saco Tragedy," *EA*, Apr. 20, 1850.

5. Roy P. Fairfield, *Sands, Spindles, and Steeples: A History of Saco, Maine* (Portland, Maine: House of Falmouth, 1956), 146. A public sewer system was not available in Saco until the 1870s.

6. "The Murder at Saco," *FC*, Apr. 25, 1850, *Early American Newspapers*, series 1. University of New England, Biddeford, Maine, http://info.web.newsbank.com/ (accessed February 9, 2006). *Early American Newspapers* is a digital collection available at the American Antiquarian Society (Worcester, Mass.) or by institutional subscription from Readex, a division of NewsBank. See the collection description and access information at www.americanantiquarian.org/digital2.htm.

7. Fairfield, *Sands, Spindles, and Steeples*, 45. On the history of Saco see also Jacques Downs, *The Cities on the Saco: A Pictorial History* (Norfolk, Va.: Donning, 1985); Peter N. Scontras, *Saco: Then and Now* (Saco, Maine: Scontras Publishing, 1994); Dane Yorke, *A History and Stories of Biddeford* (Biddeford, Maine: McArthur Library, 1994); and Fellowship Class of the United Baptist Church of Saco, comp., *A Folklore History of Saco Bay, 1629–1976* (Portland, Maine: House of Falmouth, 1976).

8. "Saco and Biddeford—Their Progress," *SU*, Feb. 2, 1849; also quoted in Yorke, *History and Stories*, 19.

9. Yorke, *History and Stories*, 37; Fairfield, *Sands, Spindles, and Steeples*, 50.

10. Fairfield, *Sands, Spindles, and Steeples*, 48–49.

11. Asa Wentworth to J. H. Brown, circa 1846, quoted in "Report of the Examination of Asa & Henry Wentworth," *MD*, May 14, 1850.

12. Fairfield, *Sands, Spindles, and Steeples*, 59, 391.

13. *The Business Directory of Saco and Biddeford. For the Year 1849* (Saco, Maine: L. O. Cowan and A. A. Hanscom, 1849), [2].

14. Fairfield, *Sands, Spindles, and Steeples*, 63.

15. On the rise of the police department in Saco, see Fairfield, *Sands, Spindles, and Steeples*, 67, 144. See also Roger Lane, *Policing the City: Boston 1822–1885* (Cambridge, Mass.: Harvard Univ. Press, 1967), 6; and Lane, *Murder in America: A History* (Columbus: Ohio State Univ. Press, 1997), 102.

16. John D. Beatty, *Vital Records of Biddeford, Maine, Prior to 1856* (Camden, Maine: Picton Press, 1998); E. P. Burnham, "Miscellaneous Notes and a Brief Diary, 1853–1865," typescript, DL; E. P. Burnham, "Saco Families," typescript, DL; "Deaths from the Original Records at Saco City Hall," vol. 2, Nov. 3, 1840, to Dec. 29, 1867. Photocopy, DL; "Marriages from the Original Records at Saco City Hall," vol. 1: Nov. 18–Dec. 28, 1850, and vol. 2: Feb. 18, 1851–Mar. 3, 1867, DL; Melvil F. Meeds, comp., "Intentions and Return of Marriages from the Original Records at City Hall," vol. 1, 1832–1851, typescript ca. 1952, MHS; "Records of Births, Book 2d: 1836–1882," typescript (Mar. 1995), DL.

17. *Directory of Saco and Biddeford*, 78–93.

18. Ardis Cameron, *Radicals of the Worst Sort: Laboring Women in Lawrence,*

Massachussetts, 1860–1912 (Urbana: Univ. of Illinois Press, 1993), xvi–xvii. On the lives of factory girls see Thomas Dublin, *Women at Work: The Transformation of Work and Community in Lowell, Massachusetts, 1826–1860* (New York: Columbia Univ. Press, 1979); and Dublin, *Transforming Women's Work: New England Lives in the Industrial Revolution* (Ithaca, N.Y.: Cornell Univ. Press, 1994).

19. "Comparative Prices and Wages," Center for Lowell History, http://library.uml.edu/clh/ApC.html (accessed Aug. 9, 2006); "Weekly Wages 1824–1868," Center for Lowell History, http://library.uml.edu/clh/All/char05.htm (accessed Feb. 4, 2007).

20. Marion Hopkins, diary, Nov. 6, 1854. Tuck Library Special Collections, NHHC.

21. Ibid., Oct. 4, 1854.

22. See the extensive bibliography of stories featuring factory girls in Judith A. Ranta, *Women and Children of the Mills: An Annotated Guide to Nineteenth-Century American Textile Factory Literature* (Westport, Conn.: Greenwood Press, 1999).

23. On the literature of the Sarah Cornell case, see David Kasserman, *Fall River Outrage: Life, Murder, and Justice in Early Industrial New England* (Philadelphia: Univ. of Pennsylvania Press, 1986), 255–57; see also William G. McLoughlin, "Untangling the Tiverton Tragedy: The Social Meaning of the Terrible Haystack Murder of 1833," *Journal of American Culture* 7 (1984): 75–84; and Catherine Williams, *Fall River: An Authentic Narrative*, ed. Patricia Caldwell (New York: Oxford Univ. Press, 1993).

24. Orrilla Durrell was said to have been from Maine. "Love and Suicide," *AA*, Jan. 25, 1849; "The Ruined Girl," *LL*, July 14, 1849; an advertisement for the publication of *Love and Suicide* is found in *LL*, Aug. 25, 1849.

25. "Another Horrible Mystery," *MD*, Feb. 19, 1850; also reported in the *SU*, Feb. 1850.

26. *AA*, Apr. 25, 1850.

27. *BT*, Apr. 15, 1850; *DJ*, Apr. 16, 1850, uses the same headline.

28. This advertisement appeared in the *MD* throughout the spring of 1849.

29. "James W. Smith, Remarkable Penman," newspaper article circa 1931, clippings file, DL. I am grateful to the late Alexander Cumming for alerting me to this resource. On the Smith family see the entry for James H. Smith in the United States census records at Ancestry.com, 1850 United States Federal Census, roll M432_275, page 303 and roll M432_276, page 192 [online database] (Provo, Utah: The Generations Network, 2004), http://www.ancestry.com/ (accessed January 8, 2003). For Sarah Dresser Smith, see "Dresser Family Genealogy: Main Line," Ancestry World Tree Project [online database], Ancestry.com, http://www.ancestry.com/ (accessed January 8, 2003).

30. James H. Smith to Moses Woodsum, June 26, 1849, Records of Mortgages, Deeds and Bills of Sale, vol. 8, 1843–1852, DL; James H. Smith to Rufus M. Lord and George Stuart, Mar. 8, 1850, Records of Mortgages, Deeds and Bills of Sale, vol. 8, 1843–1852, DL; James H. Smith to Francis A. Boothby, May 13, 1854, Records

of Mortgages, Deeds and Bills of Sale, vol. 9, 1852–1860, DL; Writ #436 Leland v. James H. Smith, Western District Court Writs, Feb. Term 1850, box 241 Agency Y-C, MSA.

31. On Smith's involvement in the Parker murder case and 1849 investigation, see *MD*, Feb. 13, 20, and 27, 1849.

32. "Report of the Examination of Asa & Henry Wentworth," *MD*, May 14, 1850.

33. *MD*, Apr. 18, 1850; reprinted in *EA*, Apr. 20, 1850.

34. "The Murder at Saco," *FC*, Apr. 25, 1850, *Early American Newspapers*, series 1. University of New England, Biddeford, Maine, http://info.web.newsbank. com (accessed Feb. 9, 2006).

35. "Verdict of Coroners Jury on the Body of Mary Bean," manuscript documents related to *State v. James H. Smith*, MSA.

36. "Dead Body Found," *SU*, Apr. 19, 1850.

37. On the concern with identity and sincerity see Karen Halttunen, *Confidence Men and Painted Women: A Study of Middle-Class Culture in America, 1830–1870* (New Haven, Conn.: Yale Univ. Press, 1982); and John F. Kasson, *Rudeness and Civility: Manners in Nineteenth-Century Urban America* (New York: Hill and Wang, 1990).

38. William Long was born December 3, 1828, the son of Isaac and Susannah Long. Biddeford Records of Birth, MHS.

39. "Examination of James H. Smith," *MD*, Apr. 30, 1850.

40. The origin of the name Berengera is found in E.G. Withycombe, *The Oxford Dictionary of English Christian Names* (New York: Oxford Univ. Press, 1997), 47. This unusual name continued into the next generation. Berengera's older sister Abigail Caswell Sleeper named a daughter Elizabeth Berengera (born 1854) and her younger brother Isaac named his first daughter (born 1862) Berengera. On Caswell genealogy see "Descendants of Abiel Chandler," http://www. geocities.com/Heartland/Plains/3975/Chandler/abiechan.html (accessed February 28, 2004); Ancestral File of "Berengera Dalton Caswell" (AFN:MKSD-ZX) and "Thais Elizabeth Caswell" (AFN:MKTB-CN), Family Search [online database], The Church of Jesus Christ of Latter-Day Saints, http://www.family search.org/ (accessed March 5, 2002); "Descendants of Nathan Caswell," Ancestry World Tree Project [online database], Ancestry.com, http://www.ancestry. com/ (accessed February 7, 2005); Richard W. Musgrove, "The Chandler Families," in *History of the Town of Bristol, Grafton County, New Hampshire* (Bristol, N.H.: R. W. Musgrove, 1904), 90–93, available http://www.persi.heritagequestonline. com [online database accessed at the Maine Historical Society, Portland, Maine] (accessed June 15, 2005). I am most grateful to the genealogical and family history information confirmed and provided by Susan Reynolds-Phaneuf, descendant of Ruth Caswell Straw Reynolds.

41. Dublin, *Women at Work*, 109.

42. Fairfield, *Sands, Spindles, and Steeples*, 47–48; "Turn Out of Female Operatives," *KG*, Apr. 3, 1841; "Saco Factories," *KG*, Apr. 10, 1841; "Higher Wages!

Better Times!" *MD*, Mar. 30, 1841; "The Factory Agent's Circular," *MD*, Apr. 6, 1841; "The Late Turn Out," *MD*, Apr. 20, 1841; "The Turnouts," *MD*, May 4, 1841; "The Late Turn Out of the Factory Girls," *YCH—Extra*, Apr. 15, 1841.

43. Francis Tamburro, "A Tale of a Song: The Lowell Factory Girl," *Southern Exposure* 2 (1974): 42–51; see also Evelyn Alloy, *Working Women's Music: The Songs and Struggles of Women in the Cotton Mills, Textile Plants, and Needle Trades* (Somerville, Mass.: New England Free Press, 1976); and Philip S. Foner, *American Labor Songs of the Nineteenth Century* (Urbana: Univ. of Illinois Press, 1975), 40–45.

44. *MD*, June 11, 1850; see also complaints in *MD*, July 30, 1850; and see the discussion of the Lowell Female Labor Reform Association and the labor press in Foner, *American Labor Songs*, 52–53.

45. On the process of carding and on weaving see Dublin, *Women at Work*, 62–64, 67. See also Jacquelyn Dowd Hall et al., *Like a Family: The Making of a Southern Cotton Mill World* (New York: Norton, 1987), 80. The Caswell sisters' payroll records are found in "Amoskeag Mfg. Co., Payroll, Mill #3, 1846–1848" and "Amoskeag Mfg. Co., Payroll, Mill #3, 1848–1850," MHA. I am very grateful to archivist Eileen O'Brien for searching through these volumes despite the temporary closure of the research library. On the history of the Amoskeag Mill, see Tamara K. Harevan and Randolph Langebach, *Amoskeag: Life and Work in an American Factory City* (New York: Pantheon Books, 1978).

46. Thais Elizabeth Caswell married Oates (variously recorded as Ortes or Orzo) in 1852. He died in a mill accident a year later. She then married Joshua Page and had three daughters in three years (Almira born in 1856, Mary Tyler in 1857, and Ida May in 1858). Page died in 1863. Thais was married once again, to George Litchfield, with whom she had a son, George, around 1870. Both father and son died before 1880, leaving Thais a three-time widow. She died in 1896. Her name is variously recorded as Thais, Thayons, Thais E., and Elizabeth.

47. Gage and Forsaith, *The Manchester Almanac and General Business Directory, for the Year 1850* (Manchester, N.H.: Printed at the Manchester Messenger Building, 1850).

48. Information on how Manchester mill girls spent their evenings is gleaned from newspapers, the Manchester city directory, and the diary of Marion Hopkins, who worked in the Amoskeag mill just a few years after the Caswell sisters. For a less successful experience at Amoskeag, see Caroline A. Graham, diary, May 24–June 3, 1854, Tuck Library Special Collections, NHHC. For a study of factory workers' leisure time in the post-bellum period, see Roy Rosenzweig, *Eight Hours for What We Will: Workers and Leisure in an Industrial City, 1870–1920* (New York: Cambridge Univ. Press, 1983).

49. "The Saco Examination," *NHD*, May 2, 1850.

50. On the history of abortion see Brodie, *Contraception and Abortion*; Linda Gordon, *Woman's Body, Woman's Right: A Social History of Birth Control in America* (New York: Grossman, 1976); Helen Lefkowitz Horowitz, *Rereading Sex: Battles over Sexual Knowledge and Suppression in Nineteenth-Century America* (New York:

Vintage, 2002), 194–209; James C. Mohr, *Abortion in America: The Origins and Evolution of National Policy, 1800–1900* (New York: Oxford Univ. Press, 1978); Leslie J. Reagan, *When Abortion Was a Crime: Women, Medicine, and Law in the United States, 1867–1973* (Berkeley: Univ. of California Press, 1997); John M. Riddle, *Eve's Herbs: A History of Contraception and Abortion in the West* (Cambridge, Mass.: Harvard Univ. Press, 1997).

51. This advertisement appears in the *MD* throughout 1852.

52. Mohr, *Abortion in America*, 62.

53. Reagan, *When Abortion Was a Crime*, 9.

54. Carol Smith-Rosenberg, *Disorderly Conduct: Visions of Gender in Victorian America* (New York: Oxford Univ. Press, 1985), 233.

55. Mohr, *Abortion in America*, 55; "Madame C. Amy," *MD*, July 2, 1850; Smith-Rosenberg, *Disorderly Conduct*, 225–26. The advertisement for Madame Amy's practice appeared shortly after the Caswell excitement filled the news; Madame Amy likely saw a profitable opportunity in Saco and Biddeford.

56. On the community of women's sexual knowledge see Horowitz, *Rereading Sex*, 194–209.

57. Dublin, *Women at Work*, 82–83.

58. On Henry Wentworth's cross-dressing see *The Parker Murder* (Manchester, N.H.: Printed by J. B. Clarke, 1886), 4.

59. "Arrest of Dr. J. A. Smith, for the Murder of an Unknown Female," *BB*, Apr. 18, 1850.

60. "Examination of James H. Smith," *MD*, Apr. 30, 1850.

61. "Dead Body Found," *SU*, Apr. 19, 1850. A year earlier the *Union* had reported the death of Mrs. Sarah Bridges "by hemorrhage and inflammation of the womb, following an abortion produced by mechanical violence." The provider was not identified. *SU*, Apr. 6, 1849.

62. Gage and Forsaith, *Manchester Almanac*, 172. The *Manchester Almanac* lists physicians by medical philosophy including a column for "regular" physicians and a second column listing the "Botanic and Thompsonian" practitioners.

63. Peter P. Good, *The Family Flora and Materia Medica Botanica, containing the Botanical Analysis, Natural History, and Chemical and Medical Properties of Plants*, 2 vols. (Elizabethtown, N.J.: Published by the author, 1847), 1: [32–36]. On savin, see Riddle, *Eve's Herbs*, 40, 54–55, 143, 200–201.

64. Good, *The Family Flora*, 1: [32–36].

65. On Maine abortion law, see Bob Michaud, comp., *Abortion in Maine: A Statutory and Legislative History from 1820 to Present*, vol. 1 (Augusta: Maine State Law and Legislative Reference Library, 1992). See also the discussion in Mohr, *Abortion in America*, 41–42.

66. "Dead Body Found," *EA*, Apr. 15, 1850.

67. "The Smith Trial," *MD*, Apr. 23, 1850.

68. Although the local newspapers stated that extras were printed daily during the examination, I have located only one of these fragile and highly ephemeral

pieces: "The Smith Trial for the Murder of Mary Bean, at Saco," *MD Extra*, Apr. 22, 1850, DL.

69. On crime literature and print culture see Albert Borowitz, *Blood and Ink: An International Guide to Fact-Based Crime Literature* (Kent, Ohio: Kent State Univ. Press, 2002); Daniel A. Cohen, *Pillars of Salt, Monuments of Grace: New England Crime Literature and the Origins of American Popular Culture, 1674–1860* (New York: Oxford Univ. Press, 1993); Karen Halttunen, *Murder Most Foul: The Killer and the American Gothic Imagination* (Cambridge, Mass.: Harvard Univ. Press, 1998); Thomas McDade, comp., *The Annals of Murder: A Bibliography of Books and Pamphlets on American Murders from Colonial Times to 1900* (Norman: Univ. of Oklahoma Press, 1961); Paul Starr, *The Creation of the Media: Political Origins of Modern Communications* (New York: Basic Books, 2004); and Andie Tucher, *Froth and Scum: Truth, Beauty, Goodness, and the Ax Murder in America's First Mass Medium* (Chapel Hill: Univ. of North Carolina Press, 1994).

70. "A Horrid Murder," *MD*, Apr. 9, 1849.

71. Simon Schama, *Dead Certainties* (New York: Vintage Books, 1992), 196. See also "American Experience: Murder at Harvard," DVD, directed by Steven Ives and Ben Loerteman (Boston, Mass.: WGBH, 2005).

72. "Examination of James H. Smith," *MD*, Apr. 30, 1850.

73. Untitled article, *PT*, May 11, 1850.

74. "Examination of James H. Smith," *MD*, Apr. 30, 1850.

75. "The Smith Trial," *MD Extra*, Apr. 22, 1850.

76. "Examination of James H. Smith," *SU*, Apr. 26, 1850.

77. "Examination of James H. Smith," *MD*, Apr. 30, 1850.

78. "Swearing to Lies," *PB*, May 2, 1850.

79. "The Saco Tragedy," *BT*, Apr. 23, 1850.

80. "Examination of Dr. Jas. H. Smith," *BB*, Apr. 23, 1850; "Examination of James H. Smith," *MD*, Apr. 30, 1850; "Committal of Dr. Smith for Trial," *BT*, Apr. 26, 1850.

81. The trial testimony was not recorded by a court official. Fortunately, the newspaper reporters were diligent in publishing the testimony. Interestingly, the attorneys' questions were not recorded, only the deponents' answers, necessitating the reader, and historian, to fill in those gaps. Comparing several different newspaper accounts of the examination, written by different reporters, allows one to gain better insight into what occurred. On the intersection of law and literature and how both narrative forms suggest, or coerce, an expectation for legal situations, see Richard Weisberg, *Poethics and Other Strategies of Law and Literature* (New York: Columbia Univ. Press, 1992).

82. "The Saco Tragedy," *EA*, Apr. 24, 1850.

83. Ibid.

84. Ibid.

85. Ibid.

86. "Examination of James H. Smith," *SU*, Apr. 26, 1850.

87. "The Saco Tragedy," *EA*, Apr. 24, 1850.

88. Ibid.

89. Ibid., Apr. 25, 1850.

90. Daniela Mascetti and Amanda Triossi, *Earrings: From Antiquity to the Present* (London: Thames and Hudson, 1990), 81. See also pages 92 and 93 for photographs of drop earrings.

91. "Examination of James H. Smith," *MD*, Apr. 30, 1850.

92. "The Saco Tragedy," *SU*, Apr. 26, 1850.

93. Ibid.

94. James Smith's threat is recorded in "Supposed Murder in Saco," *NHP*, Apr. 25, 1850, *Early American Newspapers* series 1. University of New England, Biddeford, Maine, http://info.web.newsbank.com (accessed Feb. 9, 2006); Sarah Smith's threats are alleged in "The Saco Affair," *PA*, Apr. 19, 1850.

95. "The Saco Tragedy," *EA*, Apr. 26, 1850.

96. Ibid.

97. "The Saco Murder," *NHP*, May 2, 1850, Early American Newspapers series 1. University of New England, Biddeford, Maine, http://info.webnewsbank.com (accessed Feb. 9, 2006).

98. In her study of abortion patients, Leslie Reagan describes how "dying declarations" are an exception to the hearsay rule, with the assumption that those who expect to die at any moment have little motive to lie. Leslie J. Reagan, "'About to Meet Her Maker': Women, Doctors, Dying Declarations, and the State's Investigation of Abortion, Chicago, 1867–1940," *Journal of American History* 77 (Mar. 1991): 1249. Long visited Berengera each Sunday. On December 16, Berengera had just had her abortion and though she was no doubt in great pain, her infection had not yet set in to the extent that she had thought she might die. By the next Sunday visit, Berengera was dead.

99. "The Saco Tragedy," *EA*, Apr. 26, 1850.

100. From this testimony we can estimate that Berengera was between fifteen and eighteen weeks pregnant. Counting backward, this indicates a September conception, and thus, Berengera did not yet know she was pregnant when she and Long parted in September 1849. I am grateful to Dr. Terri Vanderlinde, DO, for her assistance in deciphering Berengera's pregnancy timetable and in describing the olfactory aspects of reproduction and infection.

101. "The Saco Tragedy," *EA*, Apr. 27, 1850.

102. Ibid.

103. "Swearing to Lies," *PB*, May 2, 1850; see also "The Recent Trial in Saco," *MA*, Apr. 27, 1850.

104. "Examination of James H. Smith," *SU*, Apr. 26, 1850; "Witnesses Admitted to Bail," *MD*, Apr. 30, 1850. On the court system in Maine in 1850 see "Maine Supreme Court" and "District and Superior Courts," Department of the Secretary of State: Maine State Archives, http://www.state.me.us/sos/arc/archives/judicial/judicial.htm (accessed Aug. 12, 2006); see also "Citizen's

Guide to the Courts," State of Maine Judicial Branch, http://www.courts.state.me.us/courtservices/citizen_guide/index.html (accessed Aug. 12, 2006).

105. "More Evidence against Dr. Smith," *NHD*, May 9, 1850.

106. "Deaths from Original Records," 30, DL.

107. "More Evidence against Dr. Smith," *NHD*, May 9, 1850.

108. Ruth Caswell, who had traveled with Berengera and Thais to the Lowell mill, had married in Lowell in 1848. Her first husband, Willard (or William) Straw, a former mill worker, was arrested for burglary and died in the New Hampshire state prison. With Straw she had two sons who both died young. She married William Reynolds in 1853 and together they had three children in Manchester.

109. "A Day or Two at Alfred," *MA*, Jan. 23, 1851. See also Andrew Walker, diary, Jan. 25, 1851, in the collection of the Kennebunk (Maine) Free Library.

110. Philip Greely Clifford, *Nathan Clifford, Democrat* (New York: George Putnam's Sons, 1922), 333.

111. "Trial of James H. Smith," *MD*, Jan. 28, 1851.

112. Ibid.

113. "A Day or Two at Alfred," *MA*, Jan. 23, 1851.

114. "Examination of Dr. Jas. H. Smith," *BB*, Apr. 23, 1850.

115. In a similar highly publicized case in Boston, jurors were instructed not to read the newspapers so as to avoid influence, yet they did anyway. Mohr, *Abortion in America*, 121.

116. Brodie, *Contraception and Abortion*, 88.

117. "Trial of James H. Smith," *MD*, Jan. 28, 1851.

118. On public discussion of women's bodies, see Barbara Baumgartner, "Genderless Anatomies: The Body in Nineteenth-Century Anatomy and Physiology Texts" (paper presented at "Women, Health and Representation," a conference sponsored by the Maine Women Writers Collection, Univ. of New England, Portland, Maine, June 19, 2004); and Alison Piepmeier, *Out in Public: Configurations of Women's Bodies in Nineteenth-Century America* (Chapel Hill: Univ. of North Carolina Press, 2004). See also Halttunen, *Murder Most Foul*, 187–93.

119. "Trial of James H. Smith," *MD*, Jan. 28, 1851.

120. "Woman's Proper Sphere," *MD*, June 11, 1850.

121. "Trial of James H. Smith," *MD*, Jan. 28, 1851.

122. C. Austin, "The Factory Girl," broadside poem, circa 1852, Biddeford, Maine. Photocopy in the "Factory Island" exhibit files, SM.

123. "The Saco Tragedy," *BI*, May 8, 1850.

124. Historian Daniel A. Cohen analyzes the intersection of gender and consumption in the public portrayals of the murdered Maria Bickford. "Some accounts pictured the slain woman as a tasteful and sensitive consumer; others described her as a wasteful and undisciplined spendthrift" (p. 6). "The Murder of Maria Bickford: Fashion, Passion, and the Birth of a Consumer Culture," *American Studies* 31 (Fall 1990): 5–30.

125. "Trial of James H. Smith," *MD*, Jan. 28, 1851.

126. Ibid.

127. "The Saco Examination," *NHD*, May 2, 1850.

128. "Examination of James H. Smith," *MD*, Apr. 30, 1850.

129. "Trial of James H. Smith," *MD*, Jan. 28, 1851.

130. Ibid.

131. Ibid.

132. "State Prison," *MD*, Apr. 29, 1851. See also *Annual Report of the Inspectors of the State Prison*, 1851, and *Annual Report of the Warden of the State Prison*, 1851, bound together in *Maine Public Documents 1851*, part 1 (Augusta, Maine: William T. Johnson, 1852).

133. Documents relating to Smith's appeal are found in *"Smith as Plaintiff in Error v. State of Maine,"* box 178, MSA; "York County Supreme Judicial Court Records," microfilm roll 33, vol. 10, p. 19, 1852, MSA; *Maine Reports*, vol. 33 [33 Maine 48] (Hallowell, Maine: Masters, Smith, 1853). See also the "Index to the Cases of Law in York County, April Term 1851," vol. 14, pp. 27–30, in the papers of Ether Shepley, collection 117/A, MHS.

134. Kasserman, *Fall River Outrage*, 2–3. Lawyers for the accused murderer of Sarah Cornell attempted to besmirch her moral fiber in order to remove culpability from their client, the local minister. The attorneys, hand in hand with published trial reports and other accounts of this murder, shaped and reshaped Cornell's image, turning her from victim to vamp. Yet she found defenders in the mill owners, agents, and mill girls who saw that in defending Cornell, they defended their own lives and livelihoods. One can imagine that for Saco's elite mill owners and all who profited from the economic growth begun by Samuel Batchelder's mill, it was in their best interests to demonstrate in court and in print that mill life itself and mill towns like Saco were safe: any danger lay in the moral flaws of individual workers, not the industry as a whole.

Some women carefully managed their public persona. Prior to her murder, well-known prostitute Helen Jewett remade her own image from her early roots as Dorcas Doyen. Yet, like Berengera Caswell's, Jewett's agency vanished in the numerous accounts, reports, and fictions inspired by her death as publishers and authors claimed her story. See Patricia Cline Cohen, *The Murder of Helen Jewett: The Life and Death of a Prostitute in Nineteenth-Century New York* (New York: Knopf, 1998), 356.

135. Indictment, *State v. James H. Smith*, Superior Court Records, York County [Maine], vol. 9, Apr. 1845–Sept. 1851, 387–90, MSA; On Smith's Trial, *Maine Reports*, vol. 32 [32 Maine 369] (Hallowell, Maine: Masters, Smith, 1852), 369–74.

136. *Maine Reports* [33 Maine 48], 60.

137. "Justice Defeated," *MA*, Jan. 17, 1852.

138. Smith died April 3, 1855, and was buried in the newly opened Laurel Hill Cemetery, a tree-lined Victorian cemetery overlooking the Saco River. His wife, two children, their spouses, and an infant grandchild would eventually join him in this family plot. "Deaths from Original Records," 46, DL.

139. "The Saco Tragedy," *EA*, Apr. 20, 1850.

140. Editorial, *MD*, May 7, 1850.

141. Ibid.

142. "James H. Smith—Guilty!!" *MA*, Feb. 1, 1851.

143. Reagan, *When Abortion Was a Crime*, 10–11. See also Smith-Rosenberg, "The Abortion Movement and AMA," in *Disorderly Conduct*, 217–44.

144. Israel Thorndike Dana, "Report of the Committee on the Production of Abortion," *Transactions of the Maine Medical Association, for the Years 1866, 1867, and 1868* (Portland, Maine: Stephen Berry, printer, 1869), 41.

145. Reagan, *When Abortion Was a Crime*, 11.

146. Ibid., 12–13.

147. On the social control of women, see ibid., 13, and Mary Odem, *Delinquent Daughters: Protecting and Policing Adolescent Female Sexuality in the United States, 1885–1920* (Chapel Hill: Univ. of North Carolina Press, 1995). Another example of the newspaper serving as a means of social control is seen in Werner J. Einstadter, "Crime News in the Old West: Social Control in a Northwestern Town, 1887–1888," *Urban Life* 8 (Oct. 1979): 317–34.

148. "The Saco Tragedy," *PT*, Apr. 27, 1850.

149. Smith-Rosenberg, *Disorderly Conduct*, 226.

150. On media attention and social punishment, see Reagan, "About to Meet Her Maker," 1244, 1257–58.

151. Untitled article, *PB*, Feb. 13, 1851.

152. Carter and Long married on July 7, 1850. Beatty, *Vital Records*, 431, 461; Meeds, "Intentions and Return of Marriages," 101. Long then disappears from the local historical record. He may have been in Worcester, Massachussetts, in 1870—married with three children. Or he may have moved to California. During the Smith trial, the *Biddeford Mercantile Advertiser* was filled with news items about California, including a series of letters from the "Saco Californians," two young men who had made their way west in search of fortune. Given Long's rocky reputation, a fresh start in a new frontier may have been quite appealing. The 1880 California census identifies a William Long, born around 1830 in Maine, married and working as a laborer in the San Francisco area.

153. Cohen, *The Murder of Helen Jewett*, 356.

154. On Mary Rogers see Charles Wallace, *A Confession of the Awful and Bloody Transactions in the Life of Charles Wallace: The Fiend-like Murderer of Miss Mary Rogers, the Beautiful Cigar-Girl of Broadway, New York* (New Orleans, La.: E. E. Barclay, 1851); and Amy Gilman Srebnick, *The Mysterious Death of Mary Rogers: Sex and Culture in Nineteenth-Century New York* (New York: Oxford Univ. Press, 1995). On Pearl Bryan see *The Mysterious Murder of Pearl Bryan; or, The Headless Horror* (Cincinnati, Ohio: Barclay, [1896]); and Anne B. Cohen, *Poor Pearl, Poor Girl! The Murdered Girl Stereotype in Ballad and Newspaper*. Publications of the American Folklore Society, vol. 58 (Austin: Univ. of Texas Press, 1973).

155. Leslie Reagan notes that "periods of anti-abortion activity mark moments

of hostility to female independence." Reagan, *When Abortion Was a Crime*, 14. On hostility to laboring women see Cameron, *Radicals of the Worst Sort*. The partisan publications surrounding Sarah Cornell's death, in addition to their debate on mill life, also pitted traditional Congregationalism against the new Methodism of her alleged murderer. Mary Rogers's death became a lens for examining police reform and criminal justice in New York City, as well as the increasing criminalization of abortion. Helen Jewett's murder invited readers to see a personal face on murder and prostitution. Similarly, Berengera Caswell's demise forced a discussion on the cost of growth and prosperity, the abortion trade, and the work of women. Despite the best efforts of Miss J.A.B. and the Reverend Mr. Miller, the two novels based on Caswell's death did not gain the same notoriety or lasting impact as the multiplicity of works that grew from the murders of Cornell, Rogers, and Jewett. Still, the Caswell "murder" and the Mary Bean novels remain firmly connected to this narrative tradition of true-crime–inspired literature that instructed young women and men as it reflected the concerns of a moment in time and place.

156. Dana, "Report of the Committee on the Production of Abortion," 40.

157. John Haley, "Notes from John Haley—1913," 97, typescript, DL. In this same paragraph, Haley notes that a Doctor Stevens also died in Bacon's Court and identifies Stevens as connected to the Wentworths and the Parker murder.

158. Miss J.A.B., *Mary Bean, The Factory Girl. A Domestic Story, Illustrative of the Trials and Temptations of Factory Life. Founded on Recent Events* (Boston, Mass.: Hotchkiss, 1850), 9. Hereafter cited as *MB*. All citations are to this edition unless otherwise indicated.

159. "Just Published," *MD*, June 18 and 25, 1850.

160. "Report on the Examination of Asa & Henry Wentworth," *MD*, May 14, 1850.

161. Ibid.

162. "The Manchester Murder," *FC*, May 9, 1850; "The Manchester Murder," *EA*, May 6, 1850.

163. *The Parker Murder*, 4.

164. On the technological revolutions that facilitated the growth of reading, see Ronald Zboray, "Antebellum Reading and the Ironies of Technological Innovation," *American Quarterly* 40 (Mar. 1988): 65–82.

165. *MB*, 24, 33.

166. See the discussion of city-mysteries in David S. Reynolds, *Beneath the American Renaissance: The Subversive Imagination in the Age of Emerson and Melville* (Cambridge, Mass.: Harvard Univ. Press, 1988), 79–82. For an example of this genre see Stuart M. Blumin, ed., *New York by Gas-Light and Other Urban Sketches by George G. Foster* (Berkeley: Univ. of California Press, 1990).

167. See Shelley Fisher Fishkin, *From Fact to Fiction: Journalism and Imaginative Writing in America* (Baltimore, Md.: Johns Hopkins Univ. Press, 1985).

168. Susanna Rowson, *Charlotte Temple*, ed. Cathy Davidson (New York: Oxford Univ. Press, 1986).

169. Saco, Maine, is one hundred miles north of Boston, Massachusetts.

170. This edition, published by J. Merone, a Boston company, used the same cover image, graphics, and text as the 1850 Hotchkiss publication. With the exception of the title page and the resetting of a few lines of type to align uneven columns within the text, the Hotchkiss and Merone editions are identical.

171. On Hiram M. Rulison, see *Dictionary of Literary Biography*, vol. 49, part 2, s.v. "The Queen City Publishing House." It appears that after the late 1850s, the two Mary Bean novels ceased to be in print, and no additional elaboration of Caswell's death in fiction has been found. That Berengera's death was not a cold-blooded "murder" with a mysterious murderer, a heinous plot, and a precipitating ulterior motive may be part of the shorter life span of this true-crime tale. Unlike in the Jewett case, Caswell's "murderer" was not surprisingly respectable; in fact, he was long suspected of criminal activities. Where the Cornell and Jewett crimes were seen as rare and shocking, Caswell's death was seen at least by some as the death of yet "another factory girl." And finally, the press coverage for the New York City deaths of Jewett and Rogers was daily and intensely competitive, with multiple newspapers churning out stories for tens of thousands to read. In addition, the redefinition of the crime as manslaughter along with the ambiguity over Caswell's role in the events may have lessened the likelihood of continued, national attention. Caswell's death, however, did stimulate at least two additional tragic "factory girl" tales published and set in Maine, where issues of population growth and increasing urbanization were still very much a concern. See Fitzallen, *The Saco Factory Girl* (Saco, Maine: Harris Publishing Hall, ca. 1851), and Fitzallen, *The Biddeford Factory Girl* ([Saco], Maine: Harris Publishing Hall, 1852).

172. "Woman's Proper Sphere," *MD*, June 11, 1850.

173. Reynolds, *Beneath the American Renaissance*, 90.

174. *MB*, [5].

175. The Yale University library identifies Miss J.A.B. as J. A. Brosson. In *Women and Children of the Mills*, Judith Ranta suggests Miss J.A.B. is Johannes Adrianus Block (p. 107). David Reynolds makes the same suggestion in Reynolds, "Sensational Fiction," in *American History through Literature 1820–1870*, ed. Janet Gabler-Hover and Robert Sattelmeyer (Detroit, Mich.: Charles Scribner's Sons, 2006), 3:1054–59. Gale Virtual Reference Library. Thomson Gale. University of New England Libraries (accessed Mar. 13, 2006).

176. *MB*, [5].

177. *MB*, [39]. Italics in original.

178. *MB*, 42.

179. Fishkin, *Fact to Fiction*, 216.

180. *MB*, 22.

181. *MB*, [39].

182. *MB*, 25.

183. Rev. Mr. Miller, *A Full and Complete Confession of the Horrid Transactions in the Life of George Hamilton, The Murderer of Mary Bean, The Factory Girl* ([New

York]: [J. Merone], 1852), 12. Counterfeiting represented a parallel concern, frequently mentioned in Saco newspapers as well as on the title page of the *Life of George Hamilton*. As with interactions with confidence men, the threat of counterfeit currency cautioned readers that you could not assume the genuineness of money or those who carried it. The Wentworth brothers were accused of holding and passing counterfeit money in New Hampshire prior to their move to Maine.

184. Editorial, *SU,* reprinted in *MD,* May 7, 1850.

SOURCES

I gathered the many stories about the real Berengera Caswell and the fictional Mary Bean from a wide variety of sources. Saco and Biddeford newspapers provided detailed descriptions of the discovery of Berengera's body and the excitement of the initial examination of Dr. James Smith. During that hearing and the subsequent murder trial, newspapers from Maine, New Hampshire, and Massachusetts provided lengthy accounts of the testimony, offering us a trial transcript as set down by the numerous reporters covering this event. As no official court reporter recorded the proceedings, the newspaper accounts, with varying details, provide our only insight into what transpired in the courtroom. I found most of these newspapers in the Dyer Library in Saco, Maine, where reading the oversized bound volumes of original newspapers was a real treat. New Hampshire and Massachusetts papers survive on microfilm in the New Hampshire Historical Society and New Hampshire State Library (both in Concord), the Center for Lowell (Mass.) History, and the Boston Public Library. Although I lacked an official trial transcript, I found a wealth of court documents housed in the Maine State Archives, in Augusta. These included the verdict of the coroner's inquest jury and financial records detailing the summons issued and witnesses questioned in the quest to bring justice. Also included in the file is the initial complaint against Smith, charging him with the crime of murder, the complaint itself clipped from a newspaper and pasted into the official record. The grand jury indictment, a handwritten document in a steady neat hand several pages long, and the official report of the outcome of his murder trial documented Smith's experience in the judicial system. A year following Smith's conviction, a second file was created for his appeal. This archived record contains the handwritten argument submitted by Smith's attorney, Nathan Clifford, and the court's decision.

Court documents told only part of the story. In addition to relaying information about the examination and trial, local newspapers provided a wealth of information on life in 1850s Saco—from the items on sale in the local stores to the day's weather. The 1849 Saco-Biddeford city directory was invaluable for identifying the participants in this drama, figuring out residence patterns, and learning about Saco at the moment Berengera Caswell arrived. To learn more about the many people whose paths crossed with Caswell's, I turned to online and published genealogies; family and local history; the Manchester, New Hampshire, city directories and newspapers; and Amoskeag mill employment records, this last source housed at the Manchester Historical Society. Although I did not find any document written by a Caswell, diaries and letters from other mid-nineteenth-century factory girls lent insight into the experience the Caswell sisters shared in and out of the mills. Like the textiles Berengera helped make, these published and unpublished documents, scattered in libraries, archives, and private collections across New England, each provided an important thread that when woven together with the rest gave me insight into the short life of one woman.

As this is a story about stories, I chose to tell this tale in a more narrative form. Each detail I record, from the day's weather to the physical appearance of our characters, has a historic source (most often newspapers), and the references to those sources can be found in the notes. As a historian, I seek not only to tell a good story but also to understand what it meant to those who lived it in 1850, as well as to see how after the passage of more than a century and a half we might perceive what transpired. The life and death of Berengera Caswell touched on many social and cultural concerns. To understand the many contexts of her story, I read widely in the histories of murder, factory life, and medicine and abortion practices, as well as various genres of mid-nineteenth-century sensational literature. References to the scholarly works that informed my thinking are found in the endnotes.

Part 2 of this book presents Berengera's life reincarnated in fictional form. Surviving copies of the two ephemeral novels, *Mary Bean, The Factory Girl* (1850) and the *Life of George Hamilton* (1852), are scarce. The Borowitz Crime Collection at Kent State University has a copy of each text, as well as numerous additional nineteenth-century true-crime accounts that make for good, if a bit gruesome, comparative reading. Both novels drew on reality for story line and character and here again my sources for understanding where fiction ended and fact began included the court records and newspaper accounts of the Smith hearing and murder trial and the Wentworth brothers' examinations of 1849 and 1850. In addition to the reports filling Maine and New Hampshire newspapers, an 1880s publication on the unsolved Parker murder helped to identify the tenuous connections between the two crimes, as well as the surprising origin of Smith's selection of the Mary Bean alias.

Identifying the woman in the photograph featured in Figure 3 and on the cover of this book presented the greatest challenge of this research and still offers a bit of a mystery. The photograph has remained in the possession of Caswell-Reynolds descendants for 150 years, one in a collection of nineteenth-century family photographs, but only one of two period photographs of women that remained unidentified. One photograph showed a woman much older than Berengera at her time of death. In spirited email conversations, Caswell descendants and I reasoned that this woman may have been Abigail Caswell, Berengera's older sister who migrated to Wisconsin. Perhaps kept in the possession of Ruth Caswell Reynolds, who had no reason to label an image of her own sister, the photograph remained a mystery for subsequent generations who found they could not identify the distant aunt/great-aunt they had never met. And the other unidentified photograph was potentially Berengera's portrait—again a sister need not label and, certainly with such a shameful death, not speak often of this deceased relative. Subsequent descendants, who had never met Berengera or heard much about her, forgot her or never even knew who this attractive woman was.

If only identifying photographs was so easy. The physical descriptions of Berengera gleaned from newspapers—an attractive woman, twenty years old with a high forehead, long brown hair, drop earrings, and good teeth—match the woman in the photograph. Unfortunately, the technology of photography does not. This photograph is an ambrotype, a technology which became commercially available in 1852, two years after Berengera died. If this image were a daguerreotype, readily available during Berengera's life, my confidence in this identification would be assured. As newspapers and city directories attest, Lowell and Manchester had several daguerreotype studios where residents, including factory girls, could and did have their photograph taken for anywhere from fifty to seventy-five cents. Pricey, but not out of reach. Further, it was possible to copy a daguerreotype and create an ambrotype, and among the Caswell-Reynolds family photographs is an advertising label indicating the identity of the Manchester photographer who took at least one (or more) of the images in this collection. The business card of "M. S. Lamprey's Daguerrean Saloon" claimed "particular attention paid to copying pictures and satisfaction guaranteed." According to the online resource, Craig's Daguerreian Registry, in the 1850s Lamprey operated both a daguerreotype saloon and ambrotype gallery, likely adding the new photographic process when it became popular in the early years of that decade. Perhaps, after Berengera's death, Thais or Ruth copied her sister's daguerreotype image, sending one image home to their parents and keeping a new ambrotype for themselves as a remembrance. Possible? Perhaps.

Another clue came from the clothing in the photograph. Consulting with fashion historians produced mixed results. One indicated the clothing was representative of the mid- to late 1850s and thus too late to be Berengera. But another indicated a date a decade earlier, unless, of course, the woman was wearing clothes from the late 1840s in a photograph taken a few years later. After all, were all the clothes hanging in your closet made this very year? Yet another scholar noted the ring on the woman's finger: Is it a ring of friendship or of marriage?

If not Berengera, then who? Our most likely candidate would seem to be Thais, missing from the collection of family photographs. Thais remained in Manchester and married there in the 1850s. Does she perhaps wear Berengera's drop earrings? At the end, the pretty woman in the photograph remains stubbornly silent. The best we can say is that it is Berengera if a series of possible but not necessarily probable events fell into place, but perhaps here my wishful thinking, rather than my scholarly research, is writing yet another story about Berengera Caswell. We do learn one final lesson from this mute image: label your family photographs. Your descendants, and historians, will thank you.

INDEX